VICTORIANS IN THE MOUNTAINS

In her compelling book, Ann C. Colley examines the shift away from the cult of the sublime that characterized the early part of the nineteenth century to the less reverential perspective from which the Victorians regarded mountain landscapes. And what a multifaceted perspective it was, as unprecedented numbers of the Victorian middle and professional classes took themselves off on mountaineering holidays so commonplace that the editors of *Punch* sarcastically reported that the route to the summit of Mont Blanc was to be carpeted.

In Part One, Colley mines diaries and letters to interrogate how everyday tourists and climbers both responded to and undercut ideas about the sublime, showing how technological advances like the telescope transformed mountains into theatrical spaces where tourists thrilled to the sight of struggling climbers; almost inevitably, these distant performances were eventually reenacted at exhibitions and on the London stage. Colley's examination of the Alpine Club archives, periodicals, and other primary resources offers a more complicated and inclusive picture of female mountaineering as she documents the strong presence of women on successful expeditions in the latter half of the century. In Part Two, Colley turns to John Ruskin, Gerard Manley Hopkins, and Robert Louis Stevenson, whose writings about the Alps reflect their feelings about their Romantic heritage and shed light on their ideas about perception, metaphor, and literary style. Colley concludes by offering insights into the ways in which expeditions to the Himalayas affected people's sense of the sublime, arguing that these individuals were motivated as much by the glory of Empire as by aesthetic sensibility. Her ambitious book is an astute exploration of nationalism, as well as theories of gender, spectacle, and the technicalities of glacial movement that were intruding on what before had seemed inviolable.

Dedication

For my father, who hiked up Snowdon in a black suit; for Gwen, who climbed Mt. Kenya in the dark; for Ephraim Massey, who, risking more than any of us, repeatedly reached far beyond 20,000' in South America and the Himalaya; for intrepid Andrea Massey; for Gabriel Massey, who, as a small child with his sister, mother, and father, reached base camp of Mt. Everest and climbed Mt. Kilimanjaro, and for those who, over the years, have helped me struggle up to the base camp of Cotopaxi and Chimborazo as well as through the foothills of the Himalaya, the mountain passes of Bolivia, and innumerable other high places. The mountains are part of us.

Victorians in the Mountains

Sinking the Sublime

ANN C. COLLEY
The State University of New York,
College at Buffalo, USA

Routledge
Taylor & Francis Group

LONDON AND NEW YORK

First published 2010 by Ashgate Publishing

Published 2016 by Routledge
2 Park Square, Milton Park, Abingdon, Oxfordshire OX14 4RN
711 Third Avenue, New York, NY 10017, USA

First issued in paperback 2016

Routledge is an imprint of the Taylor & Francis Group, an informa business

British Library Cataloguing in Publication Data
Colley, Ann C.
   Victorians in the mountains : sinking the sublime.
   1. Sublime, The – History – 19th century. 2. British – Travel – Alps Region – History – 19th century – Sources. 3. Authors, English – Travel – Alps Region – History – 19th century – Sources. 4. Mountaineering expeditions – Alps – History – 19th century – Sources. 5. Sublime, The, in literature. 6. Mountains in literature. 7. English literature – 19th century – History and criticism.
   I. Title
   820.9'353'09034–dc22

Library of Congress Cataloging-in-Publication Data
Colley, Ann C.
   Victorians in the mountains : sinking the sublime / Ann C. Colley.
      p. cm.
   Includes bibliographical references and index.
   ISBN 978–1–4094–0633–4 (alk. paper) – ISBN 978–1–4094–0634–1 (eBook)
   1. English literature – 19th century – History and criticism. 2. Aestheticism (Literature) 3. Sublime, The, in literature. 4. Nature in literature. 5. Mountaineering in literature. 6. Technological innovations – History – 19th century. 7. Ruskin, John, 1819–1900 – Criticism and interpretation. 8. Hopkins, Gerard Manley, 1844–1889 – Criticism and interpretation. 9. Stevenson, Robert Louis, 1850–1894 – Criticism and interpretation. 10. Nationalism and literature – England – History – 19th century.
   I. Title.
   PR468.A33C65 2010
   820.9'36–dc22   2010025753

ISBN 13: 978-1-138-27255-2 (pbk)
ISBN 13: 978-1-4094-0633-4 (hbk)

Contents

Contents

List of Figures

Acknowledgments

Many people and places have made this book possible. I would like to thank John Bowles of the National Library of Scotland; Carol Cook and the staff of the Athenaeum Library in Providence, Rhode Island; Philip Endean, S.J. of Campion Hall, Oxford; Becky Fullerton of the Appalachian Mountain Club Library and Archives, Boston; Sue Hare of the Alpine Club Photo Library, London; Glyn Hughes, Honorary Archivist of the Alpine Club, London; Paul Smith, Archivist of the Thomas Cook Archives, Peterborough; Stephen Wildman, Director of the Ruskin Library, University of Lancaster; the Trustees and Fellows of Balliol College, Oxford, and the cheerful unnamed staff behind the Reading Room desk at the British Library. I also want to acknowledge the Cambridge University Press for giving me permission to reprint my essay "John Ruskin: Climbing and the Vulnerable Eye" from *Victorian Literature and Culture*, Volume 37 (1), 2009, pp. 43–66. In addition, I would like to express my appreciation for the support I have received from the New York State Research Council, the Provost, the UUP, and the Graduate Office at SUNY College, Buffalo. I am, as always, indebted to those individuals who take an interest in my work, among whom are Linda M. Austin of the University of Oklahoma, Anne Huberman, Joel Huberman who has done some photographic work for me, John Maynard and Adrienne Munich of *Victorian Literature and Culture*, the members of the Victorian Association of Ontario, Richard Dury of the University of Bergamo, Italy, and Kaylene Waite at Instructional Resources, SUNY College, Buffalo. I want especially to thank those who have closely and generously read each chapter more than once: Carrie Tirado Bramen, Carolyn W. Korsmeyer, Regina Grol, and Irving J. Massey.

Introduction

In the same year in which Alfred Tennyson, already schooled by Edmund Burke's *Essay on the Sublime and the Beautiful,* gazed admiringly at the lofty heights of the Jungfrau, a Presbyterian minister from New York, the Rev. George B. Cheever, traveled to Chamonix and to the Oberland Alps in search of the sublime.[1] Equipped with quotations from Coleridge, Wordsworth, and Shelley, Cheever gazed at Mont Blanc, "the monarch of the mountains," and at the "dazzling coronet" of the Jungfrau's peak so he might see the solemn mystery, savage grandeur, desolation, and awful solitude with his own eyes.

If we are to believe his 1846 narrative, *The Pilgrim in the Shadow of the Jungfrau Alp,* Cheever was not disappointed. The jagged crags, the swirling waters in the depths of a ravine, the light falling upon the mountainous ridges, and the crashing sound of avalanches, followed by a penetrating silence, deeply impressed him with their "thrilling sublimity" (71). Like many who had stood before these mountains in the late eighteenth and early nineteenth centuries, a satisfied and effusive Cheever felt as if he were in the presence of a landscape that elevated his mind and brought him closer to a sense of infinity.

A decade later, however, Cheever's sense of fulfillment and illumination was not as available. From the mid-nineteenth century on, even though a person might still travel to the mountains in order to behold their power, the feeling of being in the presence of something grand, astonishing, and uplifting became increasingly elusive. Victorian tourism with its "buzzing hives of restless strangers" (Twain 345), climbing clubs, commercialism, spectacle, nation building, and even science, compromised and interfered with the experience.[2] What people commonly understood to be the sublime seemed to be "sinking" under the weight of consumerism, sportsmanship, ambition, nationalism, and even theories of thermodynamics, as well as under the heavy burden of familiarity and the taint of staleness.

---

[1] As a young man, in 1825, Tennyson had written the poem "On Sublimity" which, as Marjorie Hope Nicolson points out, has "all the familiar themes, settings, and adjectives" associated with the cult of sublimity (371–72).

[2] It should be added that prior to the mid-century, detractions were already afoot. In the eighteenth century, tourists in search of the picturesque, traveling in Wales, the Lake District, and Scotland, invariably invaded these rural areas with their gadgets, such as the Claude Glass, colored spectacles as well as guidebooks, in order to intensify the experience. For a history of tourism see Malcolm Andrews' *The Search for the Picturesque: Landscape Aesthetics and Tourism in Britain, 1760–1800* and Esther Moir's *The Discovery of Britain: the English Tourist 1540 to 1840.*

Although the British were extending their range by climbing or settling in mountainous areas elsewhere – as far as the Himalaya – these challenges to the experience of the sublime were especially noticeable in the Alps, where, beginning in the mid 1800s, an increasing number of middle- and upper-middle-class tourists as well as climbers were invading the region and transforming it into an English-speaking preserve.[3] Such was the transformation that toward the end of the century an Alpine Club member and well-known mountaineer, J. Norman Collie, feared the mystery of the Alps was "gone, gone forever" (170). For him, and for many others, Switzerland had become a "herding place" (168).

By the end of the 1800s, the mountains that had once been thought unapproachable, even grimly horrifying, had not only been precisely measured and "conquered" but also institutionalized through maps, guidebooks, and board games that led a player all the way from London to the summit of the Matterhorn or Mont Blanc.[4] New railroad lines also made what was remote much more accessible. And certificates announcing that one had reached the summit of Mont Blanc were almost as easy to find as the sight of people trudging up and down its sometimes-dangerous routes. Moreover, the social requirements and conversation at the *table d'hôte* often threatened to eclipse any thought of the sublime view from the hotel window. In 1822, for instance, Mrs. Beecroft and her daughter had gazed in awe at the scene outside their window. Through it they had watched "the silver light of the Moon's crescent" falling upon the sides of Mont Blanc (103). But forty years later, Thomas Whitwell, though tempted to look, closed his shutters and, instead, joined his fellow climbers at the dinner table to talk about their adventures. Whitwell remarked that "scores of others" had already "gone wild about the grandeur of the mountains." By now he had read too much about the scenery "for astonishment to be any longer possible" (107).

Victorians in the Mountains: Sinking the Sublime examines this shift from the earlier cult of sublimity that continued to enchant individuals, such as the Rev. Cheever and Mrs. Beecroft, to a perspective in the second half of the nineteenth century that often diminished, compromised, and either consciously ignored or reshaped the experience. When I began writing this book, I had no intention of focusing upon the sublime. I feared getting stuck in a cliché primarily associated with Romanticism. However, as the research and writing developed, I found what I should have realized in the first place: during the second half of the nineteenth century, the popular conception of the Romantic sublime was still very much a factor to reckon with. As a result, even though this study aspires mainly to examine the ways in which members of the British Victorian middle and professional

---

[3]   Remarking upon this phenomenon, *Punch* sarcastically reported that the route up to the summit of Mont Blanc was to be carpeted. At the same time, though, others seriously talked of illuminating the Matterhorn. See "Good News for Cockney Travellers," *Punch* 27 July-December (1854): 110.

[4]   *Voyage en Suisse*, *The New Game of the Ascent of Mont Blanc*, and *Up the Matterhorn* are three Victorian board games with which I am familiar.

classes as well as leading literary figures reacted to or interacted with a mountain landscape, the book frequently finds itself diverted into a discussion of the ways in which these individuals revised the enduring, if failing, presence of the sublime – an experience that, even among the most pragmatic members of the Trigonometric Survey in the Himalaya, was ultimately neither denied nor entirely forgotten.

Because of its subject matter, this study could be thought of as a sequel to Marjorie Hope Nicolson's 1959 *Mountain Gloom and Mountain Glory: The Development of the Aesthetics of the Infinite*. In a sense, the book begins where hers ends. It takes part of its cue from her epilogue, which recognizes that the concept of the sublime was challenged during the Victorian period,[5] and that new conditions of travel altered a sense of "the old 'Sublime'" (375). *Victorians in the Mountains*, though, goes beyond the circumstances of travel that Nicolson mentions briefly, and explores the numerous pressures coming from ideas about nationalism, as well as from theories of gender, spectacle, and the technicalities of glacial movement, that were intruding upon what before had seemed inviolable.

Recent years have seen a rise of scholarly interest in mountains and mountain climbing. Impressive work has been done by critics interested in imperialism, colonialism, gender, and tourism in the context of mountaineering. *Victorians in the Mountains* is distinguished by focusing more specifically upon the aesthetic dimensions of the Victorian mountain experience. These include such categories as the reception of the sublime; the nature of perception in extreme settings; the vulgarization of the aesthetic moment; and the effect of mountains upon literary style. These issues have either been ignored or not fully addressed in such influential works as James Buzard's, Edmund Swinglehurst's, and Lynne Whitney's informative studies on tourism. Nor have they been considered in the recent and otherwise valuable critical work of Elaine Freedgood, Peter H. Hansen, and Francis O'Gorman that have tended to emphasize the cult of masculinity and nation building associated with the mountains. In this regard, it should be remembered that Geoffrey Winthrop Young, who was in a position to know, having lost a leg in World War I, rejected the argument that mountaineering was merely another form of violent imperialism or sublimated aggression. That accusation, Young says, was answered for him "decisively and always" after just a few months of war. There is no possible parallel between the "jangling monochord of death" on the battlefield and the "life-giving and humane" breath of the mountains (360).

To compensate for such omissions, *Victorians in the Mountains* investigates these aesthetic responses in both their positive and negative forms through largely unexplored sources. A good many of the diaries and narratives written by Victorian visitors to the mountains have hardly been opened and are only available because they have found their way into repository libraries, archives, special collections of

---

[5]   Nicolson observes that a traveler at the end of the nineteenth century, "armed" with the poems of Wordsworth, Byron, and Shelley, "gazed at the Alps or the lesser sublimities of the Lake District and felt, or thought he felt – or pretended to feel – as Burnet or Dennis or Wordsworth actually had felt" (372–73).

mountaineering literature, or antiquarian book shops. The present work also draws upon scrapbooks housed in the Alpine Club Archives as well as upon relevant contemporary essays in the periodical literature that often get overlooked.

Victorians in the Mountains contains three parts: Part I: "Tourists, Climbers, and the Sublime": Part II: "Literary Figures in the Alps": Part III: "Coda: The Himalaya and the Persistence of the Sublime."

Utilizing the popular understanding of the sublime in the nineteenth century as a focus and as a theoretical context, the first part of the book examines the multiple, and often complex, ways in which Victorians reacted to the assumptions and conventions attending their Romantic heritage. Reflecting upon the various forces that were bringing about change as well as upon the innumerable accounts, images, and satires (especially those that undercut the popular notions of the sublime) written and sketched by hundreds of visitors and professional writers, Part I discusses these travelers' reactions to the Alps and to the elevating events they had expected to experience.

The first chapter of Part I, "Sinking the Sublime," opens by considering what people in mid-century Britain had in mind when they looked at a panorama and exclaimed "How sublime!" Although the general public had quite predictably let expressions of the idea slip into a careless, colloquial mode, vestiges of its origins as well as remnants of its various philosophic definitions remained. The word "sublime" might have been used thoughtlessly, but it was not completely severed from its more precise applications. This opening essay examines how people in the second half of the nineteenth century reacted to these more popular conceptions of the sublime and how they tended to compromise the concept. Through tourists' diaries and letters one learns that there were many circumstances that either blocked access to the sublime or made it difficult to sustain a resonant moment that would equal the force of a Turner painting or a passage from Shelley. Similarly, climbing narratives suggest that there were any number of reasons why the concept was sometimes replaced by other more pressing matters. From these documents one learns that the mountain was no longer central to the definition of being or vital to a person's sense of worth. Every now and then the experience of the sublime was virtually lost. Although there was nostalgia for its presence, it seemed to have run its course. To illustrate this shift, the opening chapter devotes several pages to satirical cartoons, drawings, plays, and fiction poking fun at the sublime. These help demonstrate that even while the concept of the sublime seemed to be in the ascendancy, it was losing its power and sliding toward the commonplace, even toward the ludicrous.

The second chapter, "Spectators, Telescopes, and Spectacle," explores the transformation of the mountain from a solitary, sublime object to a spectacular display complete with hordes of observers. Under the influence of tourism and an active culture industry, mountains, especially notable ones such as Mont Blanc, the Jungfrau, or the Matterhorn, began to resemble a sports arena, and the drama of climbing started to take on the characteristics of the theatrical stage. Climbing attracted more and more curious and critical observers. Reading through diaries and climbing narratives, one learns that by means of well-positioned telescopes eager onlookers could trace a climb from its start to its conclusion. As a result, by mid-century, mountaineering was not as solitary an undertaking as it once had been. It was now virtually a spectator sport, complete with parades and celebrations.

"Spectators, Telescopes, and Spectacle" is about this shift and those Victorians who enjoyed the drama of the actual body in danger, and, therefore, found the sight of a struggling climber more fascinating than the lingering ideals of Romanticism. Intent upon viewing such perils, these spectators transformed themselves into voyeurs and the mountains into theatrical spaces. Eventually, under the influence of showmen, such as the exuberant Albert Smith, who in the 1850s produced the popular *Ascent of Mont Blanc*, these distant performances came down from the heights into exhibition venues and literally walked onto the London stage, complete with all the commercialism associated with spectacle. With this descent, the mountains not only left the sublime far behind; they also joined what is now referred to as the culture industry.

I argue, though, that Victorian middle-class audiences were at least partially exempt from what post-modern theorists speak of when they comment on the negative and controlling consequences of spectacle. Through their own travel experiences they were alert to the gap between the spectacle's visual fictions and their own perception of the actual mountain. For them, the mountains still had the last word. Nor, in the end, I suggest, was the Victorian public to lose all touch with the sublime. Ironically, with the coming of more efficient cameras and film in the latter part of the nineteenth century, high-altitude art photography, with its stark black and white images, reclaimed, to some extent, the mystery of the mountains that the spectacles had almost destroyed.

Because the sublime is frequently, if erroneously, thought to be a gendered notion traditionally associated with masculine power, it is only appropriate that the final chapter of Part I, "Ladies on High," should consider the ways in which women climbers were regarded in the second half of the nineteenth century. Historians of mountaineering are quick to record the prejudices that caused people to question whether a female could or should climb. Examples of discrimination are not difficult to find. In this chapter, however, I offer another perspective. I propose that when it came to climbing in the Victorian period, gender did not, as a rule, matter in the overwhelmingly debilitating way commentators have claimed. Long lists of climbs done by women in the second half of the nineteenth century as well as notices of successful expeditions in which a female mountaineer reached a significant summit remind one that women were not summarily discouraged from participating in what most recent commentators assume was solely a male-centered sport based upon power and privilege.

Even though many British Victorian women climbers faced disapproval and their achievements occasionally elicited snide remarks, these individuals also frequently benefited from a positive regard for their mountaineering ambitions. Using materials from the Alpine Club archives and references found in periodicals, letters, and climbing narratives, I explore a more complicated and inclusive picture. The evidence shows that from the mid-century on, women were being supported by, and were climbing with, the very men who supposedly were clinging to the idea of mountains as male territory. These materials challenge the more reductive histories that all too readily focus upon climbing in a skirt and emphasize a sense of social unease surrounding the phenomenon of women climbers. Victorian women mountaineers were not necessarily thought to desecrate the regions of the sublime; nor were they routinely either excluded by their Alpine Club "brothers" from expeditions or confined to paths marked especially for ladies. The sheer number of women climbers during the Victorian period, many of whom are forgotten, is striking.

Part II of *Victorians in the Mountains*, "Literary Figures in the Alps," turns away from a more general view of the Victorians' experiences with mountains and concentrates upon the individual reactions of three major literary figures to the Alpine scenery. Through much of his life, John Ruskin spent long periods of time among its mountains; Gerard Manley Hopkins enjoyed a holiday in Switzerland just before he was to enter the novitiate; and Robert Louis Stevenson, under doctor's orders, went twice to alleviate the hemorrhaging from his lungs. The physical movement of their bodies among the mountains and glaciers as well as their aesthetic and scientifically informed responses to the Alps offer a way of understanding not only their feelings about their cultural heritage but also their thoughts about the nature of perception, metaphor, and literary style. These chapters give some sense of a sublime that is altering and being accommodated to a new set of circumstances, but this part of the book also reaches beyond that concept to talk at length about the ways in which Ruskin's experiences as a climber influenced his theories of perception; the ways in which Hopkins's notebooks written during his visit to the Alps enable one to define his characteristic vision; and the ways in which landscape helped shape Stevenson's prose.

The first chapter on literary figures in the Alps, "John Ruskin: Climbing and the Vulnerable Eye," is devoted to the influence of climbing on Ruskin's theories of perception. Most readers either overlook or dismiss Ruskin's climbs in the Alps as being insignificant compared to his avid interest in geology and mountain form. However, I suggest that Ruskin's climbing – his physical and kinetic relationship to the mountains over a long period of time – is essential to his understanding of these features of nature. His numerous and repeated ascents in the Alps were not always easy. The first part of the chapter establishes just how difficult many of these scrambles were, so that the discussion can progress to the idea that these strenuous experiences influenced Ruskin's way of seeing the mountain landscape he admired.

Drawing on materials available in the Ruskin Library at Lancaster University, I argue that Ruskin's climbs in the Alps not only influenced the manner in which he regarded and represented the mountains he studied but also made him more aware of a disturbing chronic weakness in his eyes that caused floaters to interfere with his vision – a disability that contributed to his thinking frequently about the nature of interruption or obstruction, as well as about the privileges of imperfection he so admired in the Gothic details in Venetian architecture. Ruskin understood that too much clarity was unnatural. It seemed that Ruskin climbed not only for the thrill of the exertion and the rage to collect his geological specimens, but also for a perspective that reveals more than a panorama; it holds for him, in spite of the accompanying annoyances and frustrations, the privilege of the imperfect vision, which opens up a space for the imagination and leads one into the spiritual mystery of the landscape.

The second chapter of Part II, "Toothpaste and Breadcrumbs: Gerard Manley Hopkins in the Alps," is about Hopkins' reaction to that landscape as well as to his literary heritage. When Hopkins traveled to Switzerland for a holiday in 1868, he was on a different kind of journey than what most visitors to the Alps had made. Rather than succumbing to the more general cultural or traditional pressures that would have invited him to regard its mountains in the context of popular notions of the sublime, Hopkins chose, instead, to indulge his own idiosyncratic voice and vision, spiritualizing the ordinary, and articulating his sense of the energy of creation in the small as well as the immense.

To understand these preferences, I consider not only Hopkins's divergence from the more traditional ways of representing a mountainous landscape but also his reaction to contemporary scientific debates about glacial movement. The chapter opens with an examination of Hopkins's descriptions of the Alps within the context of the sublime and closes by comparing his portrayals of the glaciers to those written by John Tyndall, the famous climber and scientist, whom Hopkins met while on his Swiss holiday. What emerges is a more complete understanding of his sense of the spiritual power embedded in familiar objects as well as within the scientific. Throughout his Swiss notes, Hopkins continuously turns what scientists measure into living things. He breathes life into what is either a cliché or is reserved for what Tyndall called the "Chiefly Scientific." Through his metaphors and verbs that carry the energy of the landscape, Hopkins not only recasts the sublime – he also fuses the scientific and the spiritual. He shows how the empirical eye can be a divine way of seeing.

The last chapter of Part II, "Snowbound with Robert Louis Stevenson," concentrates upon Stevenson's negative reaction to the Alps. Given the reverential and enthusiastic regard most people had for the Alpine landscape, it is interesting to note that Stevenson chose not to partake in the popular regard for its grandeur – a noteworthy fact since he was, at this point of his life, indebted to the well-known Alpinist Leslie Stephen, his editor. His unresponsiveness separated him from a long literary tradition in which writers exulted in the sublime scenery. Particularly during his first months in the Alps, an ailing Stevenson found the snow-covered mountains surrounding Davos to be not only uninspiring but also dispiriting. In 1881, confined by doctor's orders, he was miserable and wrote little.

Stevenson's lack of productivity was not, as many have suggested, simply the consequence of his feeling unwell and discouraged by the company of others suffering from delicate health. Stevenson's negative reaction to the Alps also originated in the landscape itself. This chapter explores the ways in which the monotonous snows of Davos and the roaring sameness of its waterfall had a depressing, prison-like effect upon his imagination. In the spring, though, Stevenson started writing in earnest again, for he had gone back to the Highlands of Scotland and was surrounded once more by a varied and changing landscape.

"Snowbound with Robert Louis Stevenson" examines in what ways Stevenson's imagination was beholden to the character of the immediate scenery. The topography of Stevenson's surroundings, one might say, created the style and rhythms of his prose. The immediate landscape functioned as a kind of mirror, the reflections of which inscribed the text. Stevenson was also empowered by the sensation of traveling through a landscape. The shape of his prose depended upon that passage. In fact, the only time Stevenson came close to experiencing the sublime at Davos was when he would occasionally go tobogganing at night. During those thrilling moments, he was removed from the limits of his body and, in the spirit of Edmund Burke, could speak of the "joyful horror" when the head goes and the world vanishes. Stevenson's experience reminds one of the essential relation between bodily movement and sight, and anticipates Maurice Merleau-Ponty's understanding that the body is mediator between the world and perception. To support this discussion of Stevenson's style in the context of landscape, I not only discuss the few essays and letters Stevenson wrote while in Davos but also reflect at length upon his essays in *Memories and Portraits*, *The Silverado Squatters*, and *Travels with a Donkey in the Cévennes* as well as *The Amateur Emigrant*.

Part III or the Coda, "The Himalaya and the Persistence of the Sublime," moves to the area where British explorers, military men and their wives, and naturalists, as well as missionaries and climbers, were struggling to traverse the region's high passes during the Victorian period. Many informative studies have been written about these travelers and about early surveying and later climbing expeditions to the Himalaya. In this Coda, though, I am not interested in contributing to this well-documented and often complex history. Rather I concentrate upon how these explorations affected people's sense of the sublime. Too often this aspect of their mountain experience is ignored or forgotten, overwhelmed by critics' interest in the imperial project dedicated to surveying or crossing forbidden borders into Nepal and Tibet.

Reading through accounts of their journeys among the Himalaya, one does realize that these individuals were as much guided by an aesthetic sensibility that encouraged them to respond to the way the light played upon the landscape or to yield to the stern solitary vastness of the mountains as they were committed to the project at hand and the glory of empire. Contrary to what most might believe, the imperial imperative did not necessarily negate or replace the sublime tradition. Indeed, in some strange way, the two were linked. "The Himalaya and the Persistence of the Sublime" looks at the nineteenth-century narratives and diaries of exploration in the Himalaya that pay homage to the sublime so as to suggest that even under the most difficult and pragmatic circumstances, the concept somehow continued to play a role.

As part of this discussion, I examine the nineteenth-century convention of comparing the Alps to the Himalaya, a practice that draws attention to the fact that these Himalayan explorers were faced with a new sense of space, distance, and proportion that intensified or altered their experience of the sublime. As if these explorers not only trespassed and crossed political borders as well as physical boundaries when traversing the Himalaya, they also entered a territory where, as two early surveyors observed, "sublimity sits filtered to desolation" (Lloyd and Gerard 143). Making their way through the labyrinths of passes and immense, jagged peaks, they came face to face with the very exemplars of Burke's theory. Isolated and protected, the Himalaya made it possible, even in the late nineteenth century, to feel, for want of a better word, the presence of the Ur-sublime. The overwhelming greatness of scale and chaos surrounding those who were surveying and mapping in the Himalaya interfered with their sense of mastery. The "monarch-of-all-I see" scene that Mary Louise Pratt describes in her *Imperial Eyes: Studies in Travel Writing and Transculturation* was not to be theirs.

Aware that an invasion of tourists could spoil or compromise this experience, Victorians who had worked in and traveled to the Himalaya feared that one day too many visitors would come. Apprehensive that the Himalaya would be ruined as the Alps had been, they worried that English tourists would arrive, hot and eager with Murray (the guidebook) and alpenstock in hand. Their anxiety is proof that the sublime, though diminished, was still prized. Given such evidence of its enduring potency, we may find less cause to wonder that the sublime continues to be an active word in our vocabulary and a concept that still fascinates.

With its emphasis on both a cultural and aesthetic context, *Victorians in the Mountains* becomes a means by which one can discover a particular range of preoccupations among those who traveled to the mountains during the Victorian age. The book appears at a time when the amount of critical and historical literature on mountaineering has been remarkable. The publication of such studies as Robert Macfarlane's beautifully written *Mountains of the Mind: A History of Fascination* (Granta Books 2004), the many books about nineteenth-century women climbers (most recently, Rebecca A. Brown's *Women on High: Pioneers of Mountaineering*, published by the Appalachian Mountain Club 2002), and Helena Michie's admirable *Victorian Honeymoons: Journeys to the Conjugal* (Cambridge University Press 2006), as well as Maurice Isserman and Stewart Weaver's absorbing *Fallen Giants: A History of Himalayan Mountaineering* (Yale University Press 2008) – not to mention the recently released study of Romanticism, *The Spiritual History of Ice* by Eric G. Wilson (Palgrave 2009) – illustrates just how deeply the topic fascinates readers. Each of these has been extensively reviewed. Most recently, *Fallen Giants* was discussed in the 2 July 2009 issue of the *New York Review of Books* (Alvarez), and *Victorian Honeymoons* was featured in the year's review of nineteenth-century studies published in the Autumn 2008 *Studies in English Literature* (Colley).

These books keep company with an ever-growing market for popular books on mountain adventure as well as what some might call "coffee-table" books, such as George Band's sumptuously illustrated *Summit: 150 Years of the Alpine Club* (2006). They also keep pace with an even more popular interest in the mountains – of the sort that prompts a 17 March 2009 issue of *The New York Times* to run an article on nude hikers in the Swiss Alps (Tagliabue A8) and the outrageously satirical *Weekly World News: America's Extreme Magazine* to feature an account, complete with photograph, entitled "Gay Man Climbs Mount Everest in Mink & High Heels" (11 April 2005 36–37) – an article that reminds one of Monty Python's "The International Hairdressers Expedition on Mt. Everest."

Our own contemporary anxiety about the environment, global warming, and geology has also brought about a new interest in mountains, as sources of precious glacial ice and as major factors in the understanding of climate change. Just as I complete this introduction, I hear on the BBC that the glacial melting in the Alps is releasing toxic chemicals, such as PCBs and mercury, that are threatening animal and plant life on the mountain slopes. Now the mountain landscape seems more vulnerable than it did even during the second half of the nineteenth century.

Part I

Tourists, Climbers, and the Sublime

Richard Doyle. "A Meeting on the Mountain"

Part 1

Chapter 1
Sinking the Sublime

> The Taste of Bathos is implanted by Nature itself in the soul of man; till, perverted
> by custom or example, he is taught, or rather compelled, to relish the Sublime.
>
> (Alexander Pope, *Peri Bathous* 309)

> Mont Blanc is the Monarch of Mountains;
> They crowned him long ago;
> But who they got to put it on
> I don't exactly know.
>
> (Albert Smith as quoted in *The Baron of Piccadilly* 101)

Introduction

At the risk of oversimplifying a concept that obviously resists such an attempt, I
have decided, before commencing a discussion of the sublime in mountain scenery,
to consider what people in mid-century Britain had in mind when they looked at a
panorama and exclaimed "How sublime!" Although the general public had quite
predictably let expressions of the idea slip into a careless, colloquial mode, vestiges
of its origins as well as remnants of its various philosophic definitions remained.
The word "sublime" might have been used thoughtlessly, but it was not completely
severed from its more precise applications. As we shall see, in the 1850s, when
travelers and writers were disgruntled that they had not found anything sublime
on their trips and were beginning to question its well-established dominance in
aesthetics, they knew very well what kind of experience they were either being
denied or were choosing to leave behind and, sometimes, to denigrate.

Histories of the sublime usually begin with Longinus's eloquent recital of
the ways in which figures of speech, arrangements of words, as well as phrases
reflecting nobility of character, replicate "the grandeur of thought" and rouse the
soul "to thoughts sublime." Centuries later, Longinus's emphasis on language as
a source of the sublime was not as evident, but not forgotten. As time passed,
theorists concentrated less on rhetoric and increasingly applied their minds to vast
and majestic nature, which releases one from thoughts directed to the narrow sphere
of one's immediate surroundings. Visual representations portraying impressive
landscapes supplanted the rhetorical figures as subjects of their inquiries. In
the eighteenth and nineteenth centuries, canvases depicting imposing mountain
summits, turbulent seas, or precipitous gorges caught the popular imagination.

One need only think of Turner's paintings, whose powerful prospects liberated the observer from his finite limits. Many would have felt drawn to the earlier sentiments of Joseph Addison who, in his "The Pleasure of the Imagination" (1712), exclaimed: "Our imagination loves to be filled with an Object, or to graspe at any thing that is too big for its Capacity. We are flung into a pleasing Astonishment at such unbounded Views, and feel a delightful Stillness and Amazement in the Soul at the Apprehension of them" (412).

By the mid-nineteenth century, popular opinion about the sublime was still wedded to boundlessness, but had also been modified and schooled by Continental and British commentators, such as Kant, Schiller, and Burke, who emphasized the emotional state and disposition of mind that gave rise to and was a source of the experience.[1] Among the most prominent of the English theorists was Edmund Burke, who, in *A Philosophical Enquiry into the Origins of Our Ideas of the Sublime and the Beautiful* (1757), examined the emotional sources of the sublime and analyzed its objects. His ideas played a significant role in shaping the sensibility of the nineteenth century.

Just as it had for his predecessors, Burke's sublime had its source in what is vast or even approaches the infinite. As Burke insisted, "Greatness of Dimension is a powerful cause of the sublime" (37). Whether that greatness be attached to something that is high where one looks down from a vantage point into a grand depth, or whether the viewer be subjected to the sense of prodigious power that comes when looking up at a high mountain peak, the observer is astonished by what appears before him, even overwhelmed, so that "all [the] motions of his soul" are suspended and the mind actually loses itself (35). At a flash, the individual submits to the power of the scenery. Full of reverence, admiration, and respect, a person stands, in solitude and silence, reduced to insignificance before the sublimity of the scene. Perhaps one of Burke's most enduring suggestions was that the experience is dependent upon both pain and danger. As he explained, "Whatever is in any sort terrible, or is conversant about terrible objects, or operates in a manner analogous to terror, is the source of the *sublime*; that is, it is productive of the strongest emotion which the mind is capable of feeling" (33). Associated with the fear of death, the sublime is also replete with dark, uncertain, and confused images. Nothing can be too explicit or too vivid. In a sense, the sublime is ultimately unrepresentable. As Burke suggests, "A clear idea is therefore another name for a little idea" (36).

The sublime, though, is not only dependent on terror. As most readers of Burke and his contemporaries will recall, it also paradoxically produces delight or a feeling of exhilaration for the individual released from his or her earthly

---

[1]   In the Continental tradition, Kant is considered the major theorist of the sublime. His *Critique of the Aesthetical Judgment* reinforced the sense that the sublime does not necessarily reside in nature but is primarily found in the mind of the beholder; that an impressive mountain scene is sublime not for its own sake but for the sense of boundlessness that it creates. The mind runs the risk of sinking, of losing itself. Only through reason can the individual resist this annihilation and, thereby, discover a moral strength within him.

limits. Quite naturally, the question arises: how is it possible to mingle terror and pain with the idea of delight, especially if one understands with Burke that the two negative emotions are what he called the "emissaries" of death, "this king of terrors" (34)?[2] Burke insisted that these seemingly contradictory states of mind do indeed coexist in the sublime moment. He maintained that pain, terror, and delight occupy the same space, *if*, and this is the important caveat, the viewer keeps a certain distance from the danger. He pointed out that if one draws too near or close to death or terror, the resulting apprehension is overwhelming. It negates the effect: "When danger or pain press too nearly, they are incapable of giving any delight, and are simply terrible; but at certain distances, and with certain modifications, they may be, and they are delightful" (34).[3] In the mid-nineteenth century, tourists trudging through the Alpine regions, the climbers reaching "virgin" peaks, and those simply admiring paintings or photographs of the scenery would have been aware of these ideas in a general way, though they might not necessarily have associated them with any particular theorist. Rather, they belonged to a more popular understanding that allied profound thoughts to the inspiriting effects and overwhelming powers of the natural world. Within this context, people would have expected a certain nobility of language in descriptions of the sublime. Seeking release from the limitations of themselves, these individuals would also have hoped for the experience of astonishment as well as the mixed feeling of fear and delight when confronting natural grandeur. In a diffuse way, they would have recognized the necessity for solitude as well as the principles of obscurity and infinity, and they would have linked the sense of the vast and the remote with an exalted emotional state.

In the following pages, we shall see how people in the second half of the nineteenth century reacted to these conceptions of the sublime. In particular, I shall concentrate on the ways in which the reactions of everyday tourists and climbers were undercutting what had been a most potent aesthetic force. Through their diaries, some of which are unpublished, as well as through mid-century satires on touring and climbing, I shall explore why the sublime, at the same time as it seemed to be in the ascendancy, was losing its power and sliding towards the commonplace, even towards the ludicrous. First, I shall talk about the tourists who flocked to the

---

[2] Burke anticipates the question in Part IV, Section V, "How the Sublime is Produced." He writes, "But if the sublime is built on terror, or some passion like it, which has pain for its object; it is previously proper to enquire how any species of delight can be derived from a cause so apparently contrary to it."

[3] When writing this section, I was careful not to use the word "pleasure," for Burke was quite specific in pointing out that he distinguished between "delight" and "pleasure." In Part I, Section IV, "Of Delight and Pleasure," he explains: "As I make use of the word Delight to express the sensation which accompanies the removal of pain or danger; so when I speak of positive pleasure, I shall for the most part call it simply Pleasure."

As Joan Copjec points out in *Read My Desire*, the sublime summons the *possibility* of a terrible force and not its *existence* (236).

Alps in the second half of the nineteenth century; then, I shall concentrate on those who attempted to separate themselves from the latter by climbing thousands of feet above the snow line and seeking less well-traveled areas.[4]

Part 1: The Tourists

Even though the concept of the Sublime seems upon a cursory glance to have been flourishing in mid-nineteenth century Britain, it was suffering. In spite of the notion's recurring visibility in portrayals of wild, magnificent scenery, most of its appearances were but a shadow of what they had been several decades before. Compromised and worn down by excessive use – how could one describe a mountain without calling it sublime? – the term had begun to descend into the realm of the commonplace and into the mire of unfortunate metaphors so that the celebrated jagged peaks of Pilatus (6,995') had now, according to one of Cook's tourists, become "an incomplete set of decayed teeth" (Furby 6).

    Though no longer as informed by the reflective discourses of philosophers, weakened expressions of the sublime still lurked among the pages of texts describing Alpine scenery, waiting to do their work upon the unwary reader. Relying upon the concept's easy availability, columns in *The Illustrated London News* routinely spoke of the "sublime locality" of Mont Blanc ("The Ascent of Mont Blanc" 565), and guidebooks repeatedly called attention to "stupendously sublime" prospects (Gaze 77). Even scientific treatises prefaced their studies of glaciers with a nod to "the transcendent glory of Nature" (Tyndall, *Mountaineering in 1861* 58). John Tyndall's words echo Leslie Stephen's description of a view from a summit that "gives a most exhilarating sense of unrivalled sublimity" ("The Allelein-Horn" 274). In all these passages, the impulse to engage something larger than the Self might have been present, but so was the tendency to reach into the pockets of habit – a practice that was already established in the eighteenth century, when tourists such as Thomas Gray and Anne Radcliffe traveled to the Lake District with a guidebook in their pockets. In search of the sublime they all

---

    [4] For an interesting article about the reactions of English tourists, traveling in Britain, to the concept of the picturesque see Linda M. Austin's "Aesthetic Embarrassment: The Reversion to the Picturesque in Nineteenth-Century English Tourism." *ELH* 74 (2007): 629–53. In the essay, Austin reminds the reader of John Frow's concept of "touristic shame" and of Daniel J. Boorstin's as well as Jonathan Culler's discussion of the indictment of contemporary tourism. To consider these ideas, see, for instance, Boorstin's *The Image: A Guide to Pseudo-Events in America* (1961), Dean MacCannell's *The Tourist: A New Theory of the Leisure Class* (1976), John Ury's *The Tourist Gaze: Leisure and Travel in Contemporary Societies* (1990), and Frow's *Time and Commodity Culture: Essays in Cultural Theory and Postmodernity* (1997).

too readily borrowed the guidebook's vocabulary to describe the majestic and severe grandeur before their eyes.[5]

Mid-nineteenth century tourists were particularly vulnerable to the charms connoted by the term "sublime." Tutored by Alpine Handbooks riddled with clichés about the grandeur of the mountainous landscape, sightseers felt compelled to declare that they too had observed "stupendous scenes of desolate magnificence" (Cole 130). Even though there is no reason to doubt that most of the travelers had some authentic experience of the mountains, they felt required to fill their Alpine diaries with hackneyed declarations of the landscape's "overwhelming sublimity" (*A Budget of Letters* 19). Obliged to remark upon the "sublime snow of the Alps" (S.W. King 553), holidaymakers dutifully registered "every varying aspect of stupendous sublimity" (Yates 1:209). *Switzerland: How to See It for Ten Guineas*, a guidebook appropriately written by one Henry *Gaze* (italics mine), taught its readers exactly how to view the Alps. Its pages directed the tourists' eyes toward the spectacle of Mont Blanc. Think of the disappointment, perhaps even the anxiety, if these travelers had not found, as Gaze said they must, that the scene before them was "stupendously sublime" and that "these rugged mountain walls – those pinnacles like Gothic towers" produced "a sensation that will never be obliterated" (77).

Still other mid-century tourists were encouraged to think in terms of the sublime through the enduring popularity of the Romantic poets (Wordsworth, of course, had only recently died). It is as if this cultural inheritance – what Marjorie Hope Nicolson identifies as the "Mountain Glory" of the late seventeenth and eighteenth centuries – and the pressures exerted by the very proximity of the Alps required them to reach for the landscape of Romanticism, whether or not it was within their grasp. This obligation would effectively vitiate the experience. Typically, they positioned their descriptions of the Alps within the framework of selected passages from Wordsworth, Coleridge, Byron, Shelley, Southey, Scott, and Rogers. Baedeker's and Murray's guides (first published in the 1840s) also encouraged this practice by mingling their instructions with quotations from poetry – Karl Baedeker preferred to include German poets as well. Selected passages from these writers served as models of behavior.[6] As William Westmore Story remarks, the English tourist carried "a Murray for information, and a

---

[5] In his account of lower Borrowdale, Thomas Gray described being under Gowdarcrag: "the rocks at the top deep-cloven perpendicularly by the rains, hanging loose and nodding forwards, seem just starting from their base in shivers. The whole way down and the road on both sides is strewed with piles of fragments, strangely thrown across each other, and of dreadfull [*sic*] bulk; the place reminds me of those passes in the Alps, where the guides tell you to move with speed, and say nothing" (201). Similarly Anne Radcliffe speaks of the dark mountains and precipices that are in view as she ascends Skiddaw (454–59).

[6] In F.M. Trench's *A Journal Abroad in 1868*, the individual records her sublime reaction to the sight of the mountains and then quotes from a poem by Rogers:

Byron for sentiment, and [found] out by them what he is to know and feel at every step" (Buzard 120).[7] Emotional responses to the landscape could be as programmed as the prescribed routes that mapped the sightseers' experience of the Alps. Indeed, one tourist recognized this consequence, when he despaired, "Heigho! for Switzerland and the Alps! Travelling in Switzerland is now a hackneyed subject, and a man might well be excused, if in reply to the enquiries of his friends, he should say with Canning's razor-grinder 'Story! God bless you, I have none to tell'" (William Smith 32).

One Miss Jemima [Morrell] went on Thomas Cook's first organized trip to Switzerland in 1863 and provides an example of this tendency. Her manuscript was discovered neatly preserved in a tin box among the rubble after the Cook's offices in London were bombed during World War II. She launched her pages with lines from Byron's *Manfred* so that she might look upon Mont Blanc as "the monarch of mountains," or she selected passages from *The Prelude* as if she desired to see with Wordsworth's eyes "an unimaginable sight" (*Miss Jemima's Swiss Journal* 34). Even though her subsequent entries did not always indicate that her experience on a particular mountain or pass had matched the quotations' promise, the expectation and longing were there. Miss Jemima was not alone. Another of Cook's tourists, Alfred Miell, chose portions of Shelley's "Mont Blanc" (204–205), and in *A Budget of Letters* a holidaymaker summoned lines from one of Coleridge's poems to describe the "overpowering sublimity" of the glaciers (243). Yet another of Cook's group, C.G. Heard, reached for the heights by selecting a verse from an anonymous poem in John Murray's *A Handbook for Travellers*:[8]

> There was the whole range of snowy peaks stretched out before us – a glorious
> sight, as fine as any one has ever seen before, or ever will again.
>
> "Who first beholds those everlasting clouds,
> Those mighty hills, so shadowy, so sublime,
> As rather to belong to heaven than earth, –
> But instantly receives into his soul
> A sense, a feeling, that he loses not,
> A something that informs him 'tis an hour
> When he may date henceforward and for ever." (36)

[7]   In the satirical 1889 play *The Adventures of Mr. John Timothy Homespun in Switzerland*, Frances Anne Kemble, who had been to the Alps in the mid-1850s, makes sure that one of the English tourists, when preparing for an expedition, opens his Murray and takes his directions from that guidebook: "Listen, this is what Murray says: 'This tremendous peak assumes to those who approach it from different sides different aspect of majestic terror. Now the spectator beholds above him the enthroned image of a gigantic female mantled in snow...'" His sister responds: "What fools your guidebooks are" (55).

[8]   At other points in this journal, C.G. Heard quotes from Byron in order to describe places like the Staubbach Fall.

Above me are the Alps,
The palaces of nature, whose vast walls
Have pinnacled in clouds their snowy scalps,
And throned Eternity in icy halls
Of cold sublimity, where forms and falls
The avalanche, the thunderbolt of snow! (22)

I should add that an equal number of tourists also copied lines from even poorer poems, a rather damning symptom of the sublime's suffering. William Smith, Jr. in his *A Yorkshireman's Trip to Rome in 1866*, for instance, began one of his chapters with the following couplet: "There stood in that romantic clime,/ A mountain awfully sublime" (40).

As I have intimated, although the impulse to pay homage to the sublime and its "Greatness of Dimension" was pressing and often genuine, the actual experience of it was not always to be had. Consequently, it was not uncommon for someone like Mrs. Ashton Yates (1841) to express dissatisfaction with what she found when she crossed the Simplon Pass. Expecting to share Wordsworth's sublime moment, described in Book VI of *The Prelude*, she discovered that though the terrain was "rude and rugged," it was not grand in its dimensions: "even the water was shallow, and flowed languidly." Here the sublime had drowned in a puddle. Parodying Wordsworth, Yates sarcastically added, "the powers of nature seemed more than half suspended" (2:181). Her disillusionment was no different from that felt by another tourist, who, looking at the Matterhorn, admitted he had "heard and read too much" about the grand mountain's wildness and magnitude before coming to the Alps. As a result, he had found the actual experience, by comparison, disappointing. "Astonishment" – that essential effect of the sublime moment– was not, in his mind, "any longer possible" (Whitwell 107). The motions of his soul were not suspended, as Burke said they should be, and not even the inferior effects of "admiration, reverence, and respect" (35) were felt. In straining after transcendental description, the guidebooks and poems had effectively damaged the experience. As critics such as Jonathan Culler and Daniel Boorstin suggest, tourists want sights to look like pictures of themselves.

Undermining the Sublime

Through tourists' diaries one learns that there were many circumstances that either blocked access to the sublime or made it difficult to sustain a resonant moment that would equal the force of a Turner painting or a passage from Shelley. Their pages are replete with episodes of the resulting disharmony. Something both trivial and annoying usually intruded to undercut the sublime occasion. No sooner had sightseers marveled at the rays of the evening sun illuminating the Alpine peaks, feeling themselves removed from their earthly existence, than the mundane would interfere to compromise the moment and send it packing. Where now were the vast and the obscure landscapes, and where was that elevated feeling? In *Journals of Excursions in the Alps* (1845), William Brockedon was, at first, impressed by the savage grandeur and deep sense of solitude of Mont Blanc until he was greeted by a "fat and filthy landlady" who, "breathing the sweets of eau de vie and garlic," welcomed him to a place with dirty beds, rickety tables, and rotting food (38). And Eustace Anderson, who came to Chamonix (sometimes spelled "Chamounix" or "Chamoni") ten years later, with "romantic ideas" about the scenery, discovered that rather than staying at "the simple country inns" he "had been led to expect," there were large establishments, "with three *table d'hôtes* a day, warm baths, London porter, and every luxury" (31). Feeling confused by such circumstances, people turned to clichés they hoped would suffice and summoned them to substitute for the real sublime they had been anticipating.

The Tourist Invasion and English Preserves

One of the reasons for this disenchantment was, of course, a significant increase in the number of travelers to the Alps, from Germany, America, and Britain. People especially complained about the "British invasion" (Buzard 16). The necessary silence and solitude that were supposedly prerequisite for the sublime were no longer available. Instead, tourists were overwhelmed by their own kind as well as by the material and social practices of tourism. There was no escaping the confines of the socialized self. Such was the profusion of visitors that even the showman Albert Smith, who usually sought the attention of the populace through his books and panoramic entertainments, fled from a throng of tourists congregating in his hotel's lobby by taking refuge in the privacy of his bath (Smith, *The Story of Mont Blanc* 142). For most who journeyed to the Alps, the effect of these numbers was to compromise or enfeeble what they trusted would be a sublime experience. Crowds were disquieting to visitors who desired to leave behind the stress and business of home.

From the mid-century on there were more and more efficient ways of getting to places in the Alps – a circumstance that, according to Ruskin, metamorphosed a person into "a living parcel" (*Works* 8:159). There was, as James Buzard states, a vast infrastructure that supported tourism. And, of course, these newly opened routes disqualified these travelers' sense of the remote, the serene, and the inaccessible. Instead of having to rely upon a slow, long, and probably uncomfortable, ride in the diligence, there were now networks of railroad lines and tunnels to give easier and swifter access to the Alpine centers, such as the popular Chamonix, where people walked over the Mer de Glace, hiked or rode up the Montanvert, or admired Mont Blanc. Lynne Withey, in her study of the Grand Tour, recalls that in 1849 two Englishmen prepared a plan for a network of railways: "They proposed six main lines through the principal valleys, connected by steamboat services on the large lakes. By 1860, the basic components of this network were in place, and railroad mileage, which nearly doubled in the 1870s, continued to rise steadily." Simultaneously, she reminds us, there were schemes "to build funicular and cog railways in the high mountain regions, as well as the first tunnels through major Alpine passes" (198). It is interesting to note that one "extremely curious detail" of these plans caught the disgruntled attention of *The Alpine Journal* editors, who informed their readership of a scheme to build a tunnel up to the summit of Mont Blanc so that "a whole caravan of tourists may be transported in a few minutes without fear or fatigue." Directing their animadversions at the already overcrowded and increasingly commercialized features of the landscape, the editors sarcastically added

> Moreover it need not be thought that the enterprise would be a bad investment of capital. It is reckoned that annually 20,000 to 30,000 persons visit Chamoni; all of whom make one or more excursions to the neighbouring heights. Of this number, half at least, taking a very low estimate, would go to the top of Mont Blanc by means of the tunnel, as soon as ever it was opened. ("Observatory on the Summit of Mont Blanc," *The Alpine Journal* 2 [1865]: 221)

In response to the quantity of visitors, the number of hotels rose, many of which, as one can see from the disillusioned Eustace Anderson's complaint, were constructed with the comfort-seeking tourist in mind. Several of these, such as the Hôtel de Londres or the Hôtel d'Angleterre, were built for a British clientele. At these centers, instead of being encouraged to transcend the tawdry concerns of the everyday, guests found themselves thrown among, if not overwhelmed by, their own kind, attending English chapel and services, exchanging gossip at the *table d'hôte*, eating English mustard, and thinking about themselves almost exclusively within the social space of home. Miss Jemima, whom I have previously mentioned, was frustrated by this reality, and often found herself wedged between her desire for the boundlessness of the sublime and the considerably smaller confines of familiarity – located somewhere between the spirit and the distressingly physical. Her journal is replete with glimmerings of ethereal thought as well as devastating descriptions of tourists who were "Doing Switzerland jolly" (*Miss Jemima's Swiss Journal* 66). At one moment she is overpowered by "the grandeur of the matchless landscape," but, at another, she is soon succumbing to the pressures of her milieu that require her to make a presentable appearance out of her wet clothing at the dinner table (32). Caught between moments of exaltation and episodes of materiality, the sublime sat shriveled and limp among the folds of convention.

As Miss Jemima's dilemma suggests, these Alpine centers imposed a dreary conformity. One supposedly traveled to enter a new topography and to engage some sense of alterity, or perhaps to find an escape from the oppressive bondage of life. However, more often than not, the tourists found themselves thrust back into the realm of a social landscape they thought was across the sea and out of view. Indeed, the Alps were rapidly becoming known as an English-speaking preserve. Under these circumstances, people who were supposed to have experienced some sense of wonder or astonishment were presented with the all-too recognizable. The resulting familiarity of the hotel and its guests restricted any expansion of consciousness. One group of tourists, for instance, after viewing a thunderous avalanche (traditionally one of the most sublime experiences) from the sheltered prospect of a window at the Jungfrau Hotel, immediately turned to lunch (Bunny 26). Those, like Thomas Whitwell, who had come to the Alps with a desire to immerse themselves in the lofty and the profound – perhaps to touch the infinite –were disoriented by the hotel's visitor's book containing the names of acquaintances from home: "it felt strange to see a name one knew in such an out-of-the way place" (103).

Whitwell's discomfort was also Joseph Walker's, who was disappointed by the appearance of "a great many English," one of whom was an old Etonian he had known and who was "as mad as ever" (15 August 1850). Later, accompanied by yet another English friend, Walker ascended the Wengern Alp (6,061') and discovered two more of his countrymen on mules before him. An hour or so later, while smoking his pipe and attempting to enjoy the panoramic view of the looming Silberhorn, the Jungfrau, and the Eiger, he noticed "an invasion of English from the opposite direction" (17 September 1850). The sight of them promptly displaced what should have been majestic and transfixing. His experience resembles Whitwell's, who, in his 1860 "Alpine Log," also expressed his dismay that the chattering of his English companions about the latest opera at Covent Garden ruined the sublimity of a scene before him (29). At least neither Whitwell nor Walker had to listen, as did "Bunny," to a party of girls singing "God Save the Queen" on their way back down the glacier to the hotel (28). One also should not overlook the correspondence of Leslie Stephen's first wife, Minny, who, in 1867, wrote to her sister and complained that the place she and her husband were staying was

> swarming throughout with the most alarming kind of vermin ... to wit, fat
> sort of commercial travellers who plump into other people's chairs & yell for
> brandy & water toutdesuite, & women in scarlet with tartan petticoats of blowsy
> appearance, & a vile parson with a neckcloth like a tall white chimneypot, & a
> wretched crowd of limp beings with alpenstocks tipped with chamois horns –
> such as I never saw before in real life ... One creature said he had been driving in
> a charabanc up & down avalanches ... I am really disgusted. (Bicknell 1: 51)

Class

As Minny Stephen's biting words suggest, a predictable accompaniment to these reminders of England was the consciousness of class that was transported to these holiday centers. People continued to be entangled with the prejudices and limitations of their origins. The larger context of the sublime was not strong enough to counteract the familiar social hierarchy. Beginning in the mid-century, excursion companies made it possible for a significant number of lower-middle-class holidaymakers to find their way to the Alps – a change from the beginning of the century, when Alpine travel was still for the professional and upper-middle classes. This circumstance altered in the mid-1860s when Thomas Cook first offered Alpine tours to tradesmen as well as to the leisured classes, and especially to teetotalers. (He had originally developed these tours to keep people out of the pubs. His groups usually stayed in temperance hotels.) As the *Cook's Tourist's Handbook: Switzerland via Paris* (1874) proclaimed: "Now-a-days, everybody may travel, everybody ought to travel, – in fact, everybody does travel ... now the gentlemen of small means, the weary city clerk, the boys home for their holidays, all enter into the great highways of knowledge opened up by steam and rail" (1). Later these tourists were referred to as "common rail-borne trippers" (*The Saturday Review*, 12 August 1893. Scrapbook, Alpine Club Archives) or simply as "cockneys."

When Thomas Cook offered a new tour to Switzerland in 1863, over five hundred people applied (Swinglehurst 37). This opportunity was the beginning of a new mass market to the Alps. These groups particularly aroused class prejudices and annoyed those who despised being surrounded by mobs of "seedy-looking tourists" (*Cook's Tourist's Handbook* 66). Indeed, as a reaction, the rich began to set up their own enclaves. If one peruses mid-century issues of *The Excursionist*, Thomas Cook's magazine, one gets a sense of the growing popularity of the Alps as a holiday destination. Advertisements at the back offered descriptions of individuals seeking a traveling companion;[9] and inside there were articles announcing the building of new train routes, such as an 1868 piece on the "Mount Cenis Train." With the addition of all these excursionists, it is little wonder that people complained of how the Alps had become "a herding place" (Collie 168) and how the hotels were full of "Mr. Cook's army" (Chater 15 September 1865). The noise produced by such tourists was said to break the Romantic serenity of the night, especially when "every word, cough, or snore" was heard "through two or three rooms" (Longman and Trower 79). That night the tourist who had listed these grievances dreamed that the roofs of houses in England had become glaciers. The solitary and elevating sublime that many had been accustomed to reading about and had come to expect was receding faster than the glaciers sliding off the roofs of England (39). The excursions expunged any trace of its existence. As J. Norman Collie noted, if one chooses to

> talk about the merits of Claude and Turner as painters of hills, and even
> quote some of Ruskin's very finest passages about Alps and Archangles, your
> neighbour at *table d'hôte* will either think that you are a great bore, or, perhaps,
> an extremely clever person; but will be far more interested, when the old lady
> opposite begins to tell how Mr. Jones was caught that very afternoon proposing
> to Miss Robinson, & how the Bishop of X. is really coming to stop at the hotel
> for a few days. (169–70)

---

[9]   See advertisement in 8 July 1879 issue of *The Excurtionist*: "A Young Gentleman. Aged 19, wishes to meet with a suitable Companion to travel in Switzerland, about the middle of July, for a month or six weeks. An Oxford undergraduate preferred. Travelling expenses might be paid to an experienced man as Travelling Tutor. For particulars, address the Rev. A.G.C., 7, Lowndes Street, London, S.W."

Going up the Rigi

Of all the places that seemed in mid-century to attract the most crowds, and hence, criticism or disappointment was the Rigi (5,905') – a range near Lake Lucerne that, owing to its isolation, commands an extensive panorama and offers a magnificent view of the sunrise and sunset. Visits to the Rigi (sometimes spelled "Righi") were virtually required. It was on the route and part of an itinerary calculated to afford as many sublime sights as possible. As one tourist asserted, "it would never do for us not to ascend the Rigi. It would be like going to Rome and not seeing the Coliseum" (*Cook's Tourist's Handbook* 62). And they did go. According to the 1874 *Cook's Tourist's Handbook* "20,000 people get up it every year, one way or another" (65). Frances Ridley Havergal, the hymn composer, notes that when she went up, she was in the company of 200 people. Not surprisingly, this aspect of her trip was not "among the impressions of my life" (Crane 57). Here the sublime took one of its worst beatings.

Visitors of all shapes and sizes would either take the funicular (which opened in 1871) up to the summit or climb up the mountain on foot (it was a two hour and a quarter walk), ascend by mule or be carried in chairs, so that they might spend the night at the Rigi Kilm Hotel (5,905') and rise at 4:30 a.m.– with the help of a cow horn blown outside one's door – to see the splendor of the sun mounting over the prospect.

Then most guests would go back to bed, and, after eating breakfast, descend. *Punch's* "Almanack for 1868" features a charmingly funny sequence of cartoons depicting a "cockney" family going through these required steps and consuming the packaged view: "But when he'd got up to the top and the fog cleared off 'Lawes! It was a beautiful sight, worth all the money and trouble that it was!'"

Although holidaymakers often briefly found the view to be spectacular, more often than not, as I have said, something would intrude either to interrupt or to eradicate any trace of a sublime feeling they had been led to expect. A popular comic verse caught the resulting discontent; its lines are quoted in many of the tourists' diaries:

> Nine weary up-hill miles we sped the setting sun to see,
> Sulky and grim he went to bed, sulky and grim went we;
> Seven sleepless hours we tossed, and then the rising sun to see,
> Sulky and grim he rose again, sulky and grim rose we. (Jones 65)

The noise, the crowds, the bustle, and confusion conspired to wound or destroy any elevated feelings some might have had. The Reverend Harry Jones exclaimed, "I must confess I'm rather disappointed; I expected something more!" (*Cook's Tourist's Handbook* 66); Mrs. Robert Milne objected to the giggling of "some intense cockneys, who *would* keep chattering in a very loud tone of voice" (6), and declared that "I do think that all that is written about the Righi sunset is 'humbug'" (45) – she thought Scotland had much more to offer. Mrs. Milne and others also

Figure 1.1   Lord Pèzefort gravissant le Righi

complained of the damp sheets and the disarray of dress among the guests who
had simply jumped out of bed to see the sunrise. Milne especially objected to the
elderly ladies appearing rumpled and "without any hair but what nature had given,
or rather *left* them ... they *did* look miserable" (47). Similarly, a school teacher
who went on an 1852 summer tour of the Alps recorded that she had ascended the

Figure 1.2　　*Punch*'s Almanack for 1868

Rigi to see the sunrise, but, once there, had found herself more impressed by the guests' strange attire than by the spectacular view: "One gentleman had taken a blanket from his bed and wore it as a shawl; another had seized a counterpane … A French woman appeared with her night-cap under her bonnet." Disappointed, the school teacher confessed that although delighted with the landscape, "for the most part, I am afraid, thinking quite as much of the bitter wind and the oddity of our appearance, as of the grandeur of the scene around us" (Sewell 35). The sublime had been eclipsed by dress codes and social conventions. Her reaction is not unlike that of others who, while doing their best to appreciate the terror of the Mer de Glace – yet another required portion of the tourist's itinerary – could not help but think of how silly everyone looked, especially within the context of what should have been uplifting. In August 1844, Robert Snow, a tourist, looked about him and noted:

> Whilst we were in the middle of the glacier, I could not help remarking what ridiculous figures we all were, equipped with blouses, frieze gaiters, green spectacles, veils, and slouched hats, passing along with the most solemn gravity. Devouassoud [the guide], in particular, with huge spectacles, and his hat tied on with a handkerchief under his chin, supporting himself with his stick, was no bad representation of Mother Goose. (95)

Just as overwhelmed by the great many people staying at the Rigi Kilm Hotel, Miss Sewell in her 1852 journal grumbled:

> the hotel is so full that persons are not allowed to have separate rooms ... And such a noise and confusion! I long for it [the supper] to be over. The number of people one meets here, the guides and the ponies, the calling, and talking and the preparation for coffee, tea, and supper, and all that one requires, makes a very odd medley; and I could find it in my heart to wish that I could be on the top of the Righi alone, or at least with very few people. (34)

She was one of many tourists who had come clutching her edition of Byron. Miss Jemima, the Cook tourist, also felt dissatisfied. At first the sunrise on the Rigi was, in her eyes, "impressively sublime;" in "hushed silence" she looked upon "a scene of awful beauty! Strangely emotional you will believe, and indelible in its sublime impressions," but all disappeared when a hive of tourists arrived to swarm about her (*Miss Jemima's Swiss Journal* 86, 84). Whatever obscurity or uncertainty, which Burke had identified as being a generally necessary condition of sublimity, vanished and was replaced by the intrusive presence of the all-too familiar. These sightseers had forgotten that one does not go looking for the sublime; rather, it should descend upon one.

The necessary element of solitude was not only absent on the Rigi but in all the places invaded by tourists. The complaint was common. In Britain itself it tended to be attached to Snowdon. "Mr. Perk's Mountain Experience," Parts I and II, in the 27 September and 11 October 1856 issues of *Punch*, follows the progress of Mr. Perk's ascent up to Snowdon's summit. On the way up he stops to contemplate the mountain and imagines himself at one with nature – that is, until he reaches the top where a "crowd of cockney tourists" swarm around the peak that is itself sullied by all manner of commercial buildings. Full of contempt, he "grows scornful of his species, and sighs for solitude and determines to plunge into the bosom of the eternal hills in search of it" (130). Unlucky Mr. Perk: he eventually finds solitude, but a less than sublime version of it, when bored, lonely, and slouching in an armchair at the inn. The caption reads: "Mr. Perk continues his search after solitude. He finds it at the Pen-y-gwr-yd Inn, Nant-Gwynant, and doesn't like it at all" (150).

Selling the Sublime

As Mr. Perk's mountain experience suggests, the inevitable attendant commercialism also spoiled other occasions and kept the tourists' minds attached to the limits of their everyday lives. Miss Jemima's attempts to participate in the sublime were disqualified not only by the hordes surrounding her but also by the fact that she and her companions were continually being pressed to purchase something. As she admitted, she had come to the Alps to "leave the fashion of this world at a distance," but to her dismay, she had heard

MR. PERKS'S MOUNTAIN EXPERIENCES. PART I.

MR. PERKS DETERMINING ON A TOUR IN NORTH WALES, PURCHASES A KNAPSACK OF MOST SCIENTIFIC, BUT EXTREMELY COMPLICATED CONSTRUCTION.

MR. PERKS PRACTISES THE KNAPSACK EXERCISE: AND FINDS THE SCIENTIFIC ARTICLE HE HAS PURCHASED VERY DIFFICULT TO GET INTO, AND BY NO MEANS EASY TO GET OUT OF.

MR. PERKS LEAVES THE CARRNARVON TRAIN AT 5½ A.M., AND FINDING NO COACH, SCORNS CIVILISATION, AND DETERMINES TO START FOR THE MOUNTAINS: Air.—"'way, away, to the mountain's brow!"

MR. PERKS AND THE WIND BOTH COME ON TO BLOW.

MR. PERKS REACHES THE VICTORIA HOTEL, LLANBERRIS, AND AT SIGHT OF A WAITER AND SMELL OF BREAKFAST, ADMITS CIVILISATION HAS ITS ADVANTAGES.

MR. PERKS CONTEMPLATES THE MOUNTAINS, AND FOR A MOMENT IMAGINES HIMSELF WILLIAM TELL, IS FORMING HIS NATIVE HILLS, HE IS WITH THEM ONCE AGAIN.

MR. PERKS IN THE PRESENCE OF THE HILLS, GROWS SCORNFUL OF HIS SPECIES, AND SIGHS FOR SOLITUDE AND DETERMINES TO PLUNGE INTO THE BOSOM OF THE ETERNAL HILLS IN SEARCH OF IT. HE REACHES THE TOP OF SNOWDON BUT DOES NOT FIND SOLITUDE—ONLY A LARGE ASSORTMENT OF BEER-BOTTLES AND A CROWD OF COCKNEY TOURISTS.

Figure 1.3a Mr. Perks's Mountain Experiences, Part I

nothing but the irritating cries of the Swiss wanting to sell their cherries. The persistence of their cry, "*Vingt centimes, Vingt centimes!*" had rung in her ears and put to flight "our dreams of history, of valour, of poetry and beauty." She soon realized that "tourists are the staple commodity in the twenty-two cantons

MR. PERKS'S MOUNTAIN EXPERIENCES. PART II.

MR. PERKS TURNS HIS BACK ON SNOWDON IN DISGUST, INFORMING THE UNABASHED MOUNTAIN THAT HE CONSIDERS HIM A REGULAR DO!

MR. PERKS CONTINUES HIS SEARCH AFTER SOLITUDE. HE FINDS IT AT THE PEN-Y-GWR-YD INN, NANT-GWYNANT, AND DOESN'T LIKE IT AT ALL.

MR. PERKS FINDS THERE IS A GENTLEMAN IN THE HOUSE WHO WILL BE GLAD TO JOIN HIM IN HIS SITTING-ROOM. THE STRANGER IS GRIM AND CLERICAL, AND ENLIVENS MR. PERKS BY AN ACCOUNT OF ALL THE TOURISTS WHO HAVE FALLEN OVER THE CLIFFS FOR THE LAST TEN YEARS

MR. PERKS, NOT TO BE DAUNTED, JOINS AN ADVENTUROUS CRAGSMAN, BOTANIST, GEOLOGIST, AND FISHERMAN, IN A LITTLE WALK

OVER THE "GLYDDER VAWR" IN SEARCH OF "ANTHERICUM SABATINUM." MR. PERKS HAS PREVIOUSLY SOAPED HIS STOCKINGS INSIDE, WHICH PRODUCES A CHILLY FEELING ABOUT THE FEET.

VIEW OF MR. PERKS'S BOOTS AS THEY APPEARED BEFORE THE LITTLE WALK.

* N.B. *Mr. Punch* begs, from personal experience, to recommend this Inn to those of his numerous acquaintance who wish to explore Snowdonia. They may not find solitude, but they will find capital quarters, first-rate cookery, and a moderate bill.

Figure 1.3b Mr. Perks's Mountain Experiences, Part II

of Switzerland." Like "parasites," the people "feed upon us, or rather feed us" (*Miss Jemima's Swiss Journal* 67, 79). The anonymous author in *Curiosities of Modern Travel* (1847) also fell prey to the commercial spirit. After having remarked on the "overpowering sublimity" of the appearance of the Jungfrau and having marveled at the roar of the avalanche, he met a vender selling strawberries, cakes, and cream, and shortly became preoccupied with haggling for a good price. Losing sight of grandeur, he triumphantly noted, "For a dish of strawberries he charged only a single *batz*, or three cents" (11). Also intrigued by a little cannon that the vender carried from place to place in order to set off avalanches for tourists to see – the cost of firing was only "half the sum" of the strawberries – his attention was once more diverted to more immediate matters. This intrusion of economics into the sublime landscape also gets an airing in William Smith's 1864 *Adventures with my Alpen-Stock and Carpet-Bag*. He was disgusted when he opened the hotel's guest register and found, among various expressions extolling the sublimity of the mountain scenery, harsh complaints about the hotel's exorbitant charges (47).

The Satires

By the second half of the nineteenth century, the disparity between experience
and expectation, mentioned by so many tourists, nourished and dominated
satirical cartoons. In one of the London Alpine Club's scrapbooks, there is a late
nineteenth-century cartoon, "Un Drole [*sic*] de Cervin," that makes fun of the
disappointment suffered by those in search of the sublime. The cartoon initially
shows three people admiring an Alpine peak (the Cervin) from afar. They exclaim,
"*la superbe montagne!*" However, after rambling on a few miles and descending
to another perspective, they discover that what they had thought to be a sublime
object is merely a trivial, triangular, wooden structure, no taller than they. Their
astonishment, as well as the sublime, stands corrected, and reduced.

By exaggerating the tourists' complaints and disappointments, comic novels
and dramas about the continental tour also accelerated this deflation. These
satires made explicit what had settled uneasily just beneath the surface in
tourists' accounts of their days visiting Chamonix, spending the night at the
Great St. Bernard, ascending the Rigi, and traveling over the Splügen Pass. See,
for instance, "How, When, and Where? Or, the Modern Tourist's Guide to the
Continent" in the 31 October 1863 issue of *Punch*; books, such as Albert Smith's
The Adventures of Mr. Ledbury (1844) or his *Christopher Tadpole* (1848), Charles
Lever's *The Dodd Family Abroad* (1854), Richard Doyle's *The Foreign Tour of
Messrs Brown, Jones, and Robinson* (1855),[10] or Arthur Sketchley's *Mrs. Brown
on the Grand Tour* (1871). And take a look at Alfred Thompson's play *Linda of
Chamouni* (1869). In these scathingly funny and deliberately subversive tracts,
the sinking of the sublime had become unmistakable. Just as it had occasionally
done for the Miss Jemimas, the William Smiths, and the Miss Sewells, the lofty
descended to the level of the domestic realm. Taking advantage of this downward
course, *Punch* exaggerated the domestication of the sublime by announcing:
"Good News for Cockney Travellers," Mont Blanc was about to be carpeted
(*Punch* 27: 110).

Not surprisingly tourists caught sight of themselves among these satirical
images. E.D. Wynne Jones, for instance, in his *General Description of My Late
Tour through France, Switzerland and Germany* (1867), quite happily identified
with Arthur Sketchley's ludicrous Mrs. Brown, who sulked just as much as
he had done when the clouds blocked a view of the sun rising over the Rigi.
These sightseers would have appreciated Antonio (Linda's "heavy father" in
Thompson's *Linda of Chamouni*) grumbling about the railroads disturbing the
tranquility of the Alps and complaining about the strange noises coming from
"British Tourists" in an adjoining room. Even though they might themselves
have been among Cook's tourists, these readers would have enjoyed Antonio's
quip, "Too many *Cooks* must spoil our native potage" (33). Most of all, though,
they would have recognized the satirical texts' amplifying the commodification

---

[10]   These surnames are listed in an early Thesaurus as a synonym for "common."

of the sublime. They would have been familiar with Antonio's despair at being charged two florins to watch an avalanche – a sight, as I have pointed out, that was popularly supposed to be "truly sublime" and was thought to "awaken an impression not to be described, but never to be forgotten" (Beattie 96):

> Apartments for one week at eighty francs,
> Ten more for snow which melted thro' the planks,
> To seeing sunrise ev'ry morn; 2 florins
> To view of avalanche and mountain *Torrins*. (Thompson 8)

Recognizing just how intrusive costs could be, these tourists would have also been drawn toward the mocking humor of Albert Smith's *The Adventures of Mr. Ledbury*, especially to occasions when the annoyingly jovial voice of Mr. ("jolly cocks") Crinks deflated Mr Ledbury's enjoyment of a "sublime view" by abruptly reminding him that he needed to pay for a room at the Rigi Kilm Hotel (3: 171).[11] In other narratives, such as *Mrs. Brown on the Grand Tour, Haps and Mishaps of the Simpleton Family Abroad,* or *The Dodd Family Abroad,* much of the satire emanates from this positioning of the sublime object within an economic context. Wordsworth's anxiety about "Getting and spending" finds its comic correlative. Mrs. Dodd, for instance, even when looking upon a wild and dreadful mountainous prospect, worthy of a Turner, worries that the "the enjoyments" of gazing upon it "costs us something over eighteen pounds!" (Lever 185). The strength of the pound had easily deflated the value of the sublime.

Satirizing Terror

In addition to picking up on tourists' protests about crowds and commerce, the satires in the second half of the nineteenth century frequently concentrated upon what Burke and his contemporaries had identified as being among the essential causes of the sublime: the feelings of terror, pain, and danger accompanied by the paradoxical experience of delight. As Burke had proclaimed, "Whatever is fitted in any sort to excite the ideas of pain and danger, that is to say, whatever is in any sort terrible, or is conversant about terrible objects, or operates in a manner analogous to terror, is a source of the *sublime*" (33). In order to sink the sublime, satirists targeted this aspect of the sublime and disparaged tourists' attempts to recount precipitous, but minor, descents or frightening rides over a mountain pass.[12] Their texts mocked

---

[11]   When asked where the St. Bernard convent is, Mr. Crinks replies: "Close at hand. The Simplon convent. I've been staying there a week; jolly cocks!" (Albert Smith, *The Adventures of Mr. Ledbury* 3:234).

[12]   I should note that the satirists generally did not exercise their criticism upon climbers who were going up much higher and taking greater risks. The satirists, rather, reserved their wit for those who only flirted with danger. I should add, though, that even in the minor elevations a person was not completely free of peril.

excursionists, like Catherine Winkworth, who wrote in her journal of an Alpine road that "winds steeply down for miles between enormous precipices so high that you can see only a narrow strip of sky above you while below rushes the torrent." As if aware of Burke's or John Baillie's theories of the sublime, she added: "Really, sometimes the road was frightful – not that I felt frightened, beyond a pleasant degree, but Mamma was quite unhappy once or twice" (403). Indeed, some terrified tourists had early on blindfolded themselves so as not to tremble.

Sightseers like these were easy targets. The satirists pointed out that the intense danger their characters were supposedly subjected to had absolutely no mortal consequences; the terror was negligible and the situations were ridiculous. The Dodds caught in an avalanche thought only of their baggage that had gone hurtling down the mountainside and was now lost; they never thought of their own demise as a possibility (Lever 183). Others slipped, plummeted, and grimaced, but their condition was by no means a harbinger of death. A fall was a lark – a jolly tumble down – and a nose-dive into a crevasse was not life threatening. It was all part of what Miss Jemima had identified as "doing Switzerland Jolly." The hysterical Mrs. Brown, who feared going over the "pressypitch" that overhangs a "'undreds of thousands of miles" drop (Sketchley 41), and the stout Mrs. Simpleton who tumbled "H'over the *precious*" and into a ravine while traversing the Splügen Pass ("Bell" 62) were certainly not in any danger. Their rolling figures, their soft landings, and their floundering did them no harm. After about twenty tumbles, these "heroic" figures were hauled up again, none the worse for wear. Terror is laughed off the page.

Humorous illustrations also participated in this discrediting by highlighting broad rumps and ridiculous postures of travelers attempting to keep astride recalcitrant mules or clinging to their unsteady seats as they wound their way round a mountain pass's dangerously narrow and precipitous edges. Doyle's *The Foreign Tour of Messrs Brown, Jones, and Robinson* (1855) is replete with delicious images of three friends frantically clinging to a diligence as it rounds a sharp, steep bend on their descent of the St. Gothard. The caption ironically reads: "Having taken their places on the outside of the diligence, Brown, Jones, and Robinson can the better enjoy the grandeur of the scenery" (43). To play with Burke's phrase, their ridiculous predicament "press[es] too nearly" (34); their banal apprehension negates any sense of grandeur. In other illustrations these three slide down mountainsides with arms and legs helplessly outspread.

Doyle remarks, "the safest way of coming down a mountain" (40). And how right he is. Within the context of the humor, Brown, Jones, and Robinson will survive, get up, and start all over again.

Gender and Satire

Predictably, in these satires, gender makes its stereotypical appearance. As is widely recognized, the sublime has often been associated with masculine power, manly vigor, and depth of understanding. It has traditionally been part of a discourse of domination. However, in these satirical texts, the feminine, more often than not, has

Figure 1.4   Richard Doyle. "The Safest Way of Coming Down a Mountain"

the ascendancy. The "too ponderous" Mrs. Simpleton literally falls on top of her husband ("Bell" 6). Nearly suffocating him, she reduces him to a figure "sawing the air in wild distraction" (51). Although there are many equally ridiculous male characters in these satires, it is primarily the feminine figure who looms large to obstruct the way to what is lofty and elevated. Her hysterics block any refined response to the wild Alpine topography and interrupt any significant moment of peril. This tactic is actually one area in which the satirists do not take their cue from the tourists' diaries, for the sightseers' entries reveal little sense of a gender divide – a topic I address in Chapter 3.

In many of the comic pieces, the feminine offers no egress from the sensory world that Schiller had proposed in his thoughts about the sublime (201).[13] Young

---

[13]   As an example of these points, consider that "Mr. Simpleton ... was in a dying state, and looked quite decreased in size, from the heavy weight that had been pressing

beautiful women divert men from their elevated ambitions – like climbing a mountain or appreciating a view. Still more potent, though, are the "colossal" Mrs. Simpletons ("Bell" 56), the Mrs. Browns, and the Mrs. Dodds, who keep themselves and all around them very much in the lowlands of Parnassus. Whatever higher thoughts a person might have had are obliterated by these figures' "elephantine" presence ("Bell" 55). These matrons literally cannot ascend from the corporeal to sustain a visionary flight or to endure the trials of the sublime. (Recall, Mrs. Simpleton falls off precipices while Mrs. Dodd also falls off the sledge and takes a "header" [Lever 183].) These more than "ample form[s]" ("Bell" 51) overpower everything and literally replaces what commentators of the sublime had proposed was the vastness of Nature. Consequently, when the guides attempt to place Mrs. Simpleton back upon her mule, they cannot get hold of her: "It was a work of danger and difficulty ... four men were employed for the purpose, and even then, were half-an-hour about it" ("Bell" 52). Her beautiful daughter, Maria, also blows up into a larger size. Contrary to advice, Maria insists on wearing her crinoline while winding her way on the Mauvais Pas, a steep and narrow passage leading from the Mer de Glace. A tremendous gust of wind comes and turns her into "a species of balloon" (55).

The trope is familiar. In "Turgidus Alpinus," an 1869 satirical poem written by an undergraduate at St. John's College, Cambridge, "A matron who weighed twenty stones" (223) blocks the writer's progress on Mont Anvert, and in Albert Smith's *Christopher Tadpole*, Mrs. Gudge, with her stentorian voice on the Great Saint Bernard, threatens everyone. She becomes a deliberately preposterous version of that "mighty being" who "with her eternal motion makes/ A Sound like thunder" (from Wordsworth's "It is a beauteous Evening"). Even the cover of a board game entitled *Voyage en Suisse* (c. 1870) features a rotund, mature woman with thick woolen stockings and an alpenstock. As in the other caricatures, her "Greatness of Dimension" displaces and caricatures the "vastness of extent, or quantity" that Burke identifies as one of the most powerful causes of the sublime (37).

Language and the Sinking of the Sublime

Although these comic figures are effective in leveling or sinking the sublime, they are not nearly as efficient through their appearance as is their use – or rather, misuse – of language. One is reminded of Alexander Pope's *Peri Bathous* (*Martinus Scriblerus ... Or, Of the Art of Sinking in Poetry*, 1727). In that treatise, already well-aware that people too frequently feel compelled to praise the sublime, Pope identified the rhetorical means by which bad poets drive any lofty emotion off the heights of Parnassus down to the lowlands where Bathos is alive and well. Mrs. Simpleton's screams may wound the Alpine prospect, but her words mortify

him down" ("Bell" 52). And then consider Schiller's statement that "the sublime affords us an egress from the sensuous world in which the beautiful would 'gladly hold us forever captive'" (Schiller 201).

it. Agitated, she gazes at the grand spectacle of the Mer de Glace and exclaims, "We're not h'a-going to cross h'all that h'ere h'ice, h'are we?" ("Bell" 57). Mrs. Brown announces: "'Mountings is all werry well, but,' I says, 'level ground is quite good enough for me'" (Sketchley 104). Her bad French helps to hasten the descent, "Dela boure, sivel play" (38) – "Butter, if you please" – as does her habit of referring to the "Halps" (42). Mrs. Simpleton does not help. She comments upon the "Chair-bang" – *Char-à-bane* – and the "Spillikin" – the Splügen Pass ("Bell" 42, 50). Her husband's awful puns also speed the decline. (Pope had identified puns as being among the worst offenders.) When, with difficulty – "his face is of a highly florid character" – Mr. Simpleton crossed a mountain pass, he proclaimed, "to what a *pass* am I reduced!" ("Bell" 61). In a similar vein, Mr. and Mrs. Dodd bicker (and have thoughts of divorce courts) while crossing the Simplon Pass. After the altercation, the wife remarks, "And that's the way we crossed the Alps" (Lever 187) – another example of a satirist twisting Wordsworth's reaction to crossing the Alps in *The Prelude*, Book VI. With their nattering, the Dodds have once more distorted some of the most sublime lines in British literature.[14]

Nothing, however, presses down more heavily on the sublime than the metaphors that make, in Pope's words, "a Prince talk like a Jack-pudding" – when the profound is compared to an idea or image that is below it (314). The satirical texts are replete with these unfortunate metaphors. There is no echo of Longinus's sense of a great soul here (see Longinus 72). An avalanche is compared to the "bursting of a champagne bottle" or to "a thousand weird voices ... chuckling at some distance" (*Cook's Tourist's Handbook* 83, 115), and Mont Blanc is portrayed as smoking a cigar. More damaging is the tendency to associate the grand with the domestic, as when Mrs. Dodd gazes at the deep snow and immediately thinks of an egg-pudding (Lever 186). Even those, like the Simpletons and the Dodds, who have already descended to the plains, sink even deeper through metaphors used to describe them. After falling on the ice, Mr. Simpleton struggles wildly "with his arms and legs sticking up, like a peculiarly stout tortoise when turned over" ("Bell" 58) and his wife flounders "like a great porpoise" (6). A drunk Mr. Gudge has "fishy eyes" (Smith, *Christopher Tadpole* 292).

When the satirical texts used language as a way of deflating the sublime, they were not only recalling the Longinian model and taking their cue from texts like Pope's *Peri Bathous*; they were also continuing to pick up cues from tourists' accounts of their Alpine travel, especially the sightseers' own impatience with the clichés that tracked or hounded them wherever they might go. From time to time, a person would register frustration with the tired phrases that undercut an appreciation of the mountains. William Smith, in his *Adventures with my Alpen-Stock and Carpet-Bag* (1864), protested, for instance, that he and his fellow tourists grew weary of repeatedly using the same expressions. He admitted: "It must be

---

[14] Wordsworth wrote to his sister a few days after he first crossed the Simplon Pass: "I had not a thought of man, or a single created being, my whole soul was turned to him who produced the terrible majesty before us" (de Selincourt 279–80).

confessed that before we reached Chamouni ... our vocabulary of laudatory epithets got very threadbare, and we began mutually to bore and be bored by one another" (46). Similarly, the anonymous author of *How We Did Them in Seventeen Days!* cynically recorded:

> It has been suggested that a short list of adjectives, epithets, etc., which may be frequently heard on board Rhine steamers, or along Swiss routes, ought to be useful. I therefore readily give them according to our experience, and I will add that my readers are at liberty to insert any of them, according to circumstances, throughout the ensuing pages, at their discretion. (19)[15]

Other travelers also found fault with pompous companions who give vent to their admiration "in a ridiculously practical and prosaic manner" (Whitwell 21) or complained, as did Grace, one of the young women climbers who ascended Mont Blanc on 20 August 1874, about how "shoppy travellers do get" and how they are besieged by "small-talk" (*Swiss Notes by Five Ladies* 31).

Tourists' journals are also punctuated with conventional expressions of verbal inadequacy: "No words of mine can paint the scene, it baffles description" (Bradford 26); "Words fail me to describe the beauty of that night" (Hobday 19); "It is difficult to describe the almost awful appearance which this mountain [the Matterhorn] presents from this point where we stood" (Heath 24, 22 September 1852 letter to sister Louisa), or "one scene was spread out before our eyes, the grandeur of which no language of mine can depict" (William Smith, Jr. 52). These disclaimers prove the justice of Pope's sense that one way of sinking the sublime is to resort to the Aposiopesis, an "excellent figure for the Ignorant." One proclaims, "What shall I say?" when one has nothing to say (Pope 331). In other words, what appears to be an overwhelming reaction to a sublime landscape is really an acknowledgment of

---

[15]   The author makes three columns of adjectives:

Lovely	Picturesque	Comprehensive
Superb	Rich	Heavenly
Magnificent	Unique	Diversified
Very pretty	Interesting	Calcareous
Exceptional	Extensive	Venerable
Unexceptional	Incomparable	Impressive
Beautiful	Pleasing	Huge
Glorious	Delightful	Inaccessible
Fine	Perky	Perpendicular
Gorgeous	Awe-inspiring	Varied
Grand	Fertile	Bold
Fairy-like	Commanding	Shaded
Imposing	Grotesque	Exposed
Unequalled	Panoramic	Remarkable
Handsome	etc.	etc. (19–20)

the concept's emptiness. All that remains is the pressure to say something and the compulsion to feel a sense of grandeur, terror, delight, and loss of self. For these tourists, the sublime, as Pope had suggested, was an ideal which tradition had taught them to desire, but had indeed been "perverted by custom" (309). Language unmasked what was increasingly true: that there was a void within the experience of the sublime. The second part of this chapter tracks this phenomenon. Part 2, "Above the Snow Line," follows the sublime as it begins to lose both its meaning and its abode among the grand mountains. The discussion follows the sublime as it finally surrenders to the indifference of those more interested in power and empire as well as to those more intent on exploring the ordinary life below. Its decline is matched by the growth of the realistic novel in the second half of the nineteenth century.

Part 2: Above the Snow Line

Climbing and the Sublime

As many commentators have already observed, during the second half of the nineteenth century, the so-called "cockneys," and "common rail-borne trippers," described above were increasingly held in contempt, especially by those who were convinced of the packaged tours' inability to offer an authentic experience. Not caring to be thought of as mere sightseers, the more privileged travelers to the Alps endeavored to flee the reach of Mr. Cook's troupes. Scorning places like Chamonix, a center that Ruskin compared to a fashionable Chelsea riverside (Ring 61), or Zermatt, where, according to Leslie Stephen, there were people so boring that they seemed "ludicrously incapable of anything" (Bicknell 2: 358), they sought the more "real" or legitimate experience by either going elsewhere or ascending to higher altitudes, above the snow line. Stephen longed to separate himself from "Ladies in costumes, heavy German professors, Americans doing the Alps at a gallop" as well as the homegrown Cook's tourists (*The Playground of Europe* 287). For the most part these people were successful, for they certainly were not as subject to satire as were the more common tourists they deplored.

Starting in the 1840s, British climbers in particular wanted to assert their superiority – physically, intellectually, and morally – by climbing away from the trappings of civilization, to areas "less charged by the invading swarms of tourists crawling over and scratching their surfaces," and where, according to Clinton Dent, "Nature triumphs without an effort over the vulgarity of man" ("The Alpine Court at the Liverpool Jubilee Exhibition," *The Alpine Journal* 13 [1887]: 338). On another occasion, Dent also suggested that to find such a region was "like stepping out of a crowded ballroom on to a verandah, or gliding away in a gondola from the railway station at Venice" (*Above the Snow Line* 21). To Alfred Wills of the Alpine Club, it was as if he were donning a new self or a new body.[16]

---

[16] See "Mountaineering and Health" in Dent, *Mountaineering*, 77–94.

In their attempts to separate themselves from the common tourists, a number of British climbers chose to cling to the culture of the sublime so that they might dignify or lend a certain nobility to their expeditions. Consequently, while describing an ascent of Monte Rosa, Thomas Hinchliff emphasized "the grander and wilder features of the scenery" (vi). He urged his climbing companions to pause and gaze at the glorious spectacle of the Matterhorn behind them, "looking like a huge pyramid of beautiful fire rising out of the barren ocean of ice and rock around it" (107). In a similar mode, other mountaineers celebrated "the solitude, and inconceivable grandeur of ... mighty glaciers and thundering avalanches" (S.W. King 441); still others spoke of their "awe" as they clambered up the end of a glacier (Tyndall, *The Glaciers of the Alps* 11). Alpinists, such as Alfred Wills, wrote of the "sublime and wonderful" scenes that left one with a "profound and almost irrepressible emotion" (Lunn 46). And, as did many others, Stephen intimated that climbing was connected with "all that is noblest in human nature" (*The Playground of Europe* 65).

Any number reached for well-rehearsed clichés to extol a prospect's "savage sublimity" (Derwent Conway 118) or a mountain's "savage magnificence" (Tyndall, *The Glaciers of the Alps* 11). Not wishing to be thought of as "mere scramblers" (Stephen, *The Playground of Europe* 296), a majority of climbers also insisted that their pleasure in scaling steep ascents in no way made them "insensible of all that is beautiful in nature" (Mummery 234). Frederick Pollock rejected the caricature of the Alpinist as someone who "regarded mountains merely as objects of athletic ambition" (425). It is interesting to note that the Alpine Club also encouraged an aesthetic appreciation by sponsoring annual exhibits of mountain paintings – a practice that continues today.[17]

These climbers' desire to distinguish themselves by clambering up to the more elevated regions of the sublime was not, however, always easy to realize, nor was it ultimately guaranteed to be successful. The sublime was not necessarily awaiting their arrival. As Emily Hornby observed in her *Mountaineering Records*, in spite of going higher (to 9,625'), the "click of alpenstocks" (10) was everywhere – and so were empty champagne bottles.[18] Furthermore, as Stephen remarked, when en route to climbing the Rothhorn (9,790'), some of the paths were distressingly within "a short walk of the main post route and Mr. Cook's tourists" (*The Playground of Europe* 90).[19]

---

[17]   Recently the Keeper of Pictures of the Alpine Club, Peter Mallalieu, edited *The Artists of the Alpine Club: A Biographical Dictionary* (2007). Many of the climbers are artists.

[18]   In *The Miscellany: A Book for the Field or the Fire-side: Amusing Tales and Sketches* (1850), Albert Smith remarks: "We saw several corks and broken bottles lying about, which gave traces of former revelers having been to the Jardin" (45).

[19]   Both Hornby and Stephen might have been relieved to read in the 1865 edition of the *Guide to Cook's Tours in France, Switzerland and Italy* that at least one tour company did not "pretend to rise with those whose ambition carries them to the top of Mont Blanc"

Ultimately, though, it was not these persistently intrusive reminders of the world below the snow line that spoiled their intentions but the very nature of climbing itself. As fervently as many climbers wished to adhere to the nobility of the sublime and to stay connected to their nation's literary heritage, the overwhelming pressure to conquer summits and to tread where no person had been before at first compromised and then eventually replaced the impulse to dwell upon, or even mention, the "savage sublime." With the passing of time, whatever remnants of the sublime sensibility remained surrendered to familiarity, to technology, to the all-too-real encounters with danger and death, and, perhaps, most of all, to a nation's desire to be in control and to exhibit a self-mastery. The more pressing need for domination supplanted the condition of the sublime, which required the loss of self or the willingness to forget oneself in the presence of something greater. Although phrases such as "lofty ideas," a "Presence and a Power which are not of the earth" and "unqualified sublimity" (William H. Adams 18, 111, 112) were still circulating at the end of the century, they were uttered less frequently and, when repeated, sounded increasingly hollow. John Tyndall's earlier sense of the "transcendent glory of Nature" (*Mountaineering in 1861* 58) was rapidly fading.

Familiarity

One of the main reasons why the sublime had become elusive was that the Alps were almost too familiar; the more people came and climbed, the more obscurity and mystery were dispelled by the mundane and predictable force of the routine and the charted.[20] Looking back to the earlier days of climbing, Clinton Dent, in his presidential address to the Alpine Club, complained: "expeditions once considered formidable have now ceased to be so estimated" (*The Alpine Journal* 15 [1890]: 11). Starting in the mid-century, for instance, even ascents of Mont Blanc (15,800'), once thought of as being unreachable and majestic, had virtually become commonplace.[21] This revered mountain, described by Shelley, Byron, and Coleridge, had lost its identity as a "dread ambassador from Earth to Heav'n" (Samuel Taylor Coleridge 200) and had become the scene of many a "cockney" or merely recreational expedition, a consequence that perhaps Thomas Hood anticipated when he wrote "An Asssent to the Summut of Mount Blank" for his 1832 *Comic Annual*. In this satirical sketch, a servant, who has reluctantly followed

---

(32), but they would have been painfully aware of the railways creeping closer and closer to the foot of the mountains and even, believe it or not, threatening to reach the summits of the Wengern Alps and the Jungfrau.

[20] As an example of how meticulously the Alps were charted, see F.F. Tuckett's 29 July 1859 letter to Thomas Hinchliff (2–3) in which he meticulously draws diagrams and routes to support his description of a climb (Alpine Club Archives).

[21] One earlier account of a climb is Martin Barry's *Ascent to the Summit of Mont Blanc in 1834*.

his master to the top of the mountain, announces that all around him was: "Such Sno! And ice enuf to serve all the Fish Mungers, and the grate Routs till the end of the Wurld!" (54). For him, the sublime is comparable to "a twelf Cake" – an ornamented cake baked to celebrate the twelfth night (51).

A historian of mountaineering, Jeremy Bernstein, reckons that between 1786 and 1829, there had been only 19 recorded climbs of Mont Blanc, whereas between 1829 and 1856, there had been 75 (50). But by the time of the so-called "Golden Age" of climbing, the number of attempts had multiplied so that between the mid-1850s and the 1870s a great many more people were reaching its summit. In a sense, an ascent of Mont Blanc had become for the climbers what going up the Rigi was for the tourists' world. The Reverend G.F. Browne's account of his 1865 expedition to the top of Mont Blanc can hardly progress without his mentioning bumping into other parties or even into solitary climbers on their way up or down the mountain. He is particularly offended by their common behavior and their habit of leaving behind their debris.[22] As Anthony Trollope exclaimed in 1866: "to have gone up Mont Blanc was [formerly] a feat which almost opened the gates of society to the man who had done it; but Mont Blanc is now hardly more than equal to the golden ball on the top of St. Paul's Cathedral" ("The Alpine Club Men" 92). C.T. Dent once made fun of a pretentious young man who claimed to have completed "the thousand-and-first ascent of Mont Blanc" (*Above the Snow Line* 131). By 1892, even a honeymooning couple stood at its summit so that they might embrace and swear "eternal fidelity towards one another in presence of their guides" (Scrapbook, Alpine Club Archives).[23]

To add insult to injury, Mont Blanc had become not only increasingly accessible but also, as a consequence, marketable. The mountain that had inspired a kingdom of poets was now a product that reminded people that Britain was a commercial nation. With lay readers as well as climbers in mind, books, guides, and articles describing various ascents of the mountain appeared on booksellers' shelves; souvenir handkerchiefs and fans featuring Mont Blanc were available, and parlor amusements, such as *The New Game of the Ascent of Mont Blanc* went on sale. Plays and panoramas/dioramas featuring the mountain were also not uncommon. Henry and Athol Mayhew's satire *Mont Blanc: A Comedy in Three Acts* opened at the Theatre Royal Haymarket in 1874. The play follows the adventures of a Mr. Chirpey, whose ambition it is to put his advertisement for pickles, "Persuasive Pickles," up on the summit of Mont Blanc (35). This production had not forgotten Albert Smith's earlier spectacular and long-running entertainment, *Ascent of Mont Blanc*, in which Smith had elaborately narrated his 13 August 1851 climb of the mountain. Appropriately, the script featured a tourist parodying Byron:

---

[22] See Browne's "How We Did Mont Blanc."

[23] Upon their return to Chamonix, according to an 8 November 1897 clipping, "A Honeymoon in Mont Blanc," "a big gun was fired in their honour" (Scrapbook, Alpine Club Archives).

> Mont Blanc is the Monarch of Mountains,
> They crowned him long ago;
> But who they got to put it on,
> We don't exactly know. (Fitzsimons 30)[24]

By the 1890s, photographs of its peak had become so marketable that when Elizabeth Robins Penell traveled to Geneva on her bicycle, she wondered why she could not see Mont Blanc proudly rearing its head at the end of a particular street in that city. She had expected to find it there. She soon realized that earlier she had been looking at photographs of Geneva, upon which, for the sake of publicity, an image of the mountain had been painted (17).

Mont Blanc, though, was not the only mountain to become a victim of this more modern and commercial sensibility. One could, for instance, purchase miniature plaster casts of other Alpine summits or play the board game *Up the Matterhorn*.[25] Contaminating what had been, more or less, pristine, increasing numbers of British rushed to and spread throughout the Alps – Alfred Thompson, in his satirical drama *Linda of Chamouni* declared that they were growing "as in a hothouse" (7). The sport of climbing had become fashionable. The result was that an increasing number of well-established and diagrammed routes up many of the Alpine peaks and over the major passes (described in *The Alpine Journal* or the various guidebooks) became available. These assured the climber, even when he or she was not on Mont Blanc, of being either in the company of or within sight of another expedition or within sight of the dregs of previous achievements: a bottle here, a shoe or a rope there. In search of new routes, climbers also repeated their own successes, and so did the guides who went up and down the same peaks time and time again.

The increasing familiarity of the Alps troubled people who not only wanted to be distinguished for their mountaineering achievements but also desired to uphold the dignity of the region. In 1868, J. Norman Collie, one of the most eminent British climbers, worried that the Alps were "now degraded" (165). His anxious reaction recalls Burke's belief in the vitiating effects of custom on the sublime experience: that "Knowledge and acquaintance make the most striking causes affect but little" (Shaw 59). As Burke reminds us, "A clear idea is therefore another name for a little idea" (Burke 36). A lack of familiarity was the first prerequisite for the primitive

---

[24] Byron's lines should read:
Mont Blanc is the monarch of mountains,
They crowned him long ago
On a throne of rocks, in a robe of clouds,
With a diadem of snow.

[25] For a description of this game, see W.A.B. Coolidge's "Alpine Games."

sublime.[26] In this respect, as T.G. Bonney remarked, the Alps were "played out" (*The Alpine Journal* 11 [1884]: 380).

This unwanted popularity was severe enough on the more difficult climbs in the high Alps but was particularly galling at less ambitious heights. When Frederica Plunket reached the peak of Piz Languard (10,715'), she was horrified and astonished to discover that "the summit was literally crowded with people. There was such a coming and going, eating and drinking, questioning and answering, exclaiming and laughing, that we felt quite bewildered, and as if we had got by mistake mixed up in some garden party or picnic in a fashionable watering place." She would have rather been alone, "to admire and wonder in comparative silence, than to be surrounded by a buzz of small talk, that jars amid the grandeur of such a scene" (47). This fear of the vulgar extended to language: Clinton Dent, late President of the Alpine Club, was impatient with people who talked of "doing" a mountain (*The Alpine Journal* 15 [1890]: 11).

This sense of triviality not only compromised, for instance, Plunket's view from the top of Piz Languard, but also brought with it the damning "taint of staleness" that made both the mountains and the conquering of them seem almost trite, if not routine (Collie 165). An 1897 *Punch* cartoon catches the mood. In a men's club, a rather pompous but insignificant individual brags about his mountaineering achievements to a group of bored friends who are obviously not impressed by his hackneyed account – they have heard the language before: "There I stood, the terrible Abyss yawning." They archly reply: "Was it yawning when you got there, or did it start after you arrived!"

Seeking other places that might revive some excitement or wonder, starting in 1868, some British climbers began to leave the Alps to explore mountains farther afield: in Norway, the Caucasus, Japan, Africa, New Guinea, South America, and eventually the Himalaya. The first expedition to the Caucasus, for instance, was in 1868.

Danger, Terror, and the Sublime

If the sense of astonishment, obscurity, mystery, and grandeur formerly associated with the Alps had declined, then could not the presence of danger and terror rescue the sublime, left dangling as it were, on a weakened rope? And could not the climbers in the high Alps still rescue some feeling of nobility or sublimity? After all, no matter how familiar they were, the mountains could still be genuinely threatening.

The paradox is that, in spite of the fact that travel to the Alps had become commonplace, there was nevertheless real danger in high-altitude climbing. Familiarity did not ensure safety. In earlier years, when people had merely looked at the mountains, the danger had been more imagined than real, but once people

---

[26]   See Nicolson's chapter "The Aesthetics of the Infinite" in *Mountain Gloom and Mountain Glory*, 271–323.

Little Boreham (relating his Alpine adventures). "THERE I STOOD, THE TERRIBLE ABYSS YAWNING AT MY FEET——"
That Brute Brown. "WAS IT YAWNING WHEN YOU GOT THERE, OR DID IT START AFTER YOU ARRIVED?"

Figure 1.5 "There I stood, the terrible abyss yawning at my feet." *Punch*

ventured onto them and ascended to their heights, the hazards that had excited wonder were now more immediate and real.[27] Narratives often spoke of accidents, such as the time Frederica Plunket sank, through the soft snow, into a crevasse. Only a rope was between her and death – she was pulled out by her own exertions as well as by her guides' efforts (37). The press often carried announcements of fatal accidents, and periodically *The Alpine Journal* published charts on the number and nature of climbing disasters. "Fatal Accidents in the High Alps, 1856–62" is sobering; the section enumerates the avalanches, falls into crevasses, slips on rocks, and inferior guiding that had taken lives (11 [1882]: 86–89). In addition to these charts, notices in the periodical press frequently reported Alpine catastrophes, such as one involving three gentlemen and two ladies who "were roped together, and while ascending the eastern part of the mountain, slid down a precipitous snow field, and fell upon boulders of rocks" ("English Tourists in the Tyrol," December 1891–July 1895 Scrapbook, Alpine Club Archives), or the death of three Irish ladies who were crushed in an avalanche of falling rocks ("Fatal Accident to Irish Ladies in Switzerland," *The Alpine Journal* 2 [1866]: 367). No matter how frequently a person had climbed or how often a mountain had been "conquered," there was the knowledge that the snow could be unstable, a rope could break, a foot could slip, a hand lose its hold, or a poor or foolhardy choice made. Intimate acquaintance with routes up to the top of these peaks did not eradicate the fact that what had seemed knowable or familiar at one step could, at the next, suddenly become enigmatic and treacherous.

There was the understanding that the Alps could look different to a person who has to cut his or her way up, "step by step for hours together" (Cowell 274). Narratives could not avoid recognizing "the very spot" on Mont Blanc where two years earlier an avalanche had crashed down and swept guides, porters, and climbers away. Nor could they refrain from mentioning a place where shoes, knapsacks, and whitened bones stick out of the ice: "What a scene of suffering must have been here!" (Hinchliff 94). Even the intrepid Elizabeth Le Blond noted that on her way up Mont Blanc she had passed "the very spot" where Mrs. Marks and her porter had fallen into the "gloomy depths" of a large crevasse, an event that made her realize the "awful danger" of where she was (*The High Alps in Winter* 35).[28]

---

[27]   One person to speak of the danger is Anthony Trollope who, in his "The Alpine Club Man" from his *Travelling Sketches*, wrote that "It would be easier and much pleasanter to write of the Alpine Club man, and to describe his peculiarities and his glories, if that terrible accident had not happened on the Matterhorn … it may not be amiss to say yet a word or two as to the dangers of Alpine Club pursuits, – a word or two to be added to all those words that have been said in these and other columns on the same subject" (84–85).

[28]   It is important to understand that Elizabeth Le Blond married several times, so her books are written under various names: Elizabeth Hawkins-Whitshed (maiden name), Mrs. Fred Burnaby, Mrs. John Frederick Main, and Mrs. Aubrey Le Blond. Throughout this book I shall refer to her as Elizabeth Le Blond.

Under these circumstances, what happened to these mountaineers' sense of the sublime they seemed to seek? In 1860, a member of the Alpine Club, F. Vaughn Hawkins, addressed this question in his narrative of his partial (and unsuccessful) ascent of the Matterhorn (14,780'). Hawkins remarked that in the presence of "real danger," the feeling of "'the sublime' ... depends very much, I think, on a certain balance between the forces of nature and man's ability to cope with them; if they are too weak, the scene fails to impress; if they are too strong for him, what was sublime becomes only terrible" (299). His reflections evoke Burke's and other commentators' appreciation of the fact that if one draws too close to danger, terror, or pain, any possibility of the liberating and exhilarating sublime experience disappears; that, according to John Baillie (1747), "Fear sinks and contracts" any sense of spiritual or moral elevation (Shaw 54).[29]

This understanding was shared by other mountaineers who were all too aware that the consciousness of danger and the fear attending "one's personal safety, at a height of more than 14,000 feet," turned one's mind to disaster rather than to lofty thoughts (Tyndall, *The Glaciers of the Alps* 114). Any trace of the sublime was spoiled or the thought of it even held in contempt. For instance, the Alpinist Francis F. Tuckett, when describing his "defeat" on Mt. Rosa in an 1859 letter to Hinchliff, has little room for any profound thoughts or appreciation of grandeur. Most of his letter concentrates on terrifying moments that were all too close to him, such as the time when he watched a large mass of snow he had been traversing break away and go "crashing grandly down" over the edge of a precipice. Without a further word, he and his climbing party continued and reached the final rocks where they were all "hanging on by the eyelids." Only after he and his two companions, wrapped in a flea-ridden blanket, "curled up like 3 pigs," had spent the night in relative safety, was he able to gaze at the sunrise and admit that it and "the accompanying cloud-display were gorgeous" (MS letter, Alpine Club Archives). At best, when the sublime is not achievable, the lesser specter of a pleasing scene emerges, and, more or less, suffices to lend some amount of dignity to the experience.

Edward Whymper also gave some thought to the subject. In his *Scrambles Amongst the Alps in the Years 1860–69*, he also acknowledged how vulnerable was the delicate balance between the sublime and terror. He suggests that dangerous gullies, "so long as man feels that the difficulties are within his power," have their charm, but when "their enchantment vanishes directly they are too much for him, and when he feels they are dangerous to him" (113). It goes without saying that on his successful climb up to the "virgin" summit of the Matterhorn (July, 1865), that magic was nowhere to be seen or felt when he saw four of his colleagues fall to their death. On that fatal expedition, the rope to which the sublime was clinging had literally broken (or, as some believed, had been deliberately cut).[30]

---

[29]   The full quotation from John Baillie reads: "The Sublime dilates and elevates the Soul. Fear sinks and contracts it; yet both are felt upon viewing what is great and awful."

[30]   In 1865 Edward Whymper, accompanied by Lord Francis Douglas, Peter Taugwalder and his father, the Rev. Charles Hudson, D.R. Hadow, and Michel Croz

Burke's insistence that "When danger or pain press too nearly, they are incapable of giving any delight, and are simply terrible" (34) also resonates in a passage from "The Regrets of a Mountaineer" when Stephen proposes that

> your mind is far better adapted to receive impressions of sublimity when you are alone, in a silent region, with a black sky above and giant cliffs all round with a sense still in your mind, if not of actual danger, still of danger that would become real with the slightest relaxation of caution, and with the world divided from you by hours of snow and rock. (*The Playground of Europe* 296)

If the sublime is to survive, Stephen understood, like Burke, that danger had to be conditional and proximate rather than immediate.

Personal Vanity

Other factors weakened the prestige of the sublime. In 1865, aware that there were many more deaths in the Alps than reported, Charles Dickens criticized the "personal vanity" of those climbers who risked their lives "for the sake of scaling ... peaks and pinnacles" ("Foreign Climbs" 135). Dickens's criticism goes to the very heart of the sublime's decline. As the century progressed, because of their successes in the Alps, British mountaineers either reduced the aesthetic

---

ascended the Matterhorn. Whymper and Croz raced ahead and reached the summit. On the descent, however, there was disaster. According to F.M. Smythe:

> Here a fatal mistake occurred. There were three ropes. Two were strong and one weak. It was intended to fix the weak one to the rocks in order to facilitate the descent of the difficult section. Instead, although there was more than enough strong rope for the whole party, the weak rope was used between Lord Francis Douglas and old Peter Taugwalder. This was subsequently to lead to much acrimonious controversy and scandalous assertion ... The party were on slabs. They were going slowly, one by one, and moving with the utmost circumspection. It was particularly trying work for Hadow, and Croz, who was first man down ... was taking hold of his feet and placing them on the small holds. Croz was moving down a step himself, and had laid aside his ice-axe the better to assist Hadow, when suddenly the latter slipped ... The two men fell. Hudson who was next on the rope was unable to resist the shock and was pulled from his steps and Lord Francis Douglas was similarly dragged down. The remaining three, the Taugwalders and Whymper, when they heard Croz's startled exclamation braced themselves as well as they could. Old Peter was moderately well placed and hugged a rock with his arms. The strain came. They held, but the weak rope between Lord Francis Douglas and old Peter Taugwalder snapped in mid air. The four falling climbers were beyond aid. For a few seconds Whymper and his companions endured the terrible spectacle of seeing them sliding down the slabs, spreading out their arms in vain endeavours to save themselves. Then they disappeared and fell down the great precipices of the north face on to the Matterhorn glacier four thousand feet beneath. (24)

authority of the sublime they had habitually elicited to ennoble their activities, or they transferred some of its powers to themselves. They found satisfaction in the mere fact of possessing power and endurance, which enabled them to encounter and surmount difficulties calling for considerable physical force. By bringing the mountains into subjection, they not only diminished the strength of the sublime but also shifted its might into the arena of their own minds and bodies. The authority or greatness associated with the sublime experience now lay within rather than outside the boundaries of themselves. Consequently, instead of standing in awe before the Alps, many established mountaineers now demanded that the peaks surrender to them. Rather than being overcome by a power that was supposed to overwhelm its subjects, these climbers boasted of their own ability either to face (maybe "attack") or dominate what before had been considered to be astonishing and should have, in Burke's sense, suspended all the motions of the mind. While these mountaineers might still have admired the grandeur of the Alps or paid lip service to its traditional role in an appreciation of mountains, they also resisted its crushing or engulfing effects. With this reversal, "vanity" or at least an inflated sense of self-importance, was encouraged. One can more fully understand Ruskin's infamous comment that Alpine climbing excites more vanity than any other athletic skill (Clark 196).[31] And one has a bit more sympathy for the Cook's tourist who, after growing weary of a group of boasting mountaineers, exclaimed: "Bah! Another ice-axe! I'm sick of them" (*The Times* [1893?], Scrapbook, Alpine Club Archives).

Reading through climbers' accounts written in the second half of the century, one is conscious of their authors' rather heady desire to display their own mastery and skill. For instance, in the late 1850s, a self-satisfied J.J. Cowell brags about his triumph over the cliffs that had blocked his way and threatened to defeat his expedition to the summit (259). And later in the century, Elizabeth Le Blond, while showing off her own climbing skills and pluck, allots only a few minutes to something approaching a sublime moment: "For twenty minutes I enjoyed the magnificent view. Then [back to business] … the descent began" (*The High Alps in Winter* 53). Climbing confirmed the strength as well as the "resourcefulness" and "self-sustenance" of these determined sportsmen and women (Macfarlane 91). As Elaine Freedgood has remarked, "surviving the dangers of the Alps provided a sense of mastery and control" (103).

Many other mountaineers also emphasized their physical and mental strengths – their stouthearted efforts as well as their presence of mind – that gave them the means by which to triumph over a mountain's "Greatness of dimension." As A.F. Mummery explained, mountaineering is a sport that teaches "endurance and mutual trust, and forces men occasionally to look death in its grimmest aspect frankly and squarely in the face" (236). Confronted by the perceived and real dangers of climbing, these Alpinists celebrated their sheer perseverance, good

---

[31]   See John Ruskin's "Preface" to his *Sesame and Lilies*.

management, and, perhaps, even their own limitless power.[32] A.W. Moore's and Mummery's blow-by-blow accounts of their climbs in the Alps are typical. Moore reported that during a "stiff ascent," he was full of admiration for his colleague who, "with unerring judgement, hopped from one sharp-edged mass to the other, a manoeuvre which required a confident eye as well as a sure foot" (224). And Mummery praised his companions, who set their "utmost faculties, physical and mental, to fight some grim precipice" or "force some gaunt, ice-clad gully" (232). These and other Alpinists repositioned the reverence they would have formerly reserved for a sublime landscape so that it was now directed towards a climber's agility and courage; they transferred that external power to their own limited being. Under these circumstances, one may imagine how irrelevant the traditional concept of the sublime would have ultimately been to a determined mountaineer such as Francis Fox Tuckett who, between 1856 and 1874, climbed 165 peaks, of which 84 were of some significance and 57 of which were on completely new expeditions – not to mention to the fiercely ambitious Whymper. Although initially attracted to the "noblest" (*Scrambles Amongst the Alps* 164) panoramic views from a summit, Whymper was always eager to explain the ways in which he had conquered what before had been inaccessible. Tuckett, interestingly enough, was often quick to remark that he had "not time" on a summit "to describe the view" (*A Pioneer in the High Alps* 38). He was more intent on recalling how he escaped an avalanche or crawled out of a crevasse.

Letters between climbers describing ascents in the Alps made even less of an effort than the published accounts to celebrate the sublime strength of a vast and remote summit. Here, too, they glorified themselves by concentrating exclusively on a climber's way of managing or overcoming adversity. Their letters follow the Alpinist's trials, step by step. A 17 November 1863 letter from Dr. C.H. Pilkington to John Ball (President of the Alpine Club), for instance, carefully describes his route through soft snow, and then his cutting three hundred steps in the harsh ice so he might reach the topmost ridge that was "about the size of a moderate tent" (MS letter, Alpine Club Archives). And a 12 August 1890 communication from another Alpine Club member, Cecil Slingsby, offers a detailed account of his ascent of the Dent Blanche. Note that the report emphasizes the ways in which he and his fellow climbers overcame adversity:

> Tuesday August 12th. We started from the Stockje at 1:40, &, as there was still
> a strong wind blowing, each one of us retained the extra shirt in which he had
> slept, & was in other respects unusually well provided with warm clothing.
>   As we had, before starting, told Mr. Schuster we should cross the Col
> D'Herens, we did so, though Slingsby knew the way up the Wandfluh rocks. By
> the time we reached the col, the wind had gone down wonderfully, &, when the
> sun got up, as we had hoped, & rather expected, the wind *disappeared* altogether,

---

[32]   David Robertson, in his essay "Mid-Victorians Amongst the Alps," remarks: "What counted was right-minded management of the stout-hearted effort" (130).

& we had a really glorious day. Though we lost probably 5 minutes upon the upper glacier, we reached the "*good breakfast place*" below point 3566 metres at 5:10, or in 20 mins. Longer than Mr. Conway's time by the Wandfluh.

Later in the climb, they encounter more problems:

> Solly was leading across a difficult bit of rock; Haskett-Smith was paying out the rope carefully as required, & Slingsby was sitting down & holding fast round the corner of a crag above them with the rope properly hitched, all were working steadily, & most carefully expecting in a few minutes to clear their last difficulty, when, all at once the whole mountain side seemed to be ablaze, & there was a muzzled, muffled, suppressed peal of thunder. Solly & Haskett-Smith each exclaimed 'my axe was struck' & naturally enough, each had lost his axe. For a moment Solly thought that he was blind. Haskett-Smith had a beard about 11/4 inches wide burnt exactly half way round his neck. Slingsby was untouched ... All the sparks had disappeared with the flash. Now the matter was serious enough, & we felt that we had a most providential escape.

After spending a night out in the cold and after retrieving two of their lost ice axes, Slingsby wrote: "Having now two we were able to work again with renewed confidence in our powers" (MS letter, Alpine Club Archives).

Later, in a 4 September 1899 letter to her father, Gertrude Bell continues the pattern and gives a blow-by-blow account of one of her climbs in the Ecrins Range of the French Alps. She goes into great detail:

> The guides went awfully slowly and stopped to rest several times, which was boring. We roped on the glacier, it was precious cold with wind. Presently the peaks on the opposite side of the valley turned scarlet, but we got no sun until we came onto a snow col between the Ecrins and a peak called the Fifre – the Col des Avalanches, it is called. An extraordinarily steep slope of ice, which has only been done once, leads down onto the Glacier Noir ... We turned to the left, crossed a little schrund and got onto the rock where we sat down ... It was awfully cold, we didn't linger to digest, but skirts off and straight up the rock, Mathon still leading. When we were about 10 minutes up Marius dropped his axe. It fortunately stuck on the edge of the schrund and Prince Louis's porter went down to fetch it. It was a most disagreeable 10 minutes. I doubled up and sat on my hands and my feet, and froze at discretion. (The Gertrude Bell Archive)

These sentences are a long way from the correspondent who fifty years earlier had exclaimed: "Now we are in Switzerland, that glorious land of Switzerland, amid the most sublime scenes the world can produce" (A *Budget of Letters* 19).

Gear

A by-product of this glorified attention to the self was that mountaineers started to lend more prominence to the material side of climbing – to their gear (Freedgood 2). While traveling in the Alps during the 1870s, Mary Taylor and her party, for instance, observed that among climbers there was "Always the same kind of small talk; the comparative excellence of this or that maker of mountain-boots, the best kind of ice-axe, alpenstock etc., as if there were no further interest in life" (*Swiss Notes by Five Ladies* 31). In the climbers' publications, pages that had formerly been dedicated to passages about the "Magnificence of Nature" or the "Aesthetics of Infinity" were now dedicated to equipment (Nicolson). Advertisements for mountain boots, the best kind of ice-axes, the highest quality rope, and Burberry's weatherproofing mountain kit were everywhere. *The Alpine Journal* was full of reports on equipment, such as the "Report of the Special Committee on Ropes, Axes, and Alpenstocks" read before the Alpine Club on 5 July 1864. The Club also had periodic exhibits displaying the latest gear. Books on mountaineering featured chapters on "Equipment and Outfit" in which the reader could learn, for instance, that soaping and greasing of stockings proved an effective, but unpleasant, way to prevent blisters (C.T. Dent, *Mountaineering*). And, most significantly, instead of allotting space to quotations from the Romantic poets, guidebooks were editing them out and, in their place, filling their pages with equipment lists, practical suggestions, and advertisements. By 1905, Edward Whymper's *A Guide to Chamonix* had not one word of poetry. Instead, it was full of advice about clothing, ropes, ice-axes, and soap.

As usual, the satirists picked up on the trend. In Fanny (Frances Anne) Kemble's five-act farce, *The Adventures of Mr. John Timothy Homespun in Switzerland* (1889), a foolish young man assembles iron clamps, shoes, gaiters, goggles, worsted caps, three blue veils, an alpenstock, an ice-axe, and a coil of rope – all in preparation for his climbs in the Alps. But what he succeeds in doing with this equipment is looking ridiculous and making holes in the living room carpet with his crampons. And one cannot overlook Mark Twain's *A Tramp Abroad* (1880), in which the traveler prepares to ascend the Riffelberg (a mere 8,429'). He equips 154 men with tents, scientific instruments, 40-foot ladders, miles of rope, and umbrellas. Even before they leave the hotel, he ropes his extraordinary troupe together, and with their umbrellas unfurled, they process into the street in a line stretching for half a mile.

National Vanity

More noteworthy than these British climbers' almost exclusive attention to gear, as well as to themselves, was their participation in the fantasy of their nation's superiority. When celebrating their mastery in mountaineering or touting their self-importance, these climbers eagerly appropriated the language of conquest and adventure. They set their "utmost faculties, physical and mental, to fight some grim precipice" (Mummery 232), and they habitually "attacked," "conquered," and "defeated" a pass or a summit as if they were engaging in battle or embarking upon a daring expedition into the deepest and darkest regions of the world. As historians of mountaineering recognize, metaphors of military campaigns and exploration were pervasive. The practice reflects a sense of national pride and power that was often enhanced by the fact that British climbers were, indeed, extending their reach and actually placing their feet on territory where other nations had not trod. For instance, by 1865 more than a score of the major Alpine summits that had defied the native Swiss were, if I may use the metaphor, beaten into submission by British climbers and their guides. Innumerable new routes were opened. As one historian puts it, "of the thirty-nine major peaks climbed during the Golden Age, thirty-one were first ascended by British amateurs" (Lunn 46). Not only had Whymper reached the top of the Matterhorn, but Richard Barrington had made the first ascent of the Eiger (11,875'). Significantly, Barrington's account emphasizes his determination to continue when his Swiss guides, Christian Almer and Peter Bohren, were insisting that to press forward was "impossible" (Lunn 49). Moreover, rugged ranges in areas beyond the Alps were falling to people like Edward Fitzgerald, who was the first to reach the summit of Aconcagua, the highest mountain in the Americas; to Mary Kingsley, who, basically on her own, reached the top of Mount Cameroon in West Africa; to Le Blond, who accomplished the first ascent of the formidable Titinden in Northern Norway, and to Francis Younghusband, who succeeded in crossing the uncharted Mustagh Pass in the Himalaya. In addition, British alpinists were taking their Swiss guides with them to attack many of the great peaks in South America, or, as in the case of Collie, to the Himalaya. The sport and the triumph of climbing in the Alps were being transplanted to more distant and exotic regions.[33]

As Peter H. Hansen suggests in his study of mountaineering, this language of empire and exploration "enabled mountaineers to defend their sport with patriotism" ("Albert Smith," 319). To reach the summit or, especially, to complete a virgin ascent, was not just a personal victory but also one for the nation. For instance, Edward Whymper's conquest of the Matterhorn was even more notable because he had beaten an Italian expedition to the top. Members of the Alpine Club as well as members of the general public equated the English dominance of Alpine climbing with the English-British national character. They thought that these climbers afforded a striking example of the pre-eminence of their own countrymen over all situations requiring determination, intrepidity, and skill. Sometimes this sense of superiority was petty and nasty. Thomas Hinchliff, for instance, was delighted to point out that he had passed a fat German whose arms were flailing and who, made awkward by his crampons, was "as graceful as a black swan" (109). Other climbers sounded more high-minded when they would express their

---

[33]   In the final chapter, I shall be discussing the experiences of those whose mountaineering expeditions in the Himalaya were dedicated to gaining more control over China, Tibet, Pakistan, and India.

belief that an Englishman's ability to explore the earth and to subdue it has "made England the great colonizer of the world, and has led individual Englishmen to penetrate the wildest recesses of every continent" (George, *The Oberland and its Glaciers* 197). Not surprisingly, boys' adventure stories echoed this chauvinism. In R.M. Ballantyne's *Rivers of Ice* (1875), the inexperienced young Lewis shows his British pluck after his Swiss guide falls into a crevasse and dies. Displaying an "indomitable perseverance" and courage (172), Lewis alone battles his way over unbridged fissures and sheer ice-precipices, down from the summit of Mont Blanc. Through these feats, Lewis becomes truly British; he has conquered the very elements that destroyed Le Croix, his native guide.

Britain exploited and annexed its mountaineers' accomplishments to further the reach of empire and to assert its authority over other nations. No longer was the act of climbing embedded within an awesome religious or transcendental sublime; toward the end of the century, that lofty character of the sublime itself seems to have fallen hostage not only to the hubris of individuals who sought to dominate nature, but also to the psychology of a colonizing nation. The mountains that had once been regarded as the last bastion of the sublime were more and more seen as having succumbed to the imagined sense of Britain's imperial power. No wonder that cannons regularly announced a successful ascent, that mountaineers on the heights burst into a rendition of "God Save the Queen," or drank a toast to the Queen. On top of the mountain, such fantasies could seem more real than they could below the snow line. Perhaps, it is not surprising that people like Robert Louis Stevenson turned their back on these aspirations and, instead, celebrated the quiet corners of their lower world.

What Now Had Happened to the Sublime?

As I have suggested, by the end of the nineteenth century it was no longer mandatory to describe the Alps "as transcending all mere earthly functions, existing not to submit to human work and routines but to inspire human spirit" ("Aesthetics Among the Alps" 272). Attitudes had altered so that by then it would have been deemed inappropriate, even foolish, to write, as had the Alpinist Derwent Conway in 1831, that at high altitudes "the pleasure we enjoy has little to do with the world below: we commune with Heaven rather than with earth"; or to insist that we stand where "the mind refuses to take cognisance of things so insignificant as man and his petty domain" below (156). Thirty years later, that high-minded position was not as convincing, so that when John Tyndall reached the summit of the Weisshorn (14,813'), only for a minute did he "forget myself as man" (*Mountaineering in 1861* 58) and submit to the overwhelming view before him. He chose instead to dwell upon his own mastery and his power to survive and succeed. That decision was similar to one he had made in an earlier account of an ascent up Monte Rosa (1858), when he had also replaced a potentially sublime moment with a reminder of his own physical and mental might:

I thought of my position: it was the first time that a man had stood alone upon that wild peak, and were the imagination let loose amid the surrounding agencies, and permitted to dwell upon the perils which separated the climber from his kind, I dare say curious feelings might have been engendered. But I was prompt to quell all thoughts which lessen my strength. (Tyndall, *The Glaciers of the Alps* 157)

Toward the end of the century, the experience of the sublime was virtually beside the point. In his popular book on mountaineering, the Alpinist C.T. Dent casually, yet pointedly, remarked: "The drama of romance must be excluded from [a climber's] répertoire" (*Above the Snow Line* 32). Later he was more explicit when he observed: "There are times ... when the security of the party is of more consequence than the aesthetic gratification of the individual" (*Mountaineering* 78). What had happened to the sublime? In short, the concept seemed to have been virtually abandoned. It was no longer as useful either to justify, to dignify, or for that matter, to account for the experience of looking at or climbing up a peak; it appeared to have run its course. The emptiness that the language of the sublime had masked was now even more exposed than when, at mid-century, various tourists and satirists had mocked its mundane epithets, such as "How grand!" or "How sublime!" What had been considered beneficial, grand, and uplifting had now been transferred, in part, to the power of the individual and to the boundlessness of empire. One might be tempted here to recall Kant's understanding that "true sublimity must be sought only in the mind of the judging person" and not in the object, such as "shapeless mountain masses piled on one another in wild disarray, with their pyramids of ice" (Kant 95). In a sense that he could not have foreseen, Kant catches what transpired when these mountaineers thought more immediately of their own judgment and power and less of the grand forms before their eyes.[34]

Not only did many of the mountaineers consider the sublime to be passé, but so too did some figures in the literary world. Samuel Butler, for instance, scathingly disparaged his grandfather's (George Pontifex's) diary recording a trip to the Alps shortly after the defeat of Napoleon (some time after 1815). From the grandson's point of view, the journal appears to be nothing more than "a characteristic document" of its time, replete with empty expressions of "conventional ecstasy" (45). From Butler's late-century perspective, Pontifex's astonishment as he gazes at the "sublime spectacle" of Mont Blanc or the Mer de Glace is nothing but fluff, and the verses he entered into the visitors' book, meaningless. Full of the commonplaces associated with the Romantic sublime, their lines are as "groggy about the knees" (46) as his grandfather had been after walking several miles in the region of Chamonix:

Lord, while these wonders of thy hand I see,
My soul in holy reverence bends to thee.
These awful solitudes, this dread repose,

---

[34]   I am grateful to Carolyn W. Korsmeyer for pointing out this passage to me.

> Yon pyramid sublime of spotless snows,
> These spiry pinnacles, those smiling plains,
> This sea where one eternal winter reigns,
> These are they works, and while on them I gaze
> I hear a silent tongue that speaks thy praise. (46)

Much later, when his grandson visited the region, he dropped all such pretensions; in the plain style of the modernist tradition, he emptied out all the decorative phrases and simply wrote: "I went up to the Great St. Bernard and saw the dogs" (47).[35]

Dickens is yet another instance of a writer who resisted the fantasy of the sublime in favor of a disenchanted community below the snow line. As George Levine points out in his study of nineteenth-century fiction, the realistic imagination no longer required the "mythic intensity" of the mountain. In the Victorian novel "the lesser heights will do" because its fiction is grounded in the often drab give-and-take of ordinary lives: "The stage of dramatic confrontation is not some Alpine waste but the club in London, or the drawing room" (204). The disillusioned reality of the human experience must step into the space left by the sublime.

In *David Copperfield*, the Alps are off stage. David's time wandering with a guide is essentially off the pages of the text; it is, as Dickens announces, "An Absence" (*David Copperfield* 748–52) which belongs to the fantasy of a dream-like landscape rather than to what makes life plausible. Thinking back to his three years away is like "recalling ... a dream" (749) In a tightly reduced, few pages – in my edition, only five and a half – Dickens describes David's travels through the Continent; he wastes little time dwelling upon the particulars and the drama of those years abroad. The boundlessness of the sublime is not relevant to his protagonist's future. David admits, "If those awful solitudes had spoken to my heart, I did not know it" (749). Even though David momentarily saw "sublimity and wonder" in the Alps, he found the experience to be neither sustaining nor inspiriting. For him, as for Dickens, the more nurturing meaning was to be found below and back home. Consequently, David descends to the valleys and hurries back to the reality of the rooms of London, to the swollen gutters of its streets, and to places like the Gray's Inn Coffee House, so that the novel can conclude within their boundaries. As Rosemary Bodenheimer suggests in her recent study *Knowing Dickens*, Dickens roamed within the living spaces of home. He was intensely involved, for instance, with his management of the Home for Homeless Women he helped sponsor as well as with his fictional depictions of the interiors of houses.[36] For Dickens, as well as for so many other Victorian novelists, the mountains are neither central to the definition of being nor vital to a person's sense of worth. According to Levine, the feelings that were once projected on the Alps are now bestowed upon the valleys, the streets, and the interiors of the human

---

[35]   I am grateful for Marjorie Hope Nicolson's study of attitudes toward mountains for reminding me of this example. See *Mountain Gloom and Mountain Glory* 373–74.

[36]   See the chapter "Manager of the House."

community below: in the drawing rooms of *Middlemarch* and *Cranford* or within the parlors of Manchester.[37]

Perhaps what Levine identifies as a quest for "the language of the ordinary" (206) in the realist novel takes one back to the satires on the tourists. The Mrs. Simpletons, the Mrs. Browns, the Timothy Homespuns, and the Dodds, discussed in Part 1 of this chapter, had it right: these comic figures were more appropriate to their world than one would like to think. Their banality, their vocabulary, their pronunciation, while struggling up the Rigi or clambering over a mountain pass, exaggerate the sense that the harsh and unaccommodating realities of life below are becoming more prominent and more pointed. Their fear that an insurance policy will not pay the expenses if one of them falls over a precipice is, in this context, more to be understood than regretted. They offer an extreme version of the ordinary. Their preoccupation with love affairs, nattering husbands or wives, commerce, and bodily comfort while in view of the mountains is very much in keeping with the raw materials – the fallout of the sublime – that novelists like Dickens, Eliot, and Gaskell had at their disposal. These materials, as Stephen Arata points out (207), were in these novelists' imaginative hands, transformed from the banal and the vulgar.[38] One might think of it as the sublime of the ordinary, or, perhaps, a version of the moral sublime. The realist novelists were actually doing what the climber Elizabeth Le Blond did when, in the 1880s, she interrupted her admiration of a view from the high Alps in winter in order to shift her gaze down to a distant view of "knapsacks" and "dinner" (*The High Alps in Winter* 53). Her altered focus prefaces her descent to the community and streets below.

The fall of the sublime, though, did not eradicate a longing for it among an older generation of the mountaineers. Some, like J. Norman Collie, worried that climbers were now too busy trying to force their surroundings into "their own small ideas" (167); others yearned for the "old romantic flavour" (Stephen, *Men, Books, and Mountains* 203), and many mourned the passing of the early days of climbing when it was less flashy and sporty. Like A.F. Mummery, they did not want to abandon "the old love of cold nights in the open, of curious meals with the hospitable curé, of hare-brained scrambles on little-known glaciers and traverses of huge unclimbed ridges" (81); they sought rather to remember the astonishment, the mystery, the joyful terror, and the vastness of their earlier experiences. These mountaineers' nostalgia, perhaps, anticipated the modernists' mourning the defeat of the sublime, and foreshadowed what was eventually to be perceived as a lack or a void in the heart of human experience and expression. Their nostalgia looked ahead to a world for which the sublime is not only an impossibility, but also, in its absence, a symptom of a traumatic loss.

---

[37]   From the point of view of the Victorian novelists of the 1880s, the philosophy of Nietzsche, who associated everything of importance with the Alpine experience, would have appeared an anachronism.

[38]   See Stephen Arata's "Realism" in *The Cambridge Companion to the Fin de Siècle*, 207.

Chapter 2
Spectators, Telescopes, and Spectacle

> The dignity of the snow-capped mountains is lost in distinction, but the joy of the
> tourist is to recognize the traveller on top. The desire to see, for the sake of seeing
> is, with the mass, alone the one to be gratified.
>
> ("The Ten O'Clock Lecture," 20 February 1885, James
> Abbott McNeill Whistler. 2067)

Introduction

In the second half of the nineteenth century, even though people came to regard mountaineering as a sport – hence, its inclusion in the admired *Badminton Library of Sports and Pastimes* series – climbing was certainly never classified as a spectator sport. As received tradition had it, to climb a mountain was to separate oneself from those below and to push on into the cold mountain solitude, into regions out of sight and out of touch, away from the eye of the observer. Down below, large and noisy crowds pressed into public spaces to watch football matches; they gathered beside the River Dee in Aberdeen to follow swimming races and observe mock drownings (as well as rescues). But such masses of spectators were seemingly absent from these higher altitudes with their desolate scenes.[1]

The growing popularity of mountaineering and the rise of tourism in the Alps, however, altered this situation. With the increasing number of visitors to the Alpine regions, climbing attracted more and more curious and critical observers. In spite of the fact that a majority of people could not follow a mountaineer through a difficult pass or up to a summit, there was still an audience – a distant but varied one, made up of the young, the old, and the infirm as well as the able. Reading through diaries and climbing narratives, one learns that by means of various telescopes enthusiastic onlookers could trace a climb from its start to its conclusion. As a result, by mid-century, mountaineering was not as solitary an undertaking as it once had been. As Paul P. Bernard remarks, "not a step was taken on the mountain that was not observed in a dozen telescopes and subjected to critical comment" (33).

This shift to mountaineering as a spectator sport altered the ways in which Victorians regarded mountains and distinguished them from observers in the late-eighteenth and early-nineteenth centuries. Beginning with the mid-nineteenth

---

[1] To learn about the swimming shows, see Siegfried Kracauer's "Sport as Spectacle; Swimming in Victorian and Edwardian Britain."

century, a burgeoning number of visitors to the Alps, all too eager to watch others take risks, almost obliterated the earlier understanding that a mountain led one beyond the confines of one's self to transcendental or spiritual heights.[2] For these Victorian spectators, the drama of the actual body in danger was far more engaging than were the lingering ideals of Romanticism and the elevation of the soul. Intent upon viewing such perils, these spectators, armed with their viewing apparatus, transformed mountains into theatrical spaces so that they might watch and even vicariously participate in the excitement of a climb. Eventually, under the influence of the showmen, such as the exuberant Albert Smith, who in the 1850s produced the popular *Ascent of Mont Blanc*, these distant performances came down from the heights into exhibition venues and literally walked onto the London stage, complete with all the vulgarisms and commercialism associated with spectacle.

With that descent, the mountains not only left the sublime far behind; they also joined what is now referred to as the culture industry. In spite of this sinking and a growing fascination with simulacra, though, the Victorians were not to forget "the real thing" entirely. The various extravagant representations of Mont Blanc, for instance, did not hold their viewers completely hostage. Victorian audiences were exempt to a considerable degree from what post-modern theorists, such as Guy Debord, Jean Baudrillard, and Theodor Adorno, speak of when they comment on the negative and controlling consequences of spectacle. Through their own travel experiences they were acutely alert to the gap or the tension between the spectacle's visual fictions and their own perception of the actual mountain. For them, the mountains still had the last word. Nor, in the end, I suggest, was the Victorian public to lose all touch with the sublime. Ironically, with the coming of more efficient cameras and film in the latter part of the nineteenth century, high altitude art photography, with its stark black and white images, reclaimed the mystery of the mountains that the spectacles had almost destroyed. In a sense, these pictures, taken by a select number of climbers who were also professional photographers, escorted the mountains off the London stage.

The discussion that follows considers these developments in the ways Victorians looked at mountains. Part 1, "Spectators and Voyeurs," focuses on the manner in which visitors observed those attempting to reach a summit and watched as these climbers risked death. Part 2, "Performance Spaces, Spectacles, and the Culture Industry," examines how the presence of these spectators helped transform mountains and mountaineering into theatre and then into an entertaining spectacle. As I have suggested above, such changes not only affected the Victorian public's responses to mountains but also contributed to a culture industry that threatened further to compromise the sublime experience.

---

2   In the discussion that follows, I am not engaging what Elaine Freedgood suggests in her *Victorian Writing about Risk: Imagining a Safe England in a Dangerous World*. I am not thinking about Freedgood's assertion that climbers seemed to have inoculated themselves against the contingencies of the future by voluntarily engaging danger, and, in such a way, colonizing the future.

Part 1: Spectators and Voyeurs

"Mont Blanc by Telescope"

People usually do not realize that mountaineering, by its very nature, involves watching and being watched. But climbing in the mid-nineteenth century attracted many onlookers. H.G. Willink's humorous sketch of a somewhat naïve tourist intently peering through a mounted telescope would be all-too familiar.

From the moment mountaineers started their ascent until their return – or their failure to return – they were under surveillance. Clusters of tourists and fellow climbers glued their eyes to telescopes set up by the hotels at Chamonix and Zermatt, as well as at other climbing centers, so that they might periodically follow a party's advance and descent. An article in *The Daily News*, aptly entitled "A Holiday in Switzerland: Mont Blanc by Telescope," describes one such assemblage of guests, staying at Chamonix, who were "buzzing like flies" around several telescopes that were supervised by hotel employees and instructed by

Figure 2.1 H.G. Willink. "They're goin' very slowly!"

those who had previously climbed at least "a third of the mountain" (Scrapbook, Alpine Club Archives). Those who waited their turn made do with opera glasses, spectacles, and field glasses. As late as 24 July 1897, the *Times*, in a piece called "Chamounix," was reporting that a group of seventeen people ascending Mont Blanc had been "eagerly watched by many through the powerful telescopes which are provided at most of the hotels in Chamounix" (Scrapbook, Alpine Club Archives). This manner of viewing was also readily available at less populated locations. For instance, in 1886 *The Alpine Journal* reported that groups of "fifteen to twenty persons" had been seen crowding around an inn's telescope in order to track those attempting to reach the summit of the Meije by the Eastern Ridge ("The Meije by the Eastern Ridge," *The Alpine Journal* 12 [1885]: 461). The Meije is in the High Alp District of Southeastern France known as the Dauphiné.

Not surprisingly, tourist diaries and letters are replete with references to this kind of activity. In an 1865 manuscript diary, a Cook's tourist, William Chater, recorded that from his hotel with the assistance of "a powerful telescope," he had seen a party on the summit of Mont Blanc (33). Another guest, Emily Hornby, noted that because of the excellence of the telescope provided, even she had been able to observe the people at the top of the famous mountain (Hornby 24). Not many years later, a group of young Yorkshire women mentioned that when they had been considering an ascent of Mont Blanc, they had first surveyed, through their hotel's telescope, a party already on its way to the summit (*Swiss Notes by Five Ladies* 12). And, in the same decade, while on a climbing holiday based in Zermatt, Frances Ridley Havergal remarked to her sister: "in the last few days all the telescopes … were at work upon the Matterhorn." Excited, yet a little skeptical, she added: "This morning Mr. W. [Whitwell] was visible not very far from the top, *i.e.*, three moveable black dots supposed to be himself and the guides" (Crane 160).[3]

Indeed, by mid-century, so accustomed were people to looking at mountains and climbers through telescopes that illustrations accompanying climbing books and diaries adopted a telescopic perspective. If one leafs through the narratives, one notices that many of the accompanying engravings and drawings attempt to depict the prospect that presents itself to the eye as if it fell within the radius of the telescopic lens. Edward Whymper's circular engravings of distant views of the mountains from his expeditions in South America (to Cotopaxi and to Chimborazo), for instance, invite the reader to join him as a spectator looking through his telescope. And so do the circular sketches interleaved among a mid-century Alpine log as well as within the 1873 *Adventures of the Economical Family*.

The illustration from the 1860 Alpine log is especially intriguing because it brings the reader's eye along with the diarist's up to the telescope so both can share a remote view of the five climbers who are descending from the summit of Mont Blanc. The image reproduces the very prospect that the writer had seen that morning through a high-powered glass:

> We were awoke in the morning by the firing of the cannon, announcing the
> arrival at the summit of Mont Blanc of the party making the ascent. I rushed to
> my window but of course could not see them with the naked eye. During our
> breakfast 2 or 3 hours later another discharge greeted their successful descent
> as far as the Grands Mulets & shortly after we went to the observatory to watch
> the progress of their descent through the telescope. We saw them very distinctly

---

[3]   In a letter to his wife, Harriet Marian Stephen, from Zermatt in August, 1870, Leslie Stephen mentions yet another way of observing climbers on the Matterhorn: "They make signals when people try the Matterhorn by lighting a fire here & an answer should be given by lighting a fire at the hut on the Matterhorn." He goes on to remark: "Well, we had lighted our fire but there was no answer & as the weather has been so bad, we began to be afraid of an accident" (Bicknell 1: 85).

Figure 2.2   Sketch from Thomas Whitwell's "Alpine Log"

Figure 2.3   Drawing from *Adventures of the Economical Family*

trudging through the snow single-file among the tremendous heaps of the Glacier du Gasconay, and very singular they looked. (Whitwell 47)

It is interesting to note that when the scenic landscape painter William Beverley accompanied the showman Albert Smith on an 1851 tour of Switzerland, he made sketches that Smith would later use as backdrops for his Mont Blanc show. As if Beverley, who did not climb, had been looking at the Alpine views through a telescope, he placed these sketches within inked circles.

An 1895 article, "Mountaineering from Grindelwald," in the *Nonconformist Independent* gives a sense of what the experience of watching a climb in this way would have been like. The piece describes those observing an ascent of the Eiger (13,040') from the valley below. One learns that the viewing was not always a fleeting event. One also comes to realize that in spite of the distances, these spectators were, on a good day, apparently able to scan details of the climb remarkably well:

> It was just after breakfast that the word was passed round that the adventurous climbers were beginning the descent of the precipitous icefield. Excitement kindled like a flame ... In a few minutes telescopes were primed and binoculars focussed [*sic*], and for the next six hours the movements of the trio were watched with keen, and, at times, excited interest ... The watchers at the telescope anxiously followed every action of the men who, fourteen thousand feet above sea-level, were invisible to the naked eye, and – even when seen with the aid of the powerful lenses of the telescope – looked like specks on the glittering snow. The two guides were the first to appear in sight ... Shortly, Mr. Macdonald crossed the ridge, and all three were within the focus of the telescopes. After a while the elder guide crawled upwards, while the son descended on hands and knees to relieve his father in the arduous work of step-cutting. It was somewhat difficult to follow the tactics adopted . We in the valley could only surmise that dangers were imminent. (Scrapbook, Alpine Club Archives)

Not all the telescopes were attached to the hotels. Carrying their portable instruments – a required, and often clumsy, part of a visitor's gear – tourists frequently left the comfort of their hotels to mount neighboring heights in order to gain a better view.

In one of Mrs. Ashton Yates' letters, written during an 1841 journey to Switzerland, she dramatically explained to her correspondent that

> When it is known that a daring youth, accompanied by guides intends making the ascent, all the inhabitants of the neighbourhood, and visiters [*sic*] from every direction, flock in crowds to those parts of the opposite mountains whence they can have the best view of the party who intend going where it would seem that the eagle might scarce dare to soar. They are watched and gazed upon with

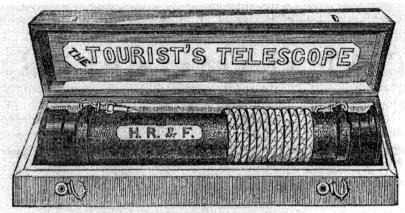

PRICE 10/6,

THE
TOURIST'S TELESCOPE

FOR SEA AND LAND,

Possessing High Magnifying Power, fine Definition, and great Portability; and is very moderate in price. Price, with Strap for suspension, enclosed in Leather Case lined with Velvet, **10/6,** per post **12/-**

This instrument is well adapted for Swiss Tourists, from its small bulk, and high magnifying power. We subjoin a few Testimonials that we have received, and shall be glad to answer any enquiries respecting the Telescope, previous to purchase.

One of the *Chamouny Guides* writes :—" They are excellent for Swiss Tourists."
" I have just returned from Switzerland, where I had one of them for my constant companion.   ·   ·   · I am sure, when still more generally known, they will command a very large sale." From the Author of " *Switzerland and How to See It.*"
" They are beautiful instruments, and marvellously cheap."—*Gloucester Chronicle.*

WHOLESALE AND RETAIL DEPÔT,

HARVEY, REYNOLDS, & FOWLER,

10, BRIGGATE, LEEDS.

LONDON AGENTS FOR TELESCOPES, W. J. ADAMS, 59, FLEET-ST. AND T. COOK, 98, FLEET STREET.

SPA LOUNGING GLASS,

POST FREE, 8s. 9d.

Shows Ships, Houses, Trees, &c., 20 miles off, a Church Clock 10 miles. Jupiter's Moons and other objects of interest are distinctly seen by it. This portable, elegant, and powerful instrument can be had only from

J. P. BROADRICK, OPTICIAN,
15, WESTBOROUGH, SCARBOROUGH.

O

Figure 2.4   1874 advertisement for portable telescope

glasses and telescopes; their ladder of ropes is anxiously descried suspended from one icy precipice to another, until the light fades; and prayers for their safety arise, mingling with those of the coming vespers. (1:175–76)

From the Gorner Grat (10,272'), a rocky ridge rising to the southeast from the plateau of Riffelberg, others might be rewarded with an exceptionally fine sight of climbers on Monte Rosa (15,217') or on the Matterhorn (14,780'). To gain this advantage was not particularly easy, but it was considered to be part of the entertainment.[4] When Mrs. Henry Freshfield went to the Alps in 1859, she, with others, hurried to the Gorner Grat so that they might follow the progress of climbers on their way down from the summit of Monte Rosa. She describes the experience as a drama that unfolds before her telescopic eye:

> In a few minutes the little *salon* [in the hotel] was cleared of its previously desponding occupants, and we were all pressing upwards to the Gorner Grat, where a numerous group were established with telescopes and glasses, watching with eager interest the movements of a party who had left the hotel in the early morning to ascend Monte Rosa, and who were now returning. Six tiny specks could be traced following each other down the steep snow slope. Now one remains stationary, and is left considerably behind; at the end of half an hour those in advance appear to hold consultation. A second black speck detaches itself, and while the others rapidly descend towards the rocks it begins to toil gradually up again, to the still motionless spot upon the snows. All was now speculation ... Was it accident or illness? One of the gentlemen watching the proceedings had two young sons among the party, and his anxiety was great until he saw the two specks were reunited; – after a short interval we watched them both descending in their companions' tracks, until all were lost among the rocks. (180)

Others scampered or rode on mules up to less ambitious heights, to places like the Montanvert (6,267') or the Bréven (7,770') for clearer images of mountaineers they knew to be either going up or coming down adjoining slopes. Because it directly faced Mont Blanc, the Bréven was a particularly popular destination for these spectators. The practice had already gotten underway earlier in the century. In a narrative of an 1827 ascent to the summit of the famous mountain, John Auldjo recalls that many people were watching his progress from that location (65). A few years later Martin Barry's relatives (he calls them "spectators") did the same thing so that they might count, with the help of their telescopes, the members of his climbing party descending Mont Blanc.

From the middle of the nineteenth century on, there were many occasions when concerned friends and family members, with telescopes "pulled out 'like the ill-fated tradesman's trousers in a pantomime'" (Dent, *Above the Snow Line* 77),

---

[4]　This ascent was considerably easier after 1898, when a cog railway was completed and took tourists up to the Gorner Grat. The trip became a popular outing.

would perch on precipices or stand on the glaciers below a mountain in order to determine how a climber was doing.

Alfred Wills' wife, Lucy, waited on a glacier running down from the Wetterhorn (12,150') until she caught sight of Wills and his guides descending from its summit. She could tell by their pace that all was right. (She had reason to be worried, for it was the first time anyone had reached that mountain's peak.) And A.F. Mummery, Lily Bristow (a formidable "lady" climber), G. Hastings, Cecil Slingsby, and J. Norman Collie on a difficult technical climb up the Grépon shouted at friends who they thought might be watching their movements from the Mer de Glace below.

Tourists were not the only spectators. Climbers also observed each other. In addition to extending their portable telescopes to survey possible routes on a mountain, they checked on the progress of other

Figure 2.5 H.G. Willink. "A lengthy observation"

mountaineering excursions. Because of the importance of the instrument and what it made possible, the narratives often contain stories of climbers carelessly dropping their telescope or the lens's protective cap in the snow.[5] Examples of

---

[5] In an article in the September 1864 issue of *The Alpine Journal*, "The Glaciers of the Bernina," E.N. Buxton speaks about one awkward moment with regard to a telescope:

> Jenni was in the habit of carrying a large nautical telescope in the side pocket of his coat, and in his struggle to keep his head uppermost it fell out, and now lay buried at an unknown depth in any part of the heap, which had become bound together and hardened into big snowballs in its descent. We probed in all directions ... it became evident what a hopeless matter it was. (Buxton 343)

In other accounts one can read about lens caps that fall off or become detached. Many climbers, though, found the portable telescopes to be most useful. Thomas W. Hinchliff, in his *Summer Months among the Alps: with the Ascent of Monte Rosa* (1857), complains about the telescope cap that slides away but also recalls that he "always carried a small folding-up telescope by Ross, which is certainly the most convenient instrument of this kind" (Hinchliff 72).

mountaineers using telescopes to keep track of each other are plentiful. It was by this means, for instance, that Edward Whymper realized that he was ahead of a competing Italian group also trying to make the first successful attempt at the Matterhorn. And through the telescope John Tyndall observed two moving objects on the glacier below and realized that another climbing party was following his tracks; Leslie Stephen shouted a loud greeting to a climbing friend he had noticed through his telescope – he received a faint echo of a reply; and Mrs. E.P. Jackson (the first woman to climb the Matterhorn) recalled that on her arrival on a summit, she and her guides were greeted by distant cheers: "looking toward the Schreckhorn we saw our companions of the morning party way down the arête on their homeward route" (*The Alpine Journal* 14 [1889]: 203). At the turn of the century, there are, of course, more examples. When Gertrude Bell was on a climbing holiday, she kept an eye on the two sons of the Comtesse d'Eu who were making a difficult traverse on the Meije. She watched them "through the telescope till a thick cloud blew across and completely hid the whole top of the Meije" (The Gertrude Bell Archive, 28 August 1899 letter to father).

"Bang! Bang! Went the guns"

At the other end of the lens, climbers were more often than not conscious of being spied upon. Especially in the more popular centers, they could not help but be aware of spectators following and "contemplating their movements" (Stephen, *The Playground of Europe* 127). Not only did the hotels provide telescopes but also, in places like Chamonix and Zermatt, the staff set off cannon shots to announce that an expedition had been seen to reach a summit or to manage a difficult pass. In response, those on the mountain would frequently raise a red handkerchief, unfurl a flag, or wave their arms as a signal to those who had been surveying their progress. In 1855, after attaining the summit of Mont Blanc, one climber recorded that as soon as he set foot upon its crown, he listened to "the faint sound of a gun fired at Chamouni, and felt proud of my success." Much to the mountaineer's delight, he heard "every discharge distinctly" (Anderson 96). When A.W. Moore reached the top of the Eiger, he also heard the celebratory guns going off below: "Bang! Bang! Went the guns at the Wengern Alp, as a sign that our progress had been watched, and our success perceived" (Moore 353). Similarly, Elizabeth Le Blond at the top of the Aiguille du Midi (12,600') saw "a puff of smoke followed some seconds later by a 'boom.'" With that signal from Chamonix, she knew "the good people below had seen our arrival, and were firing the canon in our honour" (*The High Alps in Winter* 51). Hotels sometimes activated more than one piece of artillery. In her brisk, ironic voice, Le Blond describes the tradition:

> Each hotel had two or three very diminutive cannons, which are fired by the respective porters, who give a prod with a long stick, and then turn and run, while a majestic puff, about the size of an egg, is seen to emerge from the mouth

of these warlike machines, followed by a report resembling a pistol. (*High Life and Towers of Silence* 27)

Whether or not they heard the cannons, nineteenth-century mountaineers sensed that the telescopes were directed towards them. Earlier in the 1800s, when Martin Barry had ascended Mont Blanc, he recorded hearing his guide shout "*On nous regarde.*" The guide "knew that we had just then reached a point, from which observers in the valley could, with the telescope, discern us in our snowy trail" (35). A few years before, John Auldjo had felt encouraged when he had become conscious that his efforts up Mont Blanc were being followed by "some female forms" (59) who were gazing at them from the adjoining Bréven. By mid-century such an experience was almost a commonplace. For instance, one climber remembered her guide exclaiming, "*On nous voit!*" when he realized that people in Chamonix, who had been tracking their progress up the Grands Mulets, had caught sight of them. The climber admitted, "I think we found it rather stimulating also, to know that we were being watched from below" (Crane 254).

Not everyone, however, shared the pleasures of being observed. In the early 1870s, when C.T. Dent went up the Rothorn (10,190') from Zermatt, he knew he was going to be looked at by spectators either stationed at the local hotels or scattered over the neighboring heights of the Riffel. At the moment he and his climbing partner came into view, a self-conscious Dent thought of his companion's "strange woolen garment and head-dress to match," and fretted that the onlookers might also be disapproving of his own "ancient hat." Embarrassed and "knowing full well that the exceedingly powerful telescope, with possibly a critical eye applied to it, was doubtless directed on us," he exchanged his old hat for "a species of woollen extinguisher" ("The Rothhorn from Zermatt," *The Alpine Journal* 6 [1873]: 271). Decorum, oddly enough, could still be at play in these remote regions. In an 1863 issue of *The Alpine Journal*, Leslie Stephen wrote that it was important to acknowledge being seen.[6] He recalled with distaste an Englishman who had not stopped to recognize a salute but had set straight to eating and drinking. Stephen reports that he turned to his companions and advised them not only to recognize those watching them but also to sing "God Save the Queen" ("The Joungfrau-Joch and Viescher-Joch, Two New Passes in the Oberland," *The Alpine Journal* 1 [September 1863]: 103). In an interesting counter fact, in a rather strange 1929 story, "Little Mother up the Mörderberg," H.G. Wells defiantly upsets this sense of etiquette when the narrator, a climber (who happens to be carrying his mother in

---

[6]   When H.B. George climbed in the Oberland (1866), he regretted that because he and his climbing party were "not so well provided with telescopes," they could not return the greeting to those who had been watching their proceedings on the summit. Without a telescope, he was unable to distinguish people in the cheering crowd and see that among them were "some of our friends who had only arrived from England the night before" (*The Oberland and its Glaciers* 101).

his pocket), boldly makes a "derisive gesture or so for the benefit of anyone at the telescope" watching the ascent from the hotel below (580).

Voyeuristic Pleasures

These spectators would follow with particular attention those who were engaged in a dangerous ascent. There was excitement, if not a kind of voyeuristic pleasure, in watching climbers face the possibility of death. In a sense, these observers' inclination to look at such dramas could be seen to complement Burke's understanding of one cause of the sublime that associated terror and death with the delight of being in the presence of a grand and overpowering landscape – a delight that was possible because they themselves were sufficiently removed from the danger. I suggest, though, that, for the tourists, the almost prurient pleasure of looking at something forbidden tended to work against the more elevated thoughts associated with the sublime, and that, furthermore, the diminutive and incomplete telescopic image before their eyes negated Burke's stipulation that the perspective be vast, approaching the infinite. Searching for those at risk through these optical instruments had its fascination, but it was not a fascination principally indebted to the emotional state and disposition of mind that Burke and his contemporaries associated with the sublime.

In spite of the telescope's ability to bring what is far closer to view, there are obviously moments of disjunction between the eye and the object being observed. And naturally there is a significant emotional distance between a spectator watching from the safety or comfort of a valley and a mountaineer struggling among the snows and crevasses of the higher altitudes. Leslie Stephen was fond of pointing out that a snow-slope "looks very pretty out of the valley to any one, but it will look very different to a man who has only studied it through an opera-glass, and to one who has had to cut his way up it step by step for hours together" ("The Allelein-horn" 274). Even when one could reduce the distance through a telescopic lens and bring the remote scene up to the eye, there was no way of participating in the actual physical toil of climbing. The telescope disengaged the eye from the body and thereby exempted the viewer from the sensation of actually being there. The framed image not only reduced Burke's sense of the "Greatness of Dimension" but also blocked any entrance to a climber's consciousness of his or her surroundings and difficulties. Observers were spared the discomfort of the cold winds and the icy slopes. They could loll about in cozy chairs, smoke in the lounge, or take a leisurely breakfast in between turns at peering through the lens. Even on the adjoining hills, people socialized and picnicked between views. Detached from the raw and rugged scene directly confronting the mountaineers, the framed, diminutive telescopic image shielded viewers from the painful physical effort only partially visible through its scope. Such a prospect appealed to Leslie Stephen's sister-in-law, Anne Thackeray Ritchie, who was content to see Stephen make his way up, but was even more pleased to think that she could send her eyes up mountains while she waited on "some mossy bank down below" (Ritchie 168).

Many of those tourists who searched the mountainsides through the telescope were obviously participating in a kind of vicarious experience. Even though most could not feel the pain and the struggle, they wanted to see those experiencing it. They were indulging in the pleasure of looking. In a sense, these spectators were simply another version of those "scandalized" English visitors to Geneva who were reputed to have observed Byron's and Shelley's "foibles and liaisons" through telescopes (Ring 24). Perhaps they even resembled the young woman in a *Punch* cartoon (5 September 1857) who, through a telescope held up to her eye, spied on her friend's lover, who was evidently having a good time smoking his cigar and "drinking something out of a tumbler" while away from his fiancée (Fig. 2.6).

These spectators were voyeurs watching something risky, and sometimes forbidden, as well as something thrilling, from afar. As voyeurs, they could not only enjoy the distance from a prohibited moment, but also, paradoxically, safely draw close and even become an accessory to the act. In a sense, mountains, whether near or far, were places to see what normally would be tabooed before the public eye – what was normally sternly forbidden.

Indeed, mountain tourism could lead to indecorous episodes. Eustace Anderson, once president of the Alpine Club, tells an odd anecdote. When he ascended Mont Blanc in 1855, he carried a telescope (and wore flannel cricketing trousers), but on the night before the final push, he rested in a climbing hut on the Grands Mulets with his colleagues. In the half-light, he made a point of observing what everyone else was doing. He found his attention drawn to a "facetious little guide and his friend" [another male guide] who had lain down together with their arms around each other. In the morning, he caught them "kissing one another most affectionately" (86). Days earlier, Anderson had gone in a house that kept a pet chamois. He entered only to witness a French lady "with all the vivacity of her nation" kissing the goat with her "smacking" lips and seeming to be "in ecstasies" (50).

Pleasure also came in watching oneself. A day or so after Anderson came down from the summit of Mont Blanc, he, with a "good telescope," hurried up the adjoining accent to spy the tracks he had made in the snow on Mont Blanc (107). In his book on mountaineering for the Badminton Series, C.T. Dent notes that mountaineers like to trace the marks they have imprinted on the snow the day before. A climber, he remarks, "will sweep all over the mountain with his telescope, in the hope of lighting on tracks or ice-steps" he has left behind as a mark of his presence (*Mountaineering* 138). A person could become the subject of his own voyeurism.

Considering the descriptions written by people watching climbers through a telescope, one recognizes a craving for and an involvement in the risky or even the forbidden. Tourists, rather than the climbers themselves, were more drawn to the possibility of looking at death. There were among them, no doubt, those who actually hoped to see climbers fall to their death, just as people in the eighteenth century had flocked to executions. And sometimes this fantasy came true. For

MALICIOUS.

Flora. "CAN YOU STILL SEE THE STEAMER, LUCY, DEAR?"

Lucy. "OH YES, QUITE PLAINLY!"

Flora. "AND DEAR, DEAR WILLIAM, TOO?"

Lucy. "OH, YES!"

Flora. "DOES HE SEEM UNHAPPY, NOW HE IS AWAY FROM ME?"

Lucy. "EVIDENTLY, I SHOULD SAY, DEAR; FOR HE IS SMOKING A CIGAR, AND DRINKING SOMETHING OUT OF A TUMBLER TO CHEER HIM, POOR FELLOW?"

Figure 2.6 "Malicious." *Punch*

instance, at Chamonix a tourist looked through his telescope and saw a man fall into a crevasse near the Petit Plateau.[7]

From safe places, these tourists searched for a view of danger. Protected by the lens of the telescope, visitors could peep into the treacherous regions of the high altitudes where climbers were sometimes swept away by avalanches or lost their footing and slipped to their death. Securely planted either in the villages below or at lower elevations not far from their hotels, these spectators sought a glimpse of these terrible events through the mediating view of the telescope. Detached from the possible horror and under the guise of just peeping, they could indulge their morbid interest in death while taking pleasure in the act of looking. Within the context of what many considered to be either a sublime or exquisitely beautiful landscape, they spied upon people in danger.

The thrill of spying upon someone who might be injured or who is about to die reverberates through Mrs. Henry Freshfield's account of gazing at mountaineers returning from an ascent of Monte Rosa (quoted earlier). All the "despondency" she had experienced while sitting in the hotel lounge immediately disappears when she puts the telescope to her eye. With the prospect of witnessing something terrifying, she and her fellow tourists rush to catch the drama of catastrophe. And in the passage quoted from the *Nonconformist Independent* the sense of "imminent danger" excites a cluster of spectators who are watching a group of climbers descending from the Eiger. A similar impulse motivated Francis Galton "to obtain a nearer view of the great avalanches, that rushed and roared at frequent intervals down the north face of the Jungfrau into the depths of the Trümonthal." "Seized with desire," Galton immediately snatched his telescope so that he might witness the terrifying drama ("The Avalanche of the Jungfrau," *The Alpine Journal* 1 [1863]: 184). It is not surprising that after the Matterhorn tragedy in the 1860s, when four people lost their life during Edward Whymper's descent from its peak, tourism at Zermatt increased. In the late 1860s apparently there were as many as four thousand guests in one season. This rise in numbers speaks to this attraction to disaster.

In yet another narrative, the writer speaks of interrupting his lunch so that he might look through the telescope to see two men reach the summit of the Aiguille de Charmoz (11,302'). Two hours later, he is both excited and horrified to learn that minutes after he had been watching them, these mountaineers had met with an accident and perished: He had seen them "at the foot of the couloir only a few minutes before the accident occurred." He reports that the next day "groups were to be seen around each of the hotel telescopes, waiting anxiously for the signal of the search party, while some ascended to the Plan des Aiguilles in the hope of hearing that the accident was not so serious as was feared" (*Land and Water* 24 September 1898, Scrapbook, Alpine Club Archives). Mr. Ashton

---

[7]   This incident was reported in Harold Spender's article "The Dangers of the Alps" (Mountaineering Pamphlets 258–67, Alpine Club Archives). Fortunately the observer called attention to the accident and nine guides instantly left to rescue the climber.

Binns, a member of the Alpine Club, and his guide had slid into the side of a crevasse, struck it violently, and died.

There are many accounts of events in which this tendency to voyeurism was satisfied. Henry Frith, in his mid-century narrative of hardy mountaineering, reported that on a climb of Mont Blanc, three gentleman and eight guides, after reaching the summit, were swept away in a terrific whirlwind. Their demise was not invisible, for their deaths were being watched from below through telescopes. People were attracted to the scene, partially motivated by the forbidden and partially motivated by real concern. As Frith explains: "There were anxious spectators in Chamouni watching their progress, and the last view of the unfortunate party disclosed them standing together in a group ... then the merciless snow again had them in a shroud, and they were never again seen alive" (45). A crowd of tourists, safely grounded near a refuge, following the fate of these mountaineers is also part of Elizabeth Le Blond's account of the same incident. She draws attention to "the big telescope at the Châlet of Pilan-Praz above Chamonix" which was fixed on the route of the three unfortunate climbers and their eight guides. She recalls that "the party could be seen lying down on the ground, to avoid being swept away by the hurricane" (*True Tales of Mountain Adventure* 109). Her guide, Sylvain, acting out of concern rather than from a fascination with the horrific spectacle, hurried to "an eminence not far off" where he carefully searched for tracks with the aid of his telescope. He found no traces of the climbers. When the weather cleared, Sylvain went up to the Plan-Praz once more to see if from there any traces of the lost ones could be discovered with the telescope, but "The first glance showed him five black specks near the Petit Mulets which could be nothing else but the bodies of some of the victims" (110).

From a climber's perspective, such scenes offered few voyeuristic possibilities for the dangers were and had been all too close. One does not wish to witness one's own death. The tourist as spectator, though, was another matter. For such an individual, the telescope titillated an appetite for the lurid, even when death was not necessarily the outcome; it invited one to seek a view of danger and tempted one to look. Perhaps it is no accident that the title of at least two books describing mountain travel are *A Peep at the Pyrenees by a Pedestrian. Being a Tourist's Note-Book* (1867) and *A Peep at the Mountains: The Journal of a Lady* (1871).

Part 2: Performance Spaces, Spectacles, and the Culture Industry

Performance Spaces

As the discussion on voyeurism suggests, telescopes and tourists not only transformed mountaineering into a spectator sport but also converted the landscape into a performance space of parts, arranged around dramatic scenes. Such an arrangement contributed to the Victorians' sense that the mountains were a form of theatre or places of entertainment. They were no longer primarily transcendental regions that transported the soul beyond the limits of this earth.

By the mid-nineteenth century, mountains had become "amphitheatres" (in the geographical and metaphorical senses) filled with audiences and performers. Mary Taylor, Charlotte Brontë's good friend, was not being merely conventional when she wrote from Chamonix that she seemed "to be in a vast amphitheatre of mountains" (*Swiss Notes by Five Ladies* 25). Nor was Anne Lister being simply ornamental when she asked her correspondent to imagine an "*immense* amphitheatre . . . above two miles in circumference" (Green 397). For some Victorians, mountains approached theatre. It is telling that some climbing narratives and tourist diaries of trips to the Alps would begin with a list of *Dramatis Personae* or a *Dramas* [*sic*] *Personae*. *Miss Jemima's Journal* and E. Tuckett's *How We Spent the Summer, or "A Voyage en Zigzag"* are examples. Because of this context, Leslie Stephen was not being merely metaphorical when he referred to Meta Gaskell, Elizabeth Gaskell's daughter, as "a brilliant performer" (Bicknell 1: 144). (Stephen had taken her on a 12-hour walk over a glacier pass and been impressed with her endurance.) Nor was J. Norman Collie, the accomplished climber, being simply sarcastic when he predicted that in a few years avalanches in the Alps would be timed "to be let loose only twice a day, namely at morning and afternoon *performances* [emphasis mine]" (133).

Mountains were part of an entertainment industry. As if dividing the drama of a climb into acts, hotels pointed their telescopes toward certain stages in the progress of a climb – they rarely offered random views. The view through these telescopes set the scene and the backdrop for the action. For instance, hotel telescopes often focused upon mountain huts so that guests could be sure to catch sight of climbers gathered at crucial points during their ascents or descents. In addition, hotels occasionally arranged for props associated with the drama of climbing to be clearly visible within the lens's scope. In August 1897, for instance, the *News* informed its readers that even though a ladder was no longer needed to bridge a formidable crevasse on the north-west arête of the Mönch (13,465'), it was still on show "to amuse the tourists" who were peering at the scene through a hotel telescope situated in the Scheidegg and Wengern Alps (*News* 27 August 1897, Scrapbook, Alpine Club Archives).

Spectacles

From mid-century on, mountains were not only static scenes in which perilous events occurred; they were also being transformed into theatrical spectacles with all the lavishness and commercialism accompanying such productions. A panoramic view of the mountains was referred to as a "magnificent spectacle" and was admired by visitors for being "dazzling."[8] More to the point, though, the

---

8   When, for instance, Mary De La Beche Nicholl peered through the hotel telescope to watch a giant avalanche pouring down from the Glacier Tabuchet, she exclaimed that she was witnessing "a magnificent spectacle" (Hilary M. Thomas 80). Telescopes allowed people to see brilliant details of the landscape. When, for instance, the Rev. S.W. King

sublime drama of the mountains was descending to be co-opted by the noise of celebratory parades in the streets below, and, under the direction of Albert Smith, popularized on the London stage. Obviously these developments threatened to strip away any remaining sense of an elevated or majestic point of view.

With the rise in tourism, the practice of greeting groups of climbers before and after their attempts became increasingly common. Spectators relished and took a part in these parades that were choreographed in the spirit of a spectacle. Especially in the more heavily populated climbing centers, groups of villagers and tourists lined the streets to see a mountaineering party leave – one climber wrote that he was relieved that there were few spectators watching his departure.[9] And when the mountaineers returned after conquering a summit, these same crowds, moved by the spirits of curiosity and celebration, gave them a hero's welcome. Cheers, explosions, booms from the cannons, firecrackers, marching bands, flags, pealing bells, garlands of flowers, applause, dinners, speeches, and champagne attended their re-entry. Spectacle and celebrity were fast replacing, or perhaps reformulating, the silent, solitary, and terrifying heights associated with the sublime. Now the grandeur was of another sort.

In 1853, the festivities following John MacGregor's descent from the summit of Mont Blanc overflowed with jubilation: "The bells rang a merry peal . then the cannon boomed, and the damsels of Chamounix presented bouquets." After the procession, with the showman Albert Smith presiding, there was "an excellent dinner in the open air, with all the travellers then in Chamounix as admiring spectators of the very characteristic scene." Amid the intermittent firing of guns and illuminations, "the Englishmen made speeches, and the guides sang lugubrious songs." Even the moon took a part in the production and looked upon the performance "with a calm radiance," a tranquility that did not last long under the effect of a rather potent punch (Thorington 173). In 1864, Francis Fox Tuckett and Leslie Stephen were received by a volley of guns and bouquets of flowers that, according to Tuckett, "severely" tested Stephen's modesty (F.F. Tuckett 95). The two had also just descended from the summit of Mont Blanc. Even in the less populated areas where the props and the tourists were not as readily available, there were still attempts to replicate and to participate in the customary festivities. For instance, when Tuckett came down from the Höchste Spitze, his sister wryly observed that, there being no cannon on the premises, an "intelligent native" attempted to play "See the Conquering Hero Comes" on an Alpine horn. She also made fun of their being made much of.

---

peered through his telescope pointed toward the summit of Mont Blanc, he saw "great wreaths of snow ... their long wavy ridges, fringed with enormous icicles, defined with dazzling brilliance against the dark purple sky" (82). To his eyes, the scene was dazzling and spectacular.

[9]   Before his ascent of Mont Blanc, Eustace Anderson recorded that because of trouble hiring guides, "few people were aware of our intention, and we were not troubled with many spectators at our departure" (74).

Figure 2.7   Elizabeth Tuckett. "The Return"

Figure 2.8   Elizabeth Tuckett. "At Asiago. An Ovation!"

Climbers' accounts of these events are lively. The terrors and dangers of the expedition seem momentarily to recede under the swell of the excitement. When H. Seymour King descended from the first successful attempt of the Aiguille Blanche de Peuteret (in the Italian Alps), what he hoped would be a quiet and private return after a rather treacherous climb turned out to be quite different:

> We walked briskly down the valley to Cormayeur, cheering ourselves with thoughts of soup and bed. My clothes were in rags, and my chief desire was to get

into the hotel as quietly and promptly as possible. Some one had, however, spied us on the top, and our entry into the village was signalised by the conventional cannon shots; the hotels were full, and the streets lined with groups of Italians who welcomed us with the greatest enthusiasm. We found our hotel decorated with flags ... ("The First Ascent of the Aiguille Blanche de Peuteret," *The Alpine Journal* 12 [1886]: 438)

A.F. Mummery enjoyed an even more enthusiastic welcome after he had descended from the Aiguille des Charmoz (11,302'):

Far on in the evening, the lights of the Montenvers blessed our vision. Jodels and shouts were succeeded by rockets; and, as we descended the rhododendron-covered slopes, we saw the tallest member of the Alpine Club executing a brilliant *pas seul* on a rickety table, silhouetted against the dazzling glare of red lights and other pyrotechnic displays. A tumultuous welcome greeted our arrival, and protracted festivities concluded the evening. (83)

In these spectacles, the climbers were treated as heroes. After an ascent of Mont Blanc in 1855, Richards (his full name is not given in the tourist's diary) descended into Chamonix and was welcomed by crowds who saluted him with guns. "One enthusiastic Frenchman raised him on his shoulders and begged as a memorial his Alpine stock and name" (Joseph Walker 16). In the same year, a climber who had also reached the summit returned to the courtyard of the Hôtel de Londres and was fêted with gunshots and flowers. When he retired to his bedroom, he "found the passage strewn with rose leaves and a handsome nosegay on the table" (Anderson 101). Later, in 1875, after he had climbed the Eiger, A.W. Moore heard guns firing and received enthusiastic handshaking that was "quite overpowering" (355). And, just before the turn of the century (1899), Gertrude Bell reported that, after she had come down from a difficult ascent, she "found everyone in the hotel on the doorstep, waiting for me." To her astonishment, a member of the staff let off firecrackers. She added, "A friendly old lady whom I have since discovered to be the Comtesse d'Eu, pressed my hand (– I was quite the hero! –)" (The Gertrude Bell Archive, 28 August 1899).

Given the nature of these events, it is not surprising that they were occasionally parodied. "A Boy's Ascent of Mont Blanc" (1864), supposedly written by a boy, but really composed by the man Albert Smith, mocks the traditional revelry. The boy boasts: "Never was there a grander procession than ours. Mounted on our mules, and surrounding Ralph as much as possible to conceal him from too close an inspection [Ralph is injured], we marched across the fields, the band playing with all its vigour" ("A Boy's Ascent of Mont Blanc" 143). Reflecting the dramatic character of the occasion, the young narrator offers his readers a printed program, just as if a performance were to begin:

ORDER OF PROCESSION

ON THE OCCASION OF

𝔒ur 𝔗riump𝔥ant 𝔈ntr𝔶 into 𝔠𝔥amouni.

Dogs
Gracefully waving their tails.

Boys and Girls	Villagers
Offering us their homely cheer.	pursuing us with desperate bravoes.

Band
Blowing our trumpets in unmeasured strains.

Guides	Guides
Whose poles have an electrical effect	with every eye turning on their axes.

Your Humble Servant,	Ralph Green,	Frank Kingstone,
flattered by his reception, and	looking better on his	thinking over the
delighted to get back again.	humble mule than did	expense, and wishing
	the Grands-Mulets.	he had never gone up.

Scented Pocket-Handkerchiefs	Beauty, Rank, and Fashion
Fluttering in the breeze.	Overcome by their feelings.

Guides
Overwhelmed by avalanches of children, and up to their necks in wreaths of babies.

Their Wives
In a highly dangerous state of affection.

Porters
hale and stout

More Dogs,
Majestic and solemn, but waving their tails with an enchanting grace. (143)

Henry and Athol Mayhew's *Mont Blanc: A Comedy in Three Acts* (1874) also pokes fun at these processions. In the play's lively third act, after having made an unlikely ascent of Mont Blanc, the protagonists march into Chamonix. Surrounded by flags, the firing of guns, the pealing of bells, the playing of the band, and the cheers of the public, they process through the streets. The stage directions read like a program:

Enter Procession, *with* Florence, Harold M., *and* Lord S., L.U.E.
in the following order. – It crosses behind fountain, and goes down R. to L.
1. Town Official, *bearing flag.*
2. Town Fiddler and Piper *playing a march.*
3. *Four of principal* Guides *bearing ice-axes.*
4. Florence, *with* Harold M. *on one side, and* Lord S. *on other.*
5. *Rest of* Guides *carrying axes, ropes, and lanterns.*
6. Boys *and* Girls *carrying hampers and batons of ascending party.*
7. Porters *and* Volunteers *carrying knapsack and cooking utensils.*
8. Villagers *and* Peasants *green boughs.*
(Band *plays.*) (Mayhew 47)

Albert Smith and Spectacle

Parodies of the celebrations are more often than not indebted to Albert Smith's
description of his departure and reception when, though not in good physical shape,
he had rather foolishly climbed Mont Blanc in August 1851.[10] From beginning
to end Smith's adventure aptly reflected his vocation as a popular entertainer and
prolific contributor to *Punch*. In spite of the fact that Smith had to be almost carried
to the summit during the last few hours, there were many moments of hilarity.
These difficulties were not necessarily visible to those waiting and watching
below. For them the expedition was a splendid event.[11]

---

[10]   Albert Smith was accompanied on his climb by three Oxford undergraduates:
Francis Philips, Charles G. Floyd, and the Hon. W.E. Sackville-West. The Alps had
fascinated him ever since, as a boy, he had traveled to Switzerland with his parents. As the
story goes, when Smith was younger, he had even assembled a small panoramic display,
"Alps in a Box" for his little sister. He had read the narratives of Alpine climbs, and in 1841
had composed a piece of light verse, "Ascents of Mont Blanc," that he set to the air of a
popular tune. In the poem, he proclaimed:
>   Full forty gentlemen wealthy and bold,
>   Have climbed up in spite of labour and cold;
>   But of that number there lies not one,
>   Who speaks of the journey as very good fun. (Smith, "Loose Leaves from the
>   Travellers Album at Chamouni," 579–80)

[11]   There is sometimes quite a difference between Smith's written account of his climb
and the jolly and dramatic way he eventually presented it to the public in London. For a
more thoughtful and introspective account of his climb read Smith's *The Story of Mont
Blanc*. For instance, at a particularly difficult part of the climb, he recalls:
>   From this point, on to the summit, for a space of two hours, I was in such a
>   strange state of mingled unconsciousness and acute observation – of combined
>   sleeping and waking . With the perfect knowledge of where I was, and what I
>   was about – even with such caution as was required to place my feet on particular
>   places in the snow – I conjured up such a set of absurd and improbable phantoms
>   about me . I am not sufficiently versed in the finer theories of the psychology

Word spread that the largest party ever to leave Chamonix for Mont Blanc was assembling, so crowds collected in the courtyards and streets to follow Smith, his 3 companions, his 16 guides, and his 18 porters, who were carrying, among other items, 60 bottles of vin ordinaire, 15 bottles of St. Jean, 3 bottles of Cognac, 2 bottles of champagne, 4 shoulders of mutton, and 35 small fowls. As the ascent proceeded, these spectators periodically continued to observe the group through telescopes, and, from time to time, saluted their progress with cannon fire and gunshots. During the climb, or whenever Smith felt up to it, he transformed the ascent and descent into a variety show. He led his companions in song and laughter, and, on other occasions, asked the guides to sing their Savoyard lyrics. At one point the climbing party even paused to enjoy the fun of throwing empty wine bottles down a glacier. Smith describes the sport:

> We flung them off from the rock as far as we were able, and then watched their course. Whenever they chanced to point neck first down the slope, they started off with inconceivable velocity, leaping the crevices by their own impetus, until they were lost in the distance. The excitement of the guides during this amusement was very remarkable: a stand of betting men could not have betrayed more at Derby. (As quoted in Fitzsimons 117)

Once they were on top, the champagne flowed (observed through the telescopes), the guns fired in Chamonix, and people, like Sir Robert Peel, who had just arrived for a holiday, "watched them all night through a telescope" and "kept ... everyone up drinking their health" (Fitzsimons 121). According to Smith, the descent was similar to the jolly tumble downs that satirists loved to illustrate (see previous chapter). Not at all skilled at a glissade, he and his three companions slid and slipped, or fell head over heels. Apparently spectators watching below momentarily feared these inexperienced climbers were dashing to their deaths. Smith, though, described it as a lark. Finally, the returning victorious procession brought the spectacle to a roaring close. With exuberant detail, Smith describes his triumphant entrance into Chamonix:

> We had heard the guns firing at Chamouni ever since we left the Pelerines; but as we entered the village we were greeted with a tremendous round of Alpine artillery from the roof of the new Hôtel Royal, and the garden and courtyard of the Hôtel de Londres. The whole population was in the streets, and on the bridge; the ladies at the hotels waving their handkerchiefs, and the men cheering; and a harpist and a violin player now joined the *cortège*. When we got into the court of our

---

> of sleep to know if such a state might be; but I believe for the greater part of this bewildering period I was fast asleep with my eyes open, and through them the wandering brain received external impressions; in the same manner as, upon awaking, the phantasms of our dreams are sometimes carried on . (*The Story of Mont Blanc* 196–97)

hotel, M. Edouard Tairraz had dressed a little table with some beautiful bouquets and wax candles, until it looked uncommonly like an altar, but for the half-dozen champagne that formed a portion of the ornaments; and here we were invited to drink with him, and be gazed at, and have our hands shaken by everybody. One or two enthusiastic tourists expected me there and then to tell them all about it; but the crowd was now so great, and the guns so noisy, and the heat and dust so oppressive, coupled with the state of excitement in which we all were, that I was not sorry to get away. ("Mont Blanc," *Blackwood's Magazine* 71: 54)[12]

Smith could play the part of a Romantic tourist, but he rarely let a transcendental interval compromise or obliterate his sense of the stage. For him, Mont Blanc was primarily a dramatic space. Significantly, when Smith had visited the Alps in 1849, he remarked that a view of the glacier lit by the moon had "a dioramic effect" – an observation that reveals just how vibrant the theatrical context was for him (Thorington 99). The fact that Smith could "never quite escape" this orientation did not elude the attention of an editorial writer for the *Times*, who felt annoyed that "the markers of traditional plot structure – rising action, climax, denouement" should have become the means of constructing a narrative of a climb ("Mont Blanc has Become a Positive Nuisance," *The Times* 6 October, 1856: 8).

Mont Blanc Goes to the Cities

Smith's spectacular parade was, in a sense, a major force in leading the drama of the mountains down to other arenas of performance, away from the regions of the sublime, and into the grasp of those who wanted to reconstruct its events and market its excitement.

In August 1851, Smith had actually traveled to Chamonix, determined not only to fulfill a dream of climbing Mont Blanc but also to gather materials so he might create an entertaining diorama based upon the experience.[13] When he returned to London, he began designing, with William Beverley's assistance, what was to become the most popular show in London. Seven months later, *Ascent of Mont Blanc* began its run and remained for six years at the Egyptian Hall, Piccadilly. It opened on 15 March 1852 and closed, after approximately two thousand performances, on 6 July 1858. Smith had earned a lot of money and was ready to start producing a new show on his travels in China. He had become a celebrity. Whenever he returned to Chamonix to collect more materials for his production, the cannons boomed – much to the annoyance of one mountaineer who wanted to get some sleep. In an August 1857 letter to Lucy Baile, Alfred Wills

---

[12]   Soon afterwards, a disapproving Ruskin, who was in the area, wrote to his father and declared there had been a "cockney ascent of Mont Blanc of which you are soon to hear in London" (as quoted in Fitzsimons 102).

[13]   Smith had completed a revival of his show *The Overland Mail* at the Music Hall. He was casting about for a new spectacle.

complained: "There has been a great noise today of cannons etc. Albert Smith got here last night & there was this ascent of Mont B. Happily both parties are at the other hotel ... There is not much noise now, however, & I hope to sleep" (Wills Correspondence, Alpine Club Archives).[14] Tourists also liked to visit his room in the Hôtel de Londres. When it was vacant, the room always let at a higher rate.

That Smith approached Mont Blanc as an entertainer and regarded it as theatre had a cultural precedence. Even though Smith's 1852–58 production of his ascent of Mont Blanc was to be very different – far more spectacular and entertaining – from earlier presentations of the mountain, it was indebted to them. For half a century at least, the Alps had been the subject of various public displays in city centers. In his exhaustive and enlightening study *The Shows of London*, Richard D. Altick reminds his readers that a model of the region, 20' long, 6' wide, and 8' high, had already been on exhibit at a cabinetmaker's in Piccadilly as early as 1770. By the mid-nineteenth century, because of the burgeoning interest in the Alps, representations of the region were standard fare. From the beginning of the eighteenth century, its mountains had been known to the masses through peepshows, panoramas, and dioramas, and later, by means of various optical gadgets, such as magic lanterns and stereoscopes.[15] Its imposing landscape was as enthusiastically viewed as were the splendidly large representations of exotic places, vast cityscapes, natural disasters, abbey ruins, and interiors of cathedrals, produced in the nineteenth century by such people as Robert Burford, John Burford, Robert Barker, Henry Aston Barker, Louis Jacques Mandé Daguerre, and his brother-in-law, John Arrowsmith – all designers of dioramas and panoramas.[16] Their panoramas and dioramas of these subjects were exhibited not only in London

---

[14]   Whenever tourists went to the Hôtel de Londres, they asked to see the rooms where Smith stayed. After his death, residents of Chamonix erected a slab to memorialize him. Miss Jemima, the Cook tourist we met in the previous chapter, made a point of visiting it.

[15]   For histories of these various shows and optical devices see, for instance, Richard D. Altick's *The Shows of London* (1978), Ralph Hyde's *Panoramania!* (1988), Stephan Oettermann's *The Panorama: History of a Mass Medium* (1997), and Laurent Mannoni's *The Great Art of Light and Shadow* (2000). In addition, see Vanessa R. Schwartz's *Spectacular Realities: Early Mass Culture in Fin-de-Siècle France* (1998), Helmut and Alison Gernsheim's *L.J.M. Daguerre: The History of the Diorama & the Daguerreotype* (1968), and Robert Mitchell's *Plans and Views in Perspective of Buildings Erected in England and Scotland* (1801). Isobel Armstrong's *Victorian Glassworlds* (2008) reminds us that spectacular dissolving view of volcanic eruptions were available to the public (see pp. 312–15). Also consult the web site of the Bill Douglas Centre for the History of Cinema and Popular Culture at the University of Exeter, <http://www.bftv.ac.uk/projects/Exeter.html>

[16]   For other materials on these shows, see Sophie Thomas, "Making Visible: The Diorama, the Double and the Gothic subject" <http://www.rc.umd.edu/praxis/gothic/thomas/thomas.html>; <http://blogs.princeton.edu/graphicarts/2008/10/panoramas>; "The Panorama Effect: Spectacle for the Masses" <http://newman.baruch.cuny.edu/digital/2003/panorama/new--001.htm>; and "Screen Practice Before Film" <http://www.bftv.ac.uk/projects/exeter.htm>

but also in outlying regions as well as in the major European cities: Rome, Paris, Berlin, Naples, and Florence.[17] Among the Alpine shows were Robert Burford's 1835 "Mont Blanc, the Valley of Chamounix, and the Surrounding Mountains," based on his own drawings done from the Flégère and his 1849 "Panorama from the Rigi," on view at the Panorama Royal in Leicester Square.

It is important to note that these presentations listed above were still indebted to a Romantic sensibility and, consequently, dwelt exclusively upon the sublime qualities of the Alpine landscape. They were not registering Albert Smith's sense of show or spectacle. For this reason, in the handbook accompanying the panorama of Mont Blanc, Robert Burford borrowed lines from Byron and lauded the mountain's "cold sublimity." He spoke of the vastness of the scene that "at first oppresses and overwhelms" the mind. And he drew attention to the "voluptuous and universal tranquility, the deep and solemn stillness which reigns, interrupted only by the fearful rush of the avalanche, the hollow whistling of the wind." Echoing conventional expressions describing the sublime experience, Burford spoke of how a mountain's vastness

> Impress[es] the senses in a manner that obliterates the passions and follies of
> the world, and awakens associations and feelings altogether new, disposing the
> mind to feel, in full force, the sublimity of the scene, raising the thoughts to an
> immaterial world, and inspiring emotions of religion, which the tongue cannot
> utter or the pen record. (4)

Mont Blanc was the subject of many such productions. Earlier, in 1830, the *Times* of London had announced the opening of a new representation of the famous mountain at the Diorama in Regent's Park. This diorama had been erected in 1823 and displayed pictures that were 45' by 72'. This show presented images of the Swiss Alps that had been painted on translucent material so as to produce realistic effects of light and shade that gave an illusion of depth and movement. Sophie Thomas explains that these pictures would have been presented

> in such a way that day-light from high windows and skylights invisible to the
> audience, intercepted and/or altered by "a number of coloured transparent and
> moveable blinds or curtains," could create the naturalistic illusion of three
> dimensional space. The manipulation of these blinds by an assortment of lines
> and pulleys introduced "many surprising changes in the appearance of the
> colours of the painting or scenery" – thus transforming the image from a static
> object into a site of unexpected change, often of a temporal nature (such as
> from night-time to day light). The use of both reflected and mediated light gave
> rise to the impression that the scene was brilliantly illuminated entirely from

---

[17]   From 1794 to 1863, Robert Barker and his family ran an exhibition theater, a panorama, on Leicester Square, where the largest views were about 30' high by 90' across, see <http://blogs.princeton.edu/graphicarts/2008/10/panoramas.html>.

within . One of the more innovative aspects of the building design was a rotating "saloon"; the seating area for the audience was to pivot around a central well, revolving "through an angle of 73° between scenes." A complete show would take about thirty minutes, with fifteen minutes per picture, but viewers could stay on and see the sequence repeated. (5–6)[18]

In the same year (1823), one of Louis Jacques Mandé Daguerre's dioramas, *View of Mont Blanc taken from the Valley of Chamonix*, added to these effects by placing objects in the spaces between the pictures and the audience to show scale and to give a three-dimensional appearance to the painted scenes. When Daguerre produced the show in Paris during the 1830s, he imported a chalet with barn and outhouses; he also included a live goat eating hay in a shed. The sound of the goat's bells, the blowing of an Alpen horn, and the singing of local melodies contributed to the illusion – not to mention the girls in peasant dress serving the audience a country breakfast (Sophie Thomas 11). Smith was later to copy this practice for his *Ascent of Mont Blanc* by adding three-dimensional objects and live models before the screen showing paintings of the mountain.

These performance spaces were constructed to separate their audience from their external surroundings. Just as when a person puts an eye up to a telescope and essentially shuts out all that circumscribes it, so too did the peepshows, the dioramas, and the panoramas. At the peepshows, one looked through a curtained, framed glass and saw only what was pictured through its large convex lens – all that was intrusive and extraneous to the displayed image disappeared. Similarly, a spectator entered the dioramas and panoramas through long corridors of darkness and emerged into an illuminated space that enveloped the visitor in what was normally far away and invisible. I suggest that these passages simulated the interior of the tubes belonging to an extended telescope. This time, though, the spectator entered a theatre that erased the frame of the peepshow or telescope. The viewer was transported to a seamless panoramic prospect that appeared to extend to infinity. As Altick explains, just as in most theatres, darkness removed the spectators' consciousness from all extraneous objects by which size and distance could be measured: "the limiting frame and standards of size and distance external to the picture itself – were eliminated. The intrusive elements of the spectator's

---

[18]   In contrast to dioramas, panoramas offered the spectator a 360° view of a painted scene displayed in circular rotundas. It was an all-embracing view that simulated the experience of being on the very spot – one of its inventors, Robert Barker, spoke of it as *La nature à coup d'oeil*. Sophie Thomas explains: "Viewers surveyed the scene around them from a central viewing platform, constructed in such a way as to conceal any visual borders or frames" (9). As a result, the prospect seemed to go on forever. The canvases hung suspended 30' away. One of the early more successful panoramas was one that gave the spectator the illusion of being on top of the dome of St. Paul's and seeing the landscape of London from that vantage point. The spectator ascended a series of staircases to reach the viewing platforms.

surroundings being blacked out, the world in which [the audience was] entwined consisted exclusively of the landscape or cityscape depicted on the canvas suspended thirty feet away" (132–33).[19] Appropriately, to gain admittance to Smith's *Ascent of Mont Blanc*, one had to hand over a "passport" to a ticket-taker dressed as a French gendarme. As a spectator or as a member of the audience, one literally crossed over a border into new territory. One left London behind and stepped into another world.

Ascent of Mont Blanc

Although Albert Smith's 1852–58 *Ascent of Mont Blanc* was indebted to this inheritance and, consequently, used many of the techniques and machinery from these earlier dioramas featuring Alpine scenery, the production differed in ways that remind one of how the Victorian sensibility could, to some degree, separate itself from its legacy. Now the vulgarisms and commercialism associated with spectacle replaced a taste for the mystery of the vast mountain landscape that painters, such as Turner, had represented and Ruskin admired.

To begin with, Smith's show neither dwelt on the picturesque nor devoted itself to the public taste for romantic topography. As Peter H. Hansen remarks, "Smith's Mont Blanc performances contributed to the declining cultural authority of the picturesque and the sublime in the Alps" (309). Its script turned an almost deaf ear to the sublime. Robert Burford's lugubrious sentences and the sentiments that had accompanied his 1837 Mont Blanc panorama were barely audible. Rather, almost twenty years later, Smith's production paid far more attention to the excesses that had been at play when he had actually done the climb himself and had triumphantly marched back into Chamonix. Unlike the earlier lectures on Mont Blanc that he had delivered in London in the late 1840s, Smith was now intent upon producing an active spectacle and offering his audience a lively narrative, replete with anecdotes, humor, impersonations, satirical sketches, hurdy-gurdy music of the guides, and patter songs such as "The Young English Tourist" as well as Beverley's paintings of Mont Blanc. Committed to presenting an evening of

---

[19] In 1836, Lady Morgan described what she experienced when she had watched a diorama, *The Village of Alagna, Piedmont* dramatically recreating the avalanche that had buried that Swiss village in 1820:

> First … the Alpine village and the mountains beyond were seen lying tranquil in the moonlight, with a little lake in the foreground, reflecting the glow of a hearth inside a cottage. As the moonlight diminished, the pinpoints of light elsewhere in the village became more visible. Then, as the villagers retired, the lights were extinguished, one by one. Backstage sounds of thunder and wind warned of the impending catastrophe, followed by the clangour of the church bells as someone in the village awoke (as represented by the reappearance of a single tiny light) and gave the alarm. The avalanche descended with a roar; the bell in the spire suddenly ceased ringing; and suddenly the whole picture was blacked out. (Altick 170) (Lady Morgan's account is in the *Athenaeum* [13 August 1836]: 570)

We, Albert Smith, One of Her Britannic Majesty's Representatives on the Summit of Mont Blanc, Knight of the Most Noble Order of the Grands Mulets, Baron Galignani of Piccadilly, Knight of the Grand Crossing from Burlington Arcade to the Egyptian Hall, Member of the Society for the Confusion of Useless Knowledge, Secretary for his Own Affairs, &c, &c, &c, &c, &c, &c.

Request and require, in the Name of His Majesty the Monarch of Mountains, all those whom it may concern, more especially the Police on the Piccadilly Frontier to allow

Mr Bradbury

(British Subject)

to pass freely in at the street door of the Egyptian Hall, and up stairs to the Mont Blanc Room, on the evening of Saturday, December the First 1855, at 8 P.M. and to afford him every assistance in the way of oysters, stout, champagne, soda and brandy, and other aid, of which he may stand in need.

Given at the Box Office, Piccadilly, the 28ᵗʰ day of November, 1855

Albert Smith

"God save the Queen!"

Figure 2.9   Passport to Egyptian Hall, 28 November 1855

entertainment, he was not interested in just offering views of imposing and awe-inspiring scenery. In spite of his efforts, however, there were occasionally people who appear to have been overwhelmed by an eagerness to experience the sublime. Expectations and habits from a previous generation held fast to one visitor from New York who reported that:

> On Saturday evening we attended Albert Smith's new entertainment, "The Ascent of Mont Blanc." So delighted was I with the fine graphic spirit, the charming humour of the bold tourist, and the rare beauty of his panoramic illustrations, that I fear I almost made myself ridiculous by my uncontrollable expressions of enthusiasm and pleasure. Yet I think those around me held me excused, and that our entertainer himself would have pronounced no harsh judgment upon me. I know not whether I had most delight in the tourist's wondrous power of description, which bears you with him from quiet Chamouni's quiet vale, up – up – into the awful Alpine solitude – the solemn eternity of snows – up, till you hear the avalanches thunder from the far peaks and look into the yawning fissures, the icy sepulchers of some who have gone before – up, up, till you stand with him on that stupendous dome of ice, and behold mountains, and seas, and kingdoms below, and nothing of all the earth between you and God ... (Greenwood 58)

For a majority, though, the show was merely a piece of boisterous fun that offered the illusion of travel without having to suffer the nausea of crossing the English Channel or the discomfort of trudging up steep slopes and through deep snow. On the whole, Smith's audiences eagerly embraced the spectacle and, for the moment, set aside thoughts of the sublime.

When *Ascent of Mont Blanc* opened, Smith, dressed in evening attire, stepped through a doorway of a replica of a Swiss chalet onto a raised platform and directed the entertainment. The performance began with Beverley's stationary pictures of scenes en route to Chamonix. Smith used the occasion of this journey to satirize tourists, such as Mrs. Seymour, who was always losing her luggage, and to poke fun at two old ladies, who pulled down the blinds of the diligence whenever they were near a precipice. He ridiculed young tourists such as Miss Annie Simmonds, who admired Tennyson, and he resurrected an American character, Mr. Peabody Taylor, whom he had used in previous productions. Peabody discoursed on eau de Cologne and confused Lord Byron with the Prisoner of Chillon and with Mazeppa. After an intermission, panoramas, moving vertically on the stage behind, presented Beverley's pictures of Smith and his party's ascent of Mont Blanc.

With some exaggeration, Smith described the progress of the climb, and featured fearful scenes showing his party crossing, by means of a ladder, a dangerous opening in the Glacier du Tacconay. In Smith's hyperbolic account, a single slip meant death – in reality, at that point in the climb, to lose his footing would not have been a deadly mistake. A selection from his narrative gives one a sense of how he embellished and dramatized the danger:

Figure 2.10 William Beverley. "Dangerous Crevice in the Glacier du Tacconay"

In about seven hours after leaving the Grands Mulets, is an almost perpendicular wall of ice, called the Mur de la Côte. This is about 450 feet high, and may be considered as the most difficult and really dangerous part of the whole ascension. It is bordered on the left by an awful precipice. Here the guides are compelled to cut a footing for every step in the ice, as in so hazardous a position solidity and firmness of nerve are requisite. The number of steps may be reckoned at about 260, and this short ascent requires a full hour.

He also focused upon the place where Dr. Hamel's party had perished in 1820:

We then arrive on the Grand Plateau, having on the left the Aiguille du Midi, on the right the Dome du Goûté, and in the front Mont Blanc. This plain is nearly two miles long; at its extremity is an amphitheatre of rocks and icebergs, above which the summit rises almost perpendicularly. The passage, until of late years, was two hours shorter than at present, as it led in an almost straight line from hence by the Rochers Rouges to the top; but it has been abandoned since the unfortunate ascent of Dr. Hamel in 1820, when three guides were swept away and their bodies could never be recovered. (*A Hand-Book of Mr. Albert Smith's Ascent of Mont Blanc* 22)

As if pandering to an audience eager to be among those voyeurs/tourists who watched for death through their telescopes, Smith, as did many of the earlier showmen who had mounted panoramas and dioramas that exhibited deadly avalanches or volcanic explosions, invited his audience to gawk at the inherent danger and specter of mortality lurking within the immensity of the landscape and the difficulties of the climb. In *Ascent of Mont Blanc*, however, these moments did not last long. Variety-hall songs, music, and humorous sketches, equal to any comic moment in a Dickens novel or in *Punch*, abruptly followed the climbing narrative and soon either expelled or replaced these voyeuristic moments. One amusing routine was the spoof of an Englishman attempting to speak French and order food in a Parisian café. Wanting to order a mushroom, the gentleman drew a picture of it, but the waiter, misreading the picture, offered him an umbrella instead. A spirit of fun and gaiety prevailed and obliterated any lingering sense of the terror and pain that earlier commentators on the sublime had thought integral to the experience of standing before an imposing mountain landscape.

I suppose that if there was anything that could vividly encapsulate the shift from the Romantic sensibility to the Victorian frame of mind, it might possibly be the disparity between Robert Burford's 1837 panorama of Mont Blanc and Albert Smith's 1852–58 *Ascent of Mont Blanc*.[20] Although I am usually hesitant to indulge

[20]   Of all the mountaineers I have been discussing, Albert Smith has, perhaps, received the most attention. There are many books and articles about him. My discussion of Smith is indebted to details I have garnered from these. I have also been fortunate to be in archives and libraries, such as the Alpine Club in London and the National Library of Scotland, where

in such generalities, I suggest that there is some insight to be gained through the obvious differences between these two productions. The fact that Burford's dwelt exclusively on the sublime grandeur and power of nature, whereas Smith's focused on external and practical realities as well as upon the foibles of human behavior contributes to the perception that by mid-century, the sublime was losing its imaginative power. The sublime was not only coming down from the mountains and being subjected to Dickens's sentimental, rough-and-tumble world – a point I made in the previous chapter – but was also refashioning parts of itself so that, rather than dwelling among the grand and transcendental realms, it was settling in among the excesses of spectacle. Moreover, Burke's understanding of astonishment and terror (also discussed in the previous chapter) was falling into the hands of the technological – into the machinery and gadgets of the shows – and being either compromised or supplanted by the fascination with the tangible and the useful.

Unlike Burford's more sedate panoramas, Smith's production pushed toward sensory overload and the coarseness of everyday life. The room in the Egyptian Hall resembled "a little plot of old Switzerland" (Altick 47).

Although a picture from the *The Illustrated London News* gives a good idea of what it might have been like to be there (Fig. 2.11), Richard Altick's description of the space helps us get a better view:

> Most prominent was a full-scale reproduction of the exterior of a chalet, in the center of which was a curtained window through which a cheery light shone; during the scenes the portion representing the wall was raised out of sight. The front of the hall, according to a contemporary description "was occupied by a large pool of water, surrounded by granite rocks and Alpine plants, and well stocked with some fine live fish; and from this spring clumps of bulrushes and Arum lilies, which throw water and gas from their petals. Chamois skins, Indian corn, alpenstocks, vintage baskets, knapsacks, and other appropriate matters are grouped about the balconies, and vines and creepers slung about the rafters and beams." The room was further decorated with the banners of the various cantons and "some remarkably elegant lamp-shades of hanging leaves and flowers break the light very agreeably." (47)

As the years passed, Smith kept appending extraneous matter. The more props he added, the more the show, with all its bits and pieces, exaggerated the sense of spectacle. Indulging an insatiable appetite for the accretion of objects, he brought in a model of a diligence, displayed mule bells, attempted to exhibit a pair of unfortunate chamois who had been shipped from Switzerland (and died), and imported ten St. Bernard dogs – Smith gave one to Dickens and another to the Prince Consort. Continuing to bring Mont Blanc and Chamonix onto the stage,

---

I have seen many of the objects associated with his show on Mont Blanc. One interesting article I do not mention in the course of my discussion is Peter H. Hansen's "Albert Smith, the Alpine Club, and the Invention of Mountaineering in Mid-Victorian Britain."

Figure 2.11   "Albert Smith's *Ascent of Mont Blanc*"

Smith used his guide, François Favret, to accompany the dogs to England. When one of the St. Bernards paraded during the interval, young ladies were encouraged to pet it (Fig. 2.12).

These dogs also delivered chocolates to children who sat in the front row. Smith commissioned fresh paintings, sold souvenir booklets, introduced more scenes on the journey to and from Chamonix, composed supplementary music, and offered refreshments. Moreover, he marked special occasions by presenting the audience with souvenir portraits or bouquets, and at Christmas and Twelfth-night gave out gifts.[21] One becomes almost exhausted thinking about the multitude of props, diversions, novelties, and fragments that surrounded or defined what was ostensibly a narrative of a climb. Smith's 1851 celebratory parade in Chamonix had certainly marched into London, and brought with it a lot of superfluous materials. Indeed, his friend John MacGregor wondered whether there was anything left in Chamonix – Smith had taken away so much for his show.[22]

Metallic Lilies and The Culture Industry

With its technological novelties, such as the metallic lilies in front of the stage that emitted gas and light, and the mechanisms that altered and distributed color and light onto the images, *Ascent of Mont Blanc* not only exhibited and used the machinery of spectacle but also participated in and continued the celebration of industry and commodity from the Great Exhibition of 1851. Through Smith's production, Mont Blanc had been successfully transformed into an item to be consumed. Sandwich-board men roamed the streets and spin-offs from the show popped up everywhere. Its landscape, on stage and off, was a space in which to display an abundance of products and to make a profit: the production netted £30,000. Not just Mont Blanc, but mountains in general had entered the marketplace. Advertisements for mountaineering equipment proliferated, and various exhibitions on mountaineering in London and Liverpool became more popular. The Alpine Court at the Liverpool Jubilee Exhibition in 1886 featured large panoramic views of the mountain chain as seen from the slopes of the Riffelberg, extending from the Matterhorn to the Weisshorn ("The Alpine Court at the Liverpool Jubilee Exhibition," *The Alpine Journal* 13 [1887]: 337). At the Alpine Club's annual exhibition in 1894, members displayed panoramic drawings, photographs, and models of summits, all to the accompaniment of music played by the Bijou Orchestra – "The display was exceptionally large and good; it attracted, as usual, a large attendance" ("Proceedings of the Alpine Club," *The Alpine Journal* 17 [1894]: 88).

---

[21]   For a description of his gift of the Twelfth-Night Characters see Thorington 158–64.

[22]   For more information about the friendship between Albert Smith and John MacGregor, see Thorington 169–74.

Figure 2.12 John Leech. "The St. Bernard Mastiff at the Mont Blanc Lecture. A Happy Dog – Rather"

Spectacle and Post-Modern Theory

As I pointed out in the introduction to this chapter, to a degree, these exhibits and dioramas, most especially Smith's *Ascent of Mont Blanc*, joined what post-modern theorists have come to term the culture industry – but not as wholeheartedly as these commentators on the nature and consequences of spectacle might have us believe. Guy Debord's sense of a spectacle's totalitarian rule and Theodor Adorno's despair over the defeat of reflection are not as pertinent to these displays as they are in contemporary society. Extravaganzas such as Smith's did not necessarily hold their audiences hostage to a controlling, deceptive vision. They were not substitutions for reality. In spite of various optical illusions and mechanical devices, spectators, more often than not, recognized a gap between the spectacle's visual fictions and their own perception of the actual mountain. Audiences had not yet exchanged what Jean Baudrillard refers to as the "use-value" for "sign-value." Their gestures were essentially still their own. In mid-nineteenth century, people esteemed their own particular experience and afforded it precedence, rather than surrender to a commodified, illusory world propagated by the mass media. With its mechanical techniques and marketing devices, mid-century culture was well on its way to becoming part of that industry, but it was not there yet. Sign-value was emerging but had not arrived.[23]

In Smith's show, in particular, the satirical moments preceding and concluding his narrative of the climb as well as his ironic sketches opened up a dialogic space so that people were at liberty to explore the differences between what he was presenting and reality. The audience knew that, by their very nature, his satires and songs were exaggerations; and, by extension, they understood that his images and narrative of the climb were also somewhat hyperbolic. When Henry James attended a performance of *Ascent of Mont Blanc* in the summer of 1855, he was very much aware of the disparity between Smith's affect and the gaiety of the performance. James remembers:

> I recall in especial our being arrayed, to the number of nine persons, all of our contingent, in a sort of rustic balcony or verandah which, simulating the outer gallery of a Swiss cottage framed in creepers, formed a feature of Mr. Albert Smith's once-famous representation of the Tour of Mont Blanc. Big, bearded, rattling, chattering, mimicking Albert Smith again charms my senses, though

---

[23]   My commentary on post-modern theory on the spectacle is partially founded upon my reading of: Theodor W. Adorno's *The Culture Industry: Selected Essays on Mass Culture* (1991); Jean Baudrillard's *The Spirit of Terrorism and Other Essays* (2002); "Jean Baudrillard" in the Stanford Encyclopedia of Philosophy; Richard C. Beacham's *Spectacle Entertainment of Early Imperial Rome* (1999); Jonathan Crary's "Spectacle, Attention, Counter-Memory" in *October* 50 (autumn, 1989): 96–107; Guy Debord's *The Society of the Spectacle* (1994), and Max Horkheimer and Theodor W. Adorno's *Dialectics of Enlightenment* (1969 [1944]).

subject to the reflection that his type and presence, superficially so important, so ample, were somehow at odds with such ingratiations, with the reckless levity of his performance . (Altick 475)

Douglas Freshfield, one of the leading Victorian mountaineers, also remembers being taken to the show. His account speaks of how absurd the scenes depicting Mont Blanc were, especially after he had later been able to compare them with his own ascent of that mountain:

> I was taken at the age of about nine. He [Smith] lectured in a small hall, in front of the screen was a pool of water with metal waterlilies. The pictures were small compared with what we are accustomed to. Albert Smith stood in a sort of pulpit on the right and told mildly humorous stories of old ladies wandering in pursuit of lost luggage and made the most of the incidents of the climb. I recollect particularly an absurd picture of the Mur de la Côte. I was very much disappointed ten years later by the reality! (Thorington 153)

Freshfield particularly found fault with Smith's exaggerated claim that on the Mur de la Côte "should the foot or baton slip, there is no chance for life" (Fitzsimons 148).

Once tourism, with the help of railways and relative peace in Europe after the Napoleonic wars, got underway in mid-century, and once Thomas Cook opened up Switzerland to the middle classes in the 1860s, there were more and more possibilities for people to carry out reality checks and compare what they had seen at various dioramas with what actually lay before their eyes once they were among the Alps. These spectators were not just passively confined to their revolving or static seats in a theater. As I have discussed in the previous chapter, they could travel, by ship and train, more efficiently than ever, to the very scene of the production and walk or climb among the mountains at will to gain a first-hand perspective. As a result, it is not unusual in people's travel accounts to find passages in which the individual is not only carefully examining the mountain topography through a telescope but also unfolding a circular panoramic drawing of a mountain range from a guidebook and checking meticulously to see if it is accurate. Indeed, Henry Gaze in his directions for Cook's tourists suggested that after ascending the Flégère, the traveler should look through a telescope and spend "a most interesting hour, by comparing the plan of the chain of Mont Blanc from *Murray's Handbook* with the scene before you" (79). Some tourists measured the views in the diorama against the actual scene. In *A Holiday Tour* (1868), "Bunny" speaks of first going to the Diorama of Mount Pilatus and the Rigi before ascending these mountains himself. One realizes that he is eager to place the paintings side by side with the real thing. Although there had been disappointment among tourists when the mountains themselves did not seem to measure up to the grandeur of the paintings they had previously seen, there was also satisfaction in recognizing in retrospect that once they had been among the mountains themselves, they could exercise the power to judge using their own experience and their own eyes. They did not necessarily want the sights to look like pictures as such; rather, they now preferred to have the pictures represent what they had actually seen. By no means is the diorama a substitute; it is there only to give him a sense of what he might see: "we went to see the Diorama of Mount Pilatus and the Rigi; the view of the latter gave us a good idea of the treat we should have when we made the ascent" ("Bunny" 15). The mountains themselves will have the last word. Even Smith, on an 1849 trip to the Alps, felt obligated to compare Burford's "Panorama from the Rigi" with his own experience of standing on top of the Rigi and viewing the surrounding mountain ranges. In this case, he concluded that the panorama was "singularly correct" (Thorington 94).

Redeeming Black and White Shadows

Indeed, mountains had become a spectator sport and they had joined the world of illusion and spectacle, but those phenomena never fully replaced people's awe for the unmediated wilderness of a real mountain. Large rotating or circular canvases were no substitute for "the real thing"; furthermore, the rage for panoramas and dioramas itself was dying – the Mont Blanc mania, especially, was getting to be a bit boring. Photography was now taking hold of the public imagination and replacing not only dramatic engravings of mountain scenery, such as Edward Whymper's, but also Smith's larger spectacles and entertainments. The Alpine Club started introducing art photography into its annual exhibitions, and eventually began organizing shows exclusively devoted to the skilled mountain photography of William Frederick Donkin and to the extraordinary panoramic photographs taken by Vittorio Sella, the great Italian photographer and climber. An increasing number of mountaineers were taking a serious interest in art photography. As the reviewer of the Alpine Club exhibition of pictures and photographs taken in 1892 remarked, the number and quality of submitted photographs attested to "a far-reaching and widening sphere of activity" ("The Alpine Club Exhibition of Pictures and Photographs, 1892," *The Alpine Journal* 16 [1893]: 345).

For a public who believed it to be more accurate than other forms of representation, the photograph was a more direct and convincing way of representing this wilderness. In addition to its seeming accuracy, the photograph had the advantage of reintroducing the very mystery these spectacles had destroyed. The medium's stark contrasts displayed a more severe, and, hence, daunting image, especially when displayed through gelatin prints. With the coming of photography, and not the tourist snapshot (I hasten to add), the quiet and solitary black and white world of light and shadows replaced the noise and excesses of spectacle and purged it of its plebeian aura. In a sense, serious, high-quality mountain photography in the nineteenth century reintroduced, at least temporarily, the nobility of the sublime.

When mountain photography first came into being, the equipment required was cumbersome. For instance, on Auguste Bisson's 1861 expedition to photograph the panorama from the summit of Mont Blanc, twenty-five porters were required to carry his cameras, mobile darkroom, heavy glass negatives and chemicals (de Beer 137). In mid-century, distinguished climbers, such as William Frederick Donkin, took along their cameras and carried plates that weighed between 15 and 20 pounds.[24] Donkin's work is extraordinary and captures more than the conventional sweep of a mountain range. It arrests details of light and texture visible at higher altitudes that would not be as available either in a painting or through a telescope. His photographs brought his spectator up to the sublime realm of the higher peaks. The vast and often terrifying perspective of his photographs is reflected in an Alpine Club member's remarks upon a memorial exhibition of Donkin's photographs. (Donkin and his entire party had been lost during a climb in the Caucasus on 30 August 1888. Members of the Alpine Club had desperately searched for any remains of him. In addition to retracing his steps, they also scanned the cliffs with a telescope, but they found no traces of the calamity.[25]) "H.G.W.," a member of the Alpine Club, wrote that Donkin's "exquisite photographs"

> have enabled everyone who visited the Gainsborough Gallery to study at their
> leisure the secrets of the snows. In the absence of some such opportunity most
> tourists cannot ever form any accurate idea of the great, strange world above
> their heads, a world where every prospect pleases, without a touch of vileness,
> where sky as well as earth seem to open out into "a nobler, purer air" in a never-
> ending succession of distance behind distance, and where each quality of light
> and colour seems more refined than it is below. ([Willink] "Exhibition of Mr.
> Donkin's Photographs," *The Alpine Journal* 14 [1889]: 309)

Another well-known climber and photographer was Elizabeth Le Blond, already mentioned in this chapter. She was an accomplished professional who also lugged up heavy equipment and used her macintosh as a darkroom tent so that she could secure "a picture which shall be poetic as well as true" (*Hints on Snow Photography* 8).[26] But she was fortunate to have been younger than Donkin, so she was eventually able to take full advantage of the fact that cameras were becoming smaller and easier to bear up to high altitudes. For instance, in December, 1869, the Rev. H.B. George, a member of the Alpine Club, gave a paper in which he touted the advantages of a miniature camera, measuring 7½ inches by 4 inches

---

[24]   On 28 February 1882, W.F. Donkin read a paper, "Photography in the High Alps," before the Alpine Club membership, later published in *The Alpine Journal* 11 (1882): 63–71. In the paper he talks about his experiences and his techniques.

[25]   For details about the search for Donkin and his companion H. Fox as well as for the two guides, see Clinton Dent's 1889 article "The Search Expedition to the Caucasus" in *The Alpine Journal*. Donkin's remains were eventually found.

[26]   In her *Hints on Snow Photography*, Elizabeth Le Blond remarks that her own mountain photography is "excelled by those of signor Vittoria Sella, the late W.F. Donkin, and others, that I hardly feel I have a right to give advice" (10). She knew both these photographers and climbed with them.

and weighing just over five pounds, that he could easily transport and mount on the head of his ice axe.[27]

Figure 2.13 Illustration of mounted camera

---

[27] See George, "Notes on Photography in the High Alps".

A sketch by Elizabeth (Lizzie) Tuckett depicts her brother wielding this smaller apparatus.

Figure 2.14   Elizabeth Tuckett. "Is there room up there for me and my camera?"

By 1888 there was even more flexibility, for Kodak had introduced roll film and hand-held cameras.[28] This new technology allowed Le Blond, if she so wished, to abandon the clumsy tripod and spare plates that were difficult to manipulate in freezing temperatures, and with more ease to take hundreds of photographs of mountain peaks and glaciers in all kinds of weather. Le Blond was especially famous for her winter climbs. As had Donkin's, her photographs did not keep the spectator at a respectful distance but invited the eye to be right with her solitary self in all the silence of the snows, surrounded by a purified air. She once explained:

> One of the features of the scenery of the heights of Switzerland in winter is its extraordinary clearness of atmosphere, and the consequent hardness of its outlines and the deep blue of the sky. A dark blue sky, dazzling white snow, and well-marked shadows are what we are accustomed to in the Engadine in winter. So when photographing such scenes on such a day, I try to be truthful, and if the

---

[28]   Knowing their readers' interest in mountain photography, the May 1891 issue of *The Alpine Journal* ran Walter Leaf's article "Climbing with a Hand-Camera."

result is, as I think it ought to be, a dark sky, a glittering white outline against it, and here and there an inky shadow, say, if you will, that it is not picturesque, but do not blame me for refusing to mix the characteristics of a thunderstorm on the Italian lakes with the peculiar transparency of a winter's morning in the Alps.
(*Hints on Snow Photography* 8)

Although Le Blond did eventually make a few films of people skiing (unfortunately, I understand, these are lost), she significantly never wanted to use movement in her mountain photography. She believed that it is that black and white stillness inherent in a photograph that engages the sense of the immensity and nobility of a mountain.

Figure 2.15 Elizabeth Le Blond. Alpine glacier scene

It is an odd paradox that artistic mountain photography, with all its apparatus, should briefly work to rescue the sublime from the damage inflicted by commerce, crowds, and spectacles. This phenomenon, I should explain, should not be confused with what critics, such as Darryl Slack and J. Macgregor Wise, popularly speak of as "the technological sublime" – when the machine is regarded with reverence and supplants nature. In no way do these splendid representations of the lofty mountain landscape ever take second place to the camera that registers their image.[29] Quite the contrary: the photographs release the grandeur of the mountain itself; the natural image takes full authoritative precedence over the technology.

Less than a decade after Smith's extravaganza closed, these beautifully rendered photographs had become the savior of the mountains. They reminded the spectator that, in spite of all their potential for voyeurism and spectacle, mountains could still be seen as vast, noble, astonishing, terrifying, and somehow separated from the finite everyday world that waits below. The sublime did not have to remain sunk among the machinery of commerce and stagecraft. The photograph as a work of art could restore what had been sacrificed to the illusory view and bring back a more elevated and less public sense of grandeur.

---

[29]   See Darryl Slack's and J. Macgregor Wise's *Culture and Technology: A Primer.*

Chapter 3
Ladies on High

A CLIMBING GIRL

A lady has clomb to the Matterhorn's summit
Which almost like a monument points to the sky;
Steep not very much less than the string of a plummet
Suspended, which nothing can scale but a fly.

This lady has likewise ascended the Weisshorn,
And, what's a great deal more, descended it too,
Feet foremost; which seeing it might be named lockhorn,
So slippery 'tis, no small thing to do.
No glacier can baffle, no precipice balk her,

No peak rise above her, however sublime.
Give three cheers for intrepid Miss Walker.
I say, my boys, doesn't she know how to climb!

(*Punch* 26 August 1871)

In endeavouring to keep pace with ladies' ascents an author attempts the impossible, since many ladies are too modest to record their exploits. Thus, where three ladies are named as having climbed the Finsteraarhorn [14,025'], the number ought to our knowledge to be *at least* doubled.

("Reviews and Notices," *The Alpine Journal* 11 [1883]: 306)

Introduction

While Charlotte Brontë's close friend, Mary Taylor, was escorting four young women on an 1875 Alpine climbing holiday, she was horrified when a guide refused to lead them across a certain route because, as he declared, it was not suitable for ladies. Offended and frustrated by his response, Taylor scrawled in her diary that it felt as if the guide "had just struck away the snow, and shown us a deep crevasse right before us." His response had exposed what seemed to her to be a disturbing and – both literally and metaphorically – an unbridgeable gender gap. Taylor, who earlier in her life had climbed not only in the Alps but also in New Zealand, wondered: "Was there always such a wide mental and moral separation between man and woman?" (*Swiss Notes by Five Ladies* 131)

Taylor was, among others, sensitive to this sort of discrimination. Women who wrote about their climbing experiences frequently complained of being taken up the "ladies' way."[1] Their narratives register their anger with guides who refused to accompany them by pretending that they were already engaged or saying that they had reached a certain landmark when, of course, they had not. Others catalogued their disappointments at being left behind while the men ascended higher. Mrs. H.W. Cole was envious when her male companions suggested she go back while they proceeded further up the glacier in the direction of the Jungfrau: "As they could walk faster without me, it was arranged that I should return to the hotel with one of the guides, while the other conducted them onwards; but I was so enchanted with the scene that it was with much reluctance I acceded to the arrangement" (163). On another occasion, she grudgingly accepted the fact that "No lady ... could venture upon the glacier [Unter Aar Glacier]," recently covered with snow, and spoke of having to remain "a prisoner in the Hospice" while her male friends, their guide and two young dogs bounded ahead (143).

This sort of arrangement was common. A few years later, on a tour of the Oberland and its glaciers, Hereford Brooke George planned his expeditions so that the "gentlemen" were to climb the higher peaks while the "ladies ... were to ascend as many of the minor mountains as might prove convenient" (*The Oberland and its Glaciers* 6). And when spending the summer months in the Alps, Thomas Hinchliff hired a guide whom he named "director-general of excursions for the ladies," so that he and his Alpine Club friends could, "unencumbered," ascend to greater heights (255). The ladies were to visit the Mer de Glace, the Flégère, Col de Voga, and Montanvert – all far less challenging outings.

Historians of mountaineering are quick to record the ensuing irritation and confirm the prejudices that caused people to question whether a female could or should climb. Examples of discrimination are not difficult to find. However, in spite of the authority of these histories and the readiness of evidence, I want to challenge the assumption that women climbers were routinely excluded on the grounds that the activity was unladylike or that they were considered to be incompetent. Although prejudice existed, it functioned alongside an active participation in mountaineering – so active, indeed, that the sheer number of women climbers is extraordinary. Even though I understand that it is hard to balance the general record against the individual anomaly, and that it is all too easy to impose the aspirations of the present on the past, I want to offer another perspective: when it came to climbing in the Victorian period, gender did not, as a rule, matter in the overwhelmingly debilitating way commentators have claimed. Lists of climbs done in the second half of the nineteenth century as well as notices of successful expeditions in which a lady mountaineer reached a significant summit not only

---

[1]   In an 1870 article, "The Peaks of Primiero," in *The Alpine Journal*, Leslie Stephen suggested: "Ladies who do not object to a steady climb over grass slopes and a few easy rocks, might easily reach it [Val Travitale], and could ride from Primiero to the foot of the ascent" (4 [1870]: 398).

reveal the astonishing number of women climbers but also remind the present reader that women were not summarily discouraged from participating in what most recent commentators assume was solely a male-centered sport based upon power and privilege.[2]

A closer look at British Victorian women mountaineers suggests that, even though these climbers sometimes faced disapproval and their achievements occasionally elicited snide remarks, these individuals also frequently benefited from an admiration for their mountaineering ambitions. They were often surrounded by supportive people and by an interested public. These more affirming experiences need to be part of what is a more complex picture than that which is usually assumed. Retrospective views have difficulty admitting ambiguity and too quickly settle into received opinion, and most histories of climbing are reductive. They all-too readily emphasize a sense of social unease surrounding the phenomenon of women climbers and dwell, almost exclusively, upon what they assume to be the rigid rules of Victorian society as well as upon the negative impact of gender. Contrary to what more established contemporary opinion suggests, I believe that one needs to overcome the tendency to think that to mark or distinguish a group is intrinsically a hostile act. As we shall see in this chapter, a negative remark about a lady mountaineer's knickerbockers does not always mean that the critical speaker believes that this climber does not belong upon the icy slopes. And a favorable gesture concerning such a mountaineer also does not inevitably indicate an implicit condescension.

Part 1: Should Women Climb?

Before presenting this revised or more inclusive point of view, I feel it is only honest first to examine the commonly negative attitudes that caused Taylor and her climbing colleagues discomfort, disappointment, and, occasionally, despair. It would be both foolish and deceptive to write about these women without acknowledging

---

[2] Published narratives of women's climbing holidays also support the understanding that women, if they could afford to get to these places and stay in mountainous regions for some length of time, were neither passive nor oppressed. One only has to open the pages of various travel books to sense that the presence of women up high was, from the mid-century on, an increasingly common phenomenon. Mrs. H.W. Cole's *A Lady's Tour Round Monte Rosa* (1859), Amelia B. Edwards' 1873 *A Midsummer Ramble in the Dolomites* (relating the experiences of traveling over high mountain passes in the company of her sister), Mary Taylor's anonymous *Swiss Notes by Five Ladies: An Account of Touring and Climbing in 1874* (with selections written by her four companions: Marion Neilson of Glasgow, Grace Hirst of Leeds, Marion Ross of Glasgow and Fanny Richardson of York), Anne Lister's account of her climbs in the Pyrenees, Frederica Plunket's *Here and There Among the Alps* (1875), Emily Hornby's 1907 [1873–96] *Mountaineering Records*, detailing her many notable technical climbs in the Alps, as well as Elizabeth Le Blond's numerous narratives of her ascents are some of the many examples.

the biases against them. For all the equality they discovered, by no means did any of these individuals move in a society free of criticism for their so-called "unwomanly" efforts.

In *How the English Made the Alps*, Jim Ring identifies one of the most pervasive prejudices toward lady climbers, namely that "Women were thought to have neither the physical nor the moral stamina for such activities" (104).[3] Females were said to be weaker and not vigorous enough

Figure 3.1   H.G. Willink. "Enthusiasm under difficulties"

for the higher ascents – unless, as a physician T. Clifford Allbutt quipped,

they were "endowed with a masculine frame" ("On the Health and Training of Mountaineers," *The Alpine Journal* 8 [1876]: 32). Throughout the period, climbing books displayed ludicrous drawings emphasizing the inappropriateness of the female body in a mountain setting. They often featured demeaning cartoons of stout women laboriously stumbling along, bent over an umbrella or being carried on the back of a struggling mule.[4]

In their descriptions of Alpine rambles, several club members took it for granted that certain routes would be "unpleasant of course for a lady" (MS letter from F.F.

---

[3]   At the end of the century, when the distinguished climber and Alpine Club member Martin Conway was asked "Are women ever likely to any large extent to take to mountaineering?" he alarmingly declared that a woman's lack of "staying power" could be deadly:

   I'm rather afraid that mountaineering is not well suited to women, or they to it.
   A woman lacks staying power. I mean if she were one of a party and a fall took
   place she could not be relied upon to be of much service – she would not be a
   force. She would be on the rope, but she would not strengthen the party – rather
   the reverse. Anyhow it would be so with the average woman, although I grant
   you there might be exceptions. ("How to Climb the Alps," *Daily Chronicle* 30
   December 1893. Scrapbook, Alpine Club Archives).

[4]   In a December 1869 issue of *The Eagle*, a member of St. John's College, Cambridge wrote a satirical poem about climbing in the Alps. One passage illustrates the sense of the intrusion of the female body on the mountains: "For, much to my amazement, at the steepest part I met/ A matron who weighed twenty stones, and I think must be there yet" ("Turgidus Alpinus" 223).

2. There being no proper side saddles at Pontresina. L mounts a raised seat, and finds it hard work to keep her balance in a rapid ascent.

Figure 3.2   Elizabeth Tuckett. "There being no proper side saddles at Pontresina, L. mounts a raised seat"

Tuckett to Thomas Hinchliff, Alpine Club Archives). Moreover, mountaineering narratives habitually advised that in order to conserve their limited strength, ladies should heed the "golden rule": never walk where you cannot ride (George, *The Oberland and its Glaciers* 91).[5] Believing in this principle, Leslie Stephen was among many to recommend that ladies should ride to the foot of the ascent. This requirement, though, brought the complication of finding a sidesaddle so as to insure that the lady retains her femininity and does not adopt an unbecoming masculine posture. Obtaining a sidesaddle was not always easy. Elizabeth ("Lizzie") Tuckett's sketch catches one of the many problems when the sidesaddle did not fit properly.

---

[5]   H.B. George wrote:

An English lady may not unfrequently be seen trudging laboriously up to the Bell Alp, or up the long hot valley which leads to the Grimsel. She arrives thoroughly tired, and no wonder: she finds herself unfit to join in the excursions of her companions for two or three days, and then it is time, according to previous arrangements, that they should move on elsewhere. The same strength, more judiciously expended would have taken her to the top of the Sparrenhorn or Sidethorn, a long way up the Ober Aletsch glacier, or to the Aar Pavilion. These pleasures are lost to her by disregarding the golden rule for ladies traveling in the Alps – *never walk where you cannot ride*. There is comparative little fatigue in riding on a good path, and such as there is falls mainly upon muscles different from those used in walking. (*The Oberland and its Glaciers* 92)

As Cole remarked: "One great difficulty in traveling on the Italian side is to find sidesaddles for ladies; indeed, as general rule, no horse can be obtained, usually only a mule, and sometimes nothing but a donkey, and no sidesaddle for either" (8). Such was the difficulty that when the Rev. S.W. King traveled with his wife, she took with her one of "Whippy's portable sidesaddles, which folded into a compact waterproof case, and could be adapted with equal facility to horse, mule, or donkey" (Cole 9).

The sense of a woman's physical inferiority was not only held by men, but also to some extent shared by the women themselves. In her account of exploring in the Himalaya, the Honorable Mrs. Bruce claimed, "Very few women have either the inclination or the physical strength to become earnest mountaineers" (*Twenty Years in the Himalaya* 302). In spite of her mountaineering accomplishments, Frederica Plunket also subscribed to the idea of the "inferiority of womankind" (134). As a result, in her description of climbing among the Alps, she was adamant that

> When ladies attempt any considerable ascent, their leading guide should be first-rate, as being unable to do much for themselves they depend almost entirely for safety on the assistance they receive, and a man of that class will know how to escape any difficulties that are avoidable, and how to help them over those which must be encountered. (170)

At the end of the century, although far less apologetic and more eager to admit to the strength of their own bodies, energetic and enterprising mountaineers such as the skillful Lily Bristow still seem occasionally to have deferred to the convention by mentioning the abilities of the men who were climbing with them. Bristow was periodically quick to relate how obliged she was to her male climbing companions. Although often taking the lead on rock climbs, she occasionally played the role of "inferior womankind" requiring special treatment.[6] When the expedition was over, Bristow described how A.F. [Fred] Murray, had periodically looked after her. She wrote that Murray during a particularly uncomfortable bivouac – when they were six in a tent – was a good caretaker: "Fred pulled off my boots and worried me into a wet sleeping bag, and I lay down in the shallowest part of the pool and felt heavenly comfortable and warm. The other poor devils [the men] all had to sit up" ("An Easy Day for a Lady," *The Alpine Journal* 53 [1942]: 371).

Complementing this myth of physical weakness was also the widely held assumption that lady climbers were not as morally strong or courageous as their male counterparts. Women were, therefore, less dependable in tough circumstances. If they did do well, they were praised for behaving well or being "plucky," in spite of their sex. They were sometimes said to have neither the perseverance nor the self-mastery and self-discipline necessary to complete a climb and protect themselves, as well as their fellow climbers, from danger. The predominant opinion

---

[6]   At several points Lily Bristow had taken the lead in their climbs when ascending the Grépon, the Dru, and the Rothorn.

among some of the lady climbers was that it is better to keep silent and let the men take charge. As late as 1889, Lillias Campbell Davidson, in her *Hints to Lady Travellers at Home and Abroad*, advised that "a woman's place in a moment of danger is to keep still and be ready for action … if there is a man at the head of the affair, he had better be left to manage matters without the hampering interferences of feminine physical weakness" (12). The authority of an energetic and disciplined mind was what was necessary for the challenges associated with mountaineering. These were the qualities, of course, that formed the male cult of athleticism.[7]

Because of its association with masculinity, climbing was popularly said to be an unwomanly recreation. Charles Dickens opened his article on "Foreign Climbs" (*All the Year Round* 2 September 1865) with the declaration that mountaineering "is not womanly" (137). Female climbers were often accused of being ungainly and donning unbecoming wear. A reporter for a newspaper shares the opinion and adds a dose of nationalism:

> They wear knickerbockers, which are never becoming to the sex, and look of enormous size and weight, over thick knitted stockings. As to complexion, a lady climber must abandon all idea of it … The goddess Venus would look ill with a peeled nose and a jonquil or daffodil hue … we are seriously of opinion that no lady under thirty should ever climb snow-mountains. By doing so, and taking the consequences, they lower British prestige. The alien conceives that all our women wear hideous clothes, big boots, and noses which excite compassion …
> A mountain biceps is not an excellent thing in women, and is not compensated for by thick ankles. ("Should Women Climb Snow Mountains," 26 July 1898. Scrapbook, Alpine Club Archives)

Sunburned faces were thought to be particularly unladylike.[8] Historians of mountaineering are fond of repeating the anecdote featuring Elizabeth Le Blond's

---

[7] In "Lost in the Past: A Tale of Heroes and Englishness," Susan Bassnett quotes a passage from J.E.C. Weldon, headmaster of Harrow from 1881 to 1887. His words describe the link between athleticism and the power of self-control associated with manhood: "The pluck, the energy, the perseverance, the good temper, the self-control, the discipline, the cooperation, the *esprit de corps*, which merit success in cricket or football, are the very qualities which win the day in peace or war" (Gittings 49). As James Eli Adams observes, these qualities were a defining characteristic of true manhood (*Dandies and Desert Saints: Styles of Victorian Manhood*).

[8] In 1886, *The Alpine Journal* ran an article on "The Prevention of Snow-Burning and Blistering" in which G. Scriven suggested: "The ordinary linen mask is very heating and uncomfortable, but one made of the thinnest woolen material is effectual in protecting the most delicate skin, and can be worn with little discomfort. This form of mask was used by a lady in whose company I spent a long and trying day on fresh snow this year, and, with the Lanolin ointment, entirely obviated all unpleasant effects of the snow glare" (*The Alpine Journal* 13 [1887]: 390). Around the same time, C.T. Dent pronounced: "Lady mountaineers are especially concerned [with sunburn], for the effects, like those of tattoo

Grand Aunt who sent out a frantic S.O.S. to the climber's mother: "Stop her climbing mountains. She is scandalizing all London and looks like a Red Indian" (Clark 176). Actually, like most women mountaineers, Le Blond was careful to protect her skin – but not always. A passage from her *High Life and Towers of Silence* (1886) describes the time she did a guideless climb and suffered from the sun:

> I have many times had my face badly burnt on ice and snow, but never have I experienced such agony as resulted from my walk to the Col du Tour .. A sorry spectacle we presented when at last we could leave the hotel, and I fear, from the grins of the guides, that they were not altogether sympathetic for misfortunes contracted during an excursion accomplished without their aid. (96–97)[9]

A photograph in the Film Library of the Alpine Club shows Le Blond wearing a mask, as did most women, to protect her face from the sun's harmful rays.

Fearful of being identified with muscular masculinity and of becoming thought of as "hard" (Trollope, "The Unprotected Female Tourist" 42), a number of mid-century women introduced reassuring phrases to remind their readers of their femininity. One is Mrs. Henry Freshfield, who in her *Alpine ByWays,* solicited her audience not to consider her exploits as being "unfeminine" (2). The celebrated Le Blond, however, was not to be intimidated by this label. Proposing that climbing does teach the perseverance and self-reliance associated with masculinity, Le Blond boldly opened her *True Tales of Mountain Adventure for Non-climbers Young and Old* with the assertion that "There is no manlier sport in the world than mountaineering" (ix). She did not care if others thought her skills merited her being labeled "masculine." Like many other women climbers, Le Blond found that even if there were an explicit prejudice against her activities, she was not prevented from doing what she wanted to do.

Women who climbed also risked the public's displeasure by participating in a behavior that went against the presumed moral standards of a well-bred lady, especially when, in mid-century, circumstances forced them on longer expeditions to sleep in the same mountain huts as men. (Later in the century, some huts were built that had divisions between male and female compartments.) Anticipating

---

marks, may be somewhat permanent, and have to be repented at leisure. A convenient and efficient application is 'Toilet Lanoline,' which can be purchased in small tubes ... Professor Morso advises blackening the face with burnt cork. Undoubtedly a thin layer of soot is the most efficient preventive, but on the much frequented Alps the method is unlikely to meet with favour" (*Mountaineering* 84).

[9]   Upon another occasion, with her usual snobbish, satiric humor, Le Blond recalled the time an "American lady" asked her: "Madam, will you be so very kind as to inform me if you have made your face as it is now by crossing the *glazier* this morning? Because, if our faces are likely to get so blistered and burnt, I guess we won't go over!" As if making fun of the requirement to protect one's complexion, Le Blond replied that she had blistered her face on the Dent du Géant the day before; whereupon, her questioner wanted to know "if that was as bad as the Mer de Glace," and if she and her sister wore three gauze veils, one over the other, would their complexions escape being damaged (*High Life and Towers of Silence* 25).

Figure 3.3 Elizabeth Le Blond wearing a mask

criticism of her choice to go on one of these longer climbs, Plunket felt compelled to warn her readers that the "great drawback" (174) to many of the most interesting ascents that cannot be completed in a day is the necessity of sleeping in a cave or one-roomed cabin.

Crossing into the Male Zone

Some thought, then, that ladies should be satisfied with watching a climb through a telescope from below. When Frances Ridley Havergal remarked in a letter home that she had seen two "Liverpool gentlemen" come down the Schilthorn and meet their wives, whom they had left "to amuse themselves with watching them through a telescope" (Crane 41), she was not witnessing an unusual scene. As I have pointed out in the previous chapter, in mid-nineteenth century England the presence of women in the higher mountain areas was thought to contribute to the decline of the sublime. As we have seen, especially in the satires discussed in that chapter, their attendance was perceived as being both a cause and a symptom of the sublime's "sinking." In these texts, the feminine figure looms large (literally) to obstruct the way to what is lofty and elevated. The hysterics of the Mrs. Browns or Mrs. Simpletons block any refined response to the mountains. With the exception of at least Longinus, who quoted from Sappho when giving examples of the "sublimity of style" (Longinus 76), the concept for many was a gendered notion that traditionally, if erroneously, debarred women from its heights and identified its power with the masculine concept of mind and domination.[10] By intruding upon, and therefore compromising, regions associated with the sublime, these lady mountaineers, according to a general belief, reduced the concept's potency. The actual abundant presence of women on the mountains was seen as an assault upon the theoretical imaginary of the sublime.

The momentum of this received opinion was still felt at the end of the nineteenth century, when the public was more used to the idea of female mountaineers. A symptom of this enduring attitude, perhaps, is an advertisement for a boys' book on climbing, *A Book for Boys, Young and Old: One Hundred Stories* (London: John Murray) written by the well-known mountaineer Edward Whymper. The notice for the forthcoming publication announced that the stories were "NOT TO BE READ BY WOMEN." (I have not been able to find the book. Perhaps it never appeared.)

Earlier in the century, this conviction prompted well-established climbers like John Tyndall and Leslie Stephen to think of mountains as being regionalized or stratified according to gender. As Francis O'Gorman points out, Tyndall thought of the higher Alps as a male zone "freed from female presence, a site of male friendship, facilitating the convivialities of homosociality" (137). As a consequence, on one of his expeditions Tyndall was eager to record that "A lady accompanied us on horseback to the point where the path to the Grands Mulets deviates from that to the

---

[10]   For a discussion of this concept see, the section on "Feminine Difference" in Philip Shaw's discussion of "The Romantic Sublime" (105–13).

Plan des Aiguilles; here she turned to the left, and we proceeded slowly upward"
to reach the summit of Mont Blanc (*The Glaciers of the Alps* 177). This parting or
separation marks the sense of division that can be found in many other texts. For
instance, in an August 1866 manuscript letter, A.G. Girdlestone, a member of the
Alpine Club, is keen to inform his reader that even though a woman had already
climbed the Sparrenhorn, he had ascended the mountain after a snowstorm in what
was "quite a difficult expedition" (MS letters of A.G. Girdlestone, Alpine Club
Archives). By emphasizing the difficult conditions underfoot, Girdlestone breaks
away from the lady's zone and firmly fixes his position in his rightful place.

In his popular *The Playground of Europe* (1871), Leslie Stephen reserves
the higher Alps for men. Borrowing his metaphor from biology, he secures the
higher regions for the English male and assigns the middle to the less physically
adept adventurous female. In his mind the division is organic; it is natural and
indisputable:

> Travellers, like plants, may be divided according to the zones which they reach.
> In the highest region, the English climber ... Lower down comes a region where
> he is mixed with a crowd of industrious Germans, and a few sporadic examples
> of adventurous ladies and determined sight-seers. Below this is the luxuriant
> growth of the domestic tourist in all his amazing and intricate varieties. (184)

The Alpine holidays of one of Stephen's fellow club members, Francis Fox
Tuckett, exemplify this division. Periodically between 1861 and 1870, Tuckett
took climbing holidays with "the ladies of his family and friends" (73). Typically,
he and his male companions would leave the women behind with a caretaker
(Victor Tairraz) and ascend a peak. His sister, Elizabeth Tuckett, as we have seen
in her rendition of an awkward sidesaddle, kept charming sketchbooks of these
travels: *How We Spent the Summer or "A Voyage en Zigzag" in Switzerland and
Tyrol, with Some Members of the Alpine Club* (1864), *Beaten Track, or Pen and
Pencil Sketches in Italy* (1866), *Pictures in Tyrol and Elsewhere* (1867), and
Zigzagging Amongst Dolomites (1871). Her lively, humorous sketches illustrate
this arrangement. Her drawings show the women clumsily walking through the
snow, armed with their alpenstocks, wearing face masks, sitting awkwardly on the
back of a mule or a horse, or gazing in trepidation over the side of a precipitous
drop – a posture that recalls one writer's advice that women practice looking over
such edges so that they learn not to panic (Macfarlane 85). Many depict the ladies
anxiously waiting for the men in the hostels or offering them a hero's welcome
after a successful ascent (see Fig. 3.4 overleaf).

Other narratives as well as guidebooks erect barriers separating these two
domains – what James Buzard refers to as the "masculine North and the feminine
South" (134),[11] and what Alison Blunt and Gillian Rose consider when they think

---

[11] Frances Anne Kemble's satirical play *The Adventures of Mr. John Timothy
Homespun in Switzerland* (1889) plays on this sexual division. She grounds the sister of

3. F. and E. are due at Bad Ratzes
at 2.p.m. — 3 p.m. L
becomes anxious & the
storm begins.— 5.p.m:
they read Westward Ho!
& try to forget the
Langkofel, but fail miserably.
6.p.m. they have some coffee,
C begins to be nervous — 7.p.m.
they prepare supper for 8.— 8.p.m: it
grows dark, supper postponed.— 9.L is wretched, even Mrs C's
stoicism fails.— 10. the darkness and anxiety
deepen.— 11. the supper is spoilt, L and C
are in despair, Mrs C, melancholy.

Figure 3.4   Elizabeth Tuckett. "F. and E. are due at Bad Ratizes at 2 p.m. – 3 p.m.
L. becomes anxious"

of a gendered geography in their *Writing Women and Space*. The advice of these
guides demonstrates the conviction that the lower heights and easier routes are
appropriate for the passive, weaker female. (The guidebooks characterize these
expeditions as being "an easy day for a lady.") William Longman and Henry
Trower's *Journal of Six Weeks' Adventure in Switzerland, Piedmont, and on the
Italian Lakes* (1856) suggests, for example, that both ladies and gentlemen may go
up the Rigi, "but the gentlemen may also ascend Pilate: the ladies may shelter and
row on the lake, while their companions make a day or two's excursion over the
Joch Pass" or ascend Titis (57).

Because of this gendered geographical division, it is little wonder that Havergal
recalled that she and her friends felt like "downright *boys*" (Janet Grierson 115)
when, with their alpenstocks, they "stormed" the Alpine peaks, and it is not
surprising that Ménie Muriel Norman commented that, when she had traveled
through the Carpathians, she had been "on the verge of believing myself dashing,

---

the climber in the domestic space of home, especially when the sister grows impatient with
her brother for parading over the new carpet in the living room while wearing his spiked
climbing boots. She has no enthusiasm for the mountains. He, in turn, complains what a
devilish nuisance women are.

masculine, and a monument of bravery" (vii). Both knew that by ascending certain peaks they had crossed over from the female into the male zone – a phenomenon that H.G. Willink, an Alpine Club member, noted in 1885, when he spoke of women who went higher and "dare[d] do all that may become a man" ("Alpine Sketching," *The Alpine Journal* 12 [1885]: 367). These responses are not, of course, only the property of the British. The Rev. Walter Weston (yet another Alpine Club member) who explored the Japanese mountains in the 1890s comments on the ancient belief that the higher regions of the great sacred mountains of Japan were, "until the last few years," out of bounds for women (144). He remarks on passing by the remains of the *Nionindo* ("Woman's way," a hut which marked the boundary line above which no woman could go) that had once "guarded the upper part of the mountain from the desecration of woman's tread" (210).

Even though there is really no comparison between the explicit sense of desecration and prohibition in the older Japanese culture, on the one hand, and the less restrictive as well as the more hazy understanding of the gendered strata among the Victorian climbers, on the other, the idea that a woman's presence spoils the male zone floated ambiguously in the consciousness of the English. Mountaineering narratives occasionally hint at the negative effect of a female presence upon the heroic domain of a brotherhood of men, replete with male energy.[12] They speak of being unfettered by the familial and the female, of climbing without the encumbrances of a woman's company, or of reaching heights far beyond the demands of the domestic. Hereford Brooke George was quick to note that, while exploring the Oberland glaciers, he saw two sets of gentlemen, one with ladies and the other "without encumbrances" (*The Oberland and its Glaciers* 3). And in an 1866 letter, an Alpine Club man jokes, yet reveals his anxiety, about the fact that one of his correspondent's friends is going to be climbing with a lady up the Jungfrau:

> I tremble for Fox, who it seems is going to do the polite as far as Zermatt via the Aiggischhorn, & will have his heart distracted between the two Jungfrau. I think we must have a branch of the [Alpine] club to comprise able bodied females, but it would be rather dangerous, as what mountaineer could resist a girl who has "done" the Strahleck, Géant or Weiss Thor. (F.F. Tuckett MS letter, Alpine Club Archives)

Seething beneath the humor, of course, is the threat of female invasion. Although success at mountaineering might, for some, make a woman more attractive, the overriding concern that she would distract and weaken the man, and, eventually,

---

12 Herbert Sussman, in his *Victorian Masculinities*, links the definition of maleness during this period to the possession of a distinctive, interior energy. He goes on to say: "This definition of manhood as self-discipline, as the ability to control male energy and to deploy the power not for sexual but for productive purposes was clearly specific to bourgeois man" (11).

domesticate him is ever-present.[13] These passages evoke James Eli Adams' suggestion that, for the Victorians, manhood cannot be maintained within the context of domesticity (*Dandies and Desert Saints*). They also recall Christopher E. Gittings' sense that being isolated from the subjective and emotional female presence is mandatory if one is to preserve the authority of the patriarchy (*Imperialism and Gender*).

Prejudice and the Alpine Club

Toward the end of the century some of these negative attitudes still clung to the public consciousness and occasionally found a voice among members of the Alpine Club. Mary Mummery (wife of the celebrated climber A.F. Mummery), who was herself an accomplished mountaineer – in the late 1880s she ascended the Jungfrau and the Matterhorn – in spite of her connection and successes, seems to have suffered from negative opinions against "lady" climbers. In a chapter she wrote that was included in her husband's *My Climbs in the Alps and Caucasus*, she reveals her frustration with the kinds of attitudes I have outlined above:

> The masculine mind, however, is, with rare exceptions, imbued with the idea
> that a woman is not a fit comrade for steep ice or precipitous rock, and, in
> consequence, holds it as an article of faith that her climbing should be done by
> Mark Twain's method,[14] and that she should be satisfied with watching through a
> telescope some weedy and invertebrate masher being hauled up a steep peak by
> a couple of burly guides, or by listening to this same masher when, on his return,
> he lisps out with a sickening drawl the many perils he encountered. (45)

Mary Mummery's remarks are a reminder that not all was smooth among the relationships on the mountains. Although she might have been referring to prejudices held by the general public rather than to those shared by the Alpine Club members, she does remind one that, from time to time, it was possible to bump into an annoying narrow-mindedness, and even hostility from her husband's colleagues. It should be added here that the Alpine Club, founded in 1857, did not open its doors to women until 1976. Eventually, in 1907, a group of women opened their own organization, first known as the Lyceum Club and then as the Ladies'

---

[13]   Jill Marie Maclachlan, in her dissertation "Peak Performances: Cultural and Autobiographical Constructions of the Victorian Female Mountaineer" (2004), has an interesting section on the Jungfrau and fantasies of sexual conquest (40–41).

[14]   In his *A Tramp Abroad*, Mark Twain humorously fantasized traveling on a glacier rather than taking the trouble to walk or climb through the Alps. He, however, reckoned that if a glacier moves less than an inch a day, it would take him a little over five hundred years to reach Zermatt from where he and his party were on the Gorner Glacier. Twain was well-versed in mountain literature and climbing narratives.

Alpine Club. Typical is the complaint in an article, "Alpine Club for Women," printed in an August 1907 issue of *The Standard*: "It has been a grievance that admission to the Alpine Club has been refused to women, despite the fact that Mrs. Bullock Workman holds the world's highest record in mountain climbing" (LAC Scrapbook, Alpine Club Archives). (In 1902, at the age of 47, Fanny Bullock Workman had reached the 23,300' summit of Pinnacle Peak in the Himalaya.) And characteristic is another article in the *Daily Mirror*, "Two New Clubs," that emphasizes the friction between the men and women mountaineers: "For some years women mountaineers have rebelled against their non-admittance to the sacred precincts of the Alpine Club on Savile-row. Now they have decided to start a club on their own to which men will not be admitted!" (LAC Scrapbook, Alpine Club Archives).

Privately, there could also be less generous moments, such as the time Leslie Stephen, probably in a fit of jealousy and also in keeping with his rather snippy personality, wrote to his wife from Grindelwald in January, 1888, shortly after Mrs. E.P. (Margaret Anne) Jackson had returned from traversing the Jungfrau [13,670'] from Bergh to Guggi in winter, a treacherous undertaking on ice. On her way back, Jackson had been caught overnight at between 10,000 and 11,000' on the Griggi Glacier without any protection. She and her guide, Ulrich Almer, had returned badly frostbitten. She lost several toes, and that damage put an end to her climbing career. Stephen wrote:

> Mrs. Jackson's toes are better, you will be glad to hear. I am sorry to say that two of the guides are said to be frostbitten & I would much rather that Mrs. Jackson be the sufferer. I have not seen her to my knowledge, though there was a queer dressed up little woman in the hall just now, whom I rather guess to be her. (Bicknell 1:357)[15]

Looking through the various records of the Alpine Club, I am repeatedly reminded of how inconsistent attitudes toward female mountaineers could be. If one goes back to 1866, one can find significant expressions of a desire to include women in the Club's activities and a genuine appreciation of their abilities as mountaineers. There is no reason to think that the President of the Alpine Club, F.C. Grove, was being insincere when he addressed the membership in 1887 about the recent feats of women climbers:

---

[15] Stephens' comments echo earlier malicious remarks. For instance, in an 1850 essay on "Travellers Albums," Albert Smith enjoys reprinting a comment added by a later guest to one of the entries. The entry had read: "Miss Forde, Anglaise, walked to Montanvert and from thence to the Flégère in one day – the first of her countrywomen who has performed the feat." In response the guest had written: "And it is hoped she will be the last. Let it be taken as a general rule that female striders of the above genus are seldom agreeable women and always ugly" (*The Miscellany: A Book for the Field or the Fire-side* 84).

It is pleasant to speak of these achievements, and latterly there has been another considerable one, as a lady has ascended the Aiguille du Dru; so let it be hoped that ladies will continue to climb the Alps. With women, as with men, it has been found that the best of the sex take very naturally to mountaineering, and if they come in increased numbers to the snow-line, their presence will, I am sure, be welcomed by all whose welcome they will care for. ("Address to the Alpine Club," *The Alpine Journal* 13 [1887]: 216)

Yet, a quarter of a century later, some of the older awareness of differences continues to surface, and perhaps to compromise the spirit of Grove's remarks. For instance, one year after the founding of the Ladies' Alpine Club in 1907, H. Woolley, President of the men's club, spoke at the organization's annual dinner, held 7 December 1908. On the whole his remarks were very supportive of women climbers. He defended his organization against the charge that his members had made disrespectful remarks to the ladies present: "no word of ridicule or disrespect had been uttered in the Alpine Club." He had no doubts about women's powers of physical endurance, adding that women had demonstrated they could "accomplish ascents of the very first order" and that the formation of a Ladies' Alpine Club "was only a matter of time. It was hardly to be expected that men would be allowed to have the monopoly of such a good thing as mountaineering." In the end, though, (in spite of his good intentions) he could not rid himself of the belief that women and men climbers would have a different experience on the mountain: "A lady climber could derive even greater and more lasting pleasure from mountaineering than men by reason of paying more regard to the aesthetic than to the athletic side of the question" (Lyceum Club Papers, Alpine Club Archives). His remarks were followed by those of a former President of the Alpine Club who said that years ago he had wanted to propose that women be allowed to join: "On the whole, there was a majority in favour," but because he did not want to press an "unwilling minority," he had not pursued the possibility (Lyceum Club Papers, Alpine Club Archives).

These mixed responses could create frustration. Ellen Pigeon, one of the most daunting early women climbers, is reputed to have remarked in a letter that "In days gone by many A.C.'s refused to speak to us" (Mazel 9), and the ambitious Fanny Bullock Workman is said to have spoken openly about the unfriendly reception she occasionally received in Britain. Following her death in 1925, her obituary in *The Alpine Journal* stated that she "felt that she suffered from 'sex antagonism'." The author of the obituary, J.P. Farrar, adds: "it is possible that some unconscious feeling let us say of the novelty of a woman's intrusion into the domain of exploration so long reserved to man, may in some quarters have existed ... there tended to arise ... an atmosphere shall we say of aloofness?" (Mazel 9). It is this sort of lingering edginess that prompted Adeline Edwards, Vice President of the ladies' club, publicly to challenge or embarrass Alpine Club members invited to the Ladies' Alpine Club's annual dinner (7 December 1909). In her speech, Edwards stated that not only has there been a general misunderstanding that "for every genuine woman mountaineer, there are a thousand who are carried up in chairs or on mules" but also that she has been "led to believe the Alpine Club had ridiculed their daughter [the LAC]." She added: "But I venture to think that that assertion will scarcely stand in the presence of our visitors to-night" (Lyceum Club Papers, Alpine Club Archives). Edwards's correspondence concerning the founding of the Ladies' Alpine Club also betrays some bitterness. In a 16 July 1907 letter to Miss Williams, she complained: "There is *no* woman's Alpine Club, and the club in Savile Row [The Alpine Club] will not admit them as honorary members, for I, a climber myself, have continually tried" (Lyceum Club Papers: G18, Alpine Club Archives).[16] The sting of rejection must have been all the sharper, for Edwards and many of her fellow climbers were well aware that for years, both men and women, based upon their climbing qualifications, had been admitted equally to the French Groupe de Haute Montagne (Keenlyside 63). Indeed the Ladies Alpine Club's first president was already a member of another European organization: the *Club Alpin François, Section du Mont-Blanc.*

Part 2: A Distorted History

A larger, more inclusive portrait of attitudes toward Victorian lady mountaineers has, as I have already mentioned in the introduction, either been forgotten or overlooked. It is always easier to linger upon the negative and distasteful. As a result, contemporary commentators have frequently chosen to give too much weight to the prejudices these women faced, and, consequently, have regarded those who ascended the heights as being exceptional and not part of the main culture. They become feminist heroines – exceptions. For these critics, their importance lies primarily in their overcoming the formidable obstacles of their sex. Elaine Freedgood, in her otherwise excellent study *Victorian Writing about Risk*, is one of many who has succumbed to this tendency when she asserts that even though a few women did climb, they "were simply not allowed to possess, inhabit or risk their bodies in the same ways or to the same extent as men" (120).

Current more popular representations of Victorian British women climbers have encouraged a similar point of view. They emphasize how these women managed their climbs in spite of their gender and the cultural pressure to display themselves as well-bred and proper ladies. A spring 2005 Isabella Bird catalogue (a mail order firm dedicated to women's outdoor clothing) is typical. Bird was an Englishwoman who, in 1873, with Jim Nugent, was the first woman to climb Long's Peak, one of the highest mountains in Colorado. A brief promotional message inside the catalogue's front cover declares that Bird "lived outside the boundaries. She re-defined the standards

---

[16] In response to a reporter's question about the forming of the Ladies' Alpine Club, the secretary of the men's club replied: "I think it is most excellent idea that women climbers should have a club of their own ... as to why we have never suggested them joining with us is simple on the face of it. We have no room. That is the primary reason" (*Daily Mirror*. Scrapbook, Alpine Club Archive).

for the women of her time" (Isabella Bird Catalogue insert). Other contemporary commentators contribute to this distortion by over-emphasizing the cult of masculinity attached to mountaineering in the Victorian era. Francis O'Gorman speaks of the activity as if it were exclusively male, David Robertson, in his "Mid-Victorians amongst the Alps," emphasizes the masculine idealism of the Alpine Club, and Peter H. Hansen, in his dissertation on British mountaineering, stresses the inferior status of women climbers. (292).[17] And recently, even a beautifully researched and written book, *Fallen Giants: A History of Himalayan Mountaineering from the Age of Empire to the Age of Extremes,* by Maurice Isserman and Stewart Weaver, treats nineteenth-century mountaineering as a male province of the British Empire and only grudgingly acknowledges the presence of women climbers.

Paradoxically, by emphasizing the negative reactions to women climbers, reviewed in the first part of this chapter, many well-meaning histories detailing the feats of the more famous lady mountaineers promote the very divisions they are attempting to repair. Almost exclusively, and, I think, unfairly, their authors draw attention either to what they perceive to be an all-encompassing bigotry or subscribe to a notion of a universal unbridgeable partition between the sexes.[18] In doing so, I suggest that they widen and even fall into the crevasse that Mary Taylor's guide had exposed. Jane Robinson tries to avoid this pitfall in her recent study of women travelers, *Wayward Women*, when she declares: "The female sex has always suffered from retrospective overgeneralization" (vii).

Skirts, Breeches, and Heavy Hob-nailed Boots

One of the ways in which historians have promoted a somewhat-distorted picture of difficulties facing women mountaineers during the nineteenth century is by focusing upon their supposed struggles with their climbing outfits. Many recent critics tend to concentrate upon the importance of the gendered garment. Jim Ring,

---

[17]   See Francis O'Gorman's "'The Mightiest Evangel of the Alpine Club': Masculinity and Agnosticism in the Alpine Writing of John Tyndall." For histories that tend to treat women climbers as exceptional and as victims of prejudice, see such texts as: William Davenport Adams' *Celebrated Women Travellers of the Nineteenth Century* (1903); Rebecca A. Brown's *Women on High: Pioneers of Mountaineering* (2002); Ronald Clark's *The Victorian Mountaineers* (1953); Francis Keenlyside's *Peaks and Pioneers: The Story of Mountaineering* (1975) ; Barbara T. Gates' *Kindred Nature* (1998); Arnold Lunn's *A Century of Mountaineering 1857–1957* (1900); David Mazel's *Mountaineering Women: Stories of Early Climbers* (1994); Dorothy Middleton's *Victorian Lady Travellers* (1993) [1965]; Luree Miller's *On Top of the World: Five Women Explorers in Tibet* (1965); Jim Ring's *How the English Made the Alps* (2000); Showell Styles' *On Top of the World: An Illustrated History of Mountaineering and Mountains* (1967); and James Ramsey Ullman's *The Age of Mountaineering* (1954).

[18]   Although Rebecca A. Brown's book on women climbers is helpful and informative, it does tend to emphasize the idea that these people had to be "strong and determined" in order to overcome "restrictive social conditions" (xi).

in his study of Victorian mountaineering, claims that "Women were ... obliged either to suffer the considerable inconvenience of skirts or to follow some such expedient as wearing riding breeches underneath and removing and replacing their skirts when occasion demanded." He adds menacingly, "Some were stoned for not doing so" (104). (I have not found evidence to support that assertion.) Others speak of the pressures to look ladylike and neat – they supposedly, unlike their male colleagues, could not get away with being among "the great unwashed" ("Evening Dress among the Mountains," Scrapbook, Alpine Club Archives). Showing a sensitivity to the charge that a lady climber was unwomanly, some are all too eager to point out that Lucy Walker, one of the first women to make a regular practice of climbing in the Alps, was "In every way a model Victorian lady" (Keenlyside 63). They emphasize that "Miss Lucy Walker, never used the subterfuge of men's clothes, wearing on the mountains a white print dress whose shape she carefully had 'renewed' whenever an expedition was finished" (Clark 177). And, like Claire-Elaine Engel, report that Walker, when climbing, "never dreamt of dressing like a man" (Engel 58).

Most historians dwell upon what they consider to be the loaded issue of whether or not to wear a long skirt or breeches. They describe the practice of approaching an ascent in a long skirt, which the climber would remove once away from the public eye, and upon her return, put on again. These commentators are fond of repeating the story of Elizabeth Le Blond, who once forgot to pick up her skirt that she had hidden under a stone on the far side of the mountain, and had to retrace her route to retrieve it before she could walk down toward the hotel. They forget that this was a routine matter and simply reflected a convention of the time. The question of when or whether to remove the skirt has probably done more to propagate the sense of gender difference than any other issue.

Historians also like to talk about the inconvenience of wearing a skirt in the mountains and how, attempting to maintain her femininity and decency, a woman learned to deal with this so-called inhibiting requirement by sewing rings into the hem of her skirt, passing a ribbon through them, thereby enabling her to pull her skirt up as needed – a practice that sometimes resulted in a garment's hem filling with snow and causing the skirt to become heavy and wet (Clark176). A stereoscopic slide shows one woman climbing in a ringed skirt (see Fig. 3.5 overleaf).

Some women also attached buttons to the outside of their skirt as well as hooks and eyes so that they might effect the same result. To demonstrate this practice, historians of mountaineering often recall Mrs. Cole's advice to women:

> Small rings should be sewn inside the seams of the dress, and a cord passed through them, the ends of which should be knotted together in such a way that the whole dress may be drawn up at a moment's notice to the requisite height. If the dress is too long, it catches the stones, especially when coming down hill ... A lady's dress is inconvenient for mountain traveling, even under the most careful management, and therefore every device which may render it less so should be adopted. (6)

Figure 3.5   "Vue sur la mer de glace, Chamonix"

Figure 3.6   Women in long skirts

To accommodate whatever difficulties a longer skirt might cause, during the second half of the nineteenth century many more climbers also chose to wear short skirts, and hence "skirted" what might have been cumbersome. A skirt might be an impediment, but it was minor and easily managed. A stereoscopic slide shows two women quite easily making their way across the Mer de Glace.

Significantly Kate Strasdin, who has recently researched the clothing of women climbers, claims that it is an anachronism of late twentieth-century discourse to "relate long skirts in terms of oppression and the gradual shortening of skirts as a sign of progress and female liberation" (74). She reminds readers that even toward the end of the century able mountaineers and independent females, such as Gertrude Bell, customarily climbed in a long black skirt, that is until the rock climbing and difficult scrambling began – then the skirt would be removed.[19] These examples plus numerous photographs of women mountaineers scaling heights and rocks in skirts seem to expose a faulty understanding that these garments invariably hampered their abilities to scramble, and, I believe, should make one wary of critics claiming that "the constraints of the awkward" clothing (Brown xi) were dangerous. Some women actually claimed to take pleasure in making sleds out of their petticoats.

Prompted by their attention to gendered outfits, recent commentary also tends to exaggerate the possible confusion about sexual identification that ensued when women were ascending to more adventurous heights and breaking through into the male zone, when these mountaineers were making the transition from one gendered zone to another, and appropriately shifting from their ladylike attire to short skirts or to masculine breeches. Although there is some evidence to support an unease on the part of the general public with shorter skirts, bloomers, and thick, heavy hob-nailed boots (as the cartoons in magazines such as *Punch* illustrate), there are many more examples to suggest that anxiety over this habit was not nearly as severe as recent criticism suggests. There might have been the occasional, sharp or humorous poem about ladies wearing thick mountain gloves and sturdy boots, such as the "The Walking Englishwoman on the Alps" that appeared in *The Morning Post* (1892), but there is more fun than criticism, as well as an implied pleasure in the lady's prowess (see Fig. 3.7 below).

"The Walking Englishwoman on the Alps"
You who look, at home, so charming –
Angel, goddess, nothing less –
Do you know you're quite alarming
In that dress!

Such a garb should be forbidden
Where's the grace an artist loves?
Think of dainty fingers hidden
In those gloves!

Gloves! A housemaid would not wear them,
Shapeless, brown and rough as sacks,
Thick! And yet you often tear them
With that axe!

Worst of all, unblacked, unshiny –

---

[19]   After spending several holidays in the Alps, Gertrude Bell went on eventually to become a diplomat in the Middle East. She became involved in the archaeological and political affairs of the area, and was to become instrumental in drawing the boundary lines of Modern Iraq and installing Faizel I as king. She also established the archaeological museum in Baghdad.

Greet them with derisive hoots –
Clumsy, huge! For feet so tiny!
Oh, those boots!
(Scrapbook, Alpine Club Archives)

A thorough review of mountaineering literature reveals a far less troubled picture –
so casual, indeed, that one wonders what might be the nature of present-day sexual
anxiety or ideology that causes the present to impose such distorted readings upon
the past. Rather than promoting the idea of scandal, accounts written by both male
and female climbers speak quite matter-of-factly about skirts (short or long) and
knickerbockers. Without any self-consciousness, many more mention the routine
of removing the skirt (often placing it within a knapsack) before tackling a chimney
rock or of putting the skirt on again after managing a tiresome rock climb and
negotiating a steep slope. The straightforwardness of Gertrude Bell's description
reveals just how routine the change was. There is no mystique or fraught gender
ritual attached to it:

> I did not lose my footing and it [a section up the Meije] was better than I expected.
> It took us 3 hours up and down the Dents to get to the Pic Central where we
> arrived at 2 having left the Germans far behind. We followed along the ridge,
> a precipice to the right and a steep ice slope to the left. I felt quite lighthearted
> and wondered how long I should hold out. A long tiresome bit of rock and a
> long ice slope where the steps were however already cut, down to the Glacier de
> Tabuchet. There I put on my skirt. (The Gertrude Bell Archive 27 August 1899)

Similarly, Ménie Muriel Norman observed that her knickerbockers were "no more
a matter of sex to me than my boots are" (vii). Just as uncomplicated are drawings
from *The Graphic* (13 August 1898) and *The Illustrated London News* (15 August
1901), which unselfconsciously feature women dressed in short walking skirts and
woolen stockings, with their male companions climbing the Coolin Hills in Scotland
or leaving the hut before ascending the Matterhorn (see Fig. 3.8 below).[20]
   Throughout the second half of the nineteenth century, the emphasis among the
climbers is not upon being feminine but upon being comfortable, warm, and secure.
The idea is to be sensible, practical (for instance, by having large waterproof pockets),
and protected from extremes. A man's mackintosh rather than a useless lady-like
shower-proof garment is preferable. The concern is not to find feminine footwear but
to purchase reliable boots and gaiters for steady and waterproof footing. C.T. Dent's
advice about clothing (given in 1892) has none of the concern about gender attached
to it. Following the advice of some of the more notable women climbers ("Mrs.
Jackson, Mrs. Main, and Miss Richardson"), this Alpine Club member, who wrote
one of the most widely read books on mountaineering, suggests that "Women who
climb should, like men, dress in such a manner that they are protected from extremes

---

[20]   The article that accompanies this sketch is entitled "Climbing the Matterhorn."

THE WALKING ENGLISHWOMAN
ON THE ALPS.

YOU who look, at home, so charming—
Angel, goddess, nothing less—
Do you know you're quite alarming
In that dress?

Such a garb should be forbidden;
Where's the grace an artist loves?
Think of dainty fingers hidden
In those gloves!

Gloves! A housemaid would not wear them,
Shapeless, brown and rough as sacks,
Thick! And yet you often tear them
With that axe!

Worst of all, unblacked, unshiny—
Greet them with derisive hoots—
Clumsy, huge! For feet so tiny!
Oh, those boots!

Figure 3.7   "The Walking Englishwoman on the Alps"

Figure 3.8   "The Foot of the Matterhorn: Starting from the Swiss Alpine Club Hut"

of either heat or cold. Every garment should be wool, and the softer and lighter the material the better" (*Mountaineering* 51). Dent talks about skirts, but he also, in the most routine and casual manner, mentions that the knickerbockers

> should be made of tweed, the band being lined with flannel or other woollen material. The tweed should match the skirt, and will then be found suitable either when worn, as formerly, under it, or, following the practice occasionally adopted, worn without the skirt, the latter being taken off before beginning the climb. (52)

Part 3: Acceptance

These no-nonsense comments about ladies' climbing costumes are but one example of a more general acceptance of female mountaineers. After reading the first part of this chapter reviewing the various instances of discrimination, one can understand how easy it is to dwell upon negative attitudes, and in turn, to emphasize the difficulties that women had to overcome if they were to climb. And one could, as do critics such as Freedgood, Hansen, O'Gorman, and Robertson, stress the masculine ideals of the London Alpine Club that encouraged its members to think of their more strenuous climbs as a projection of a certain kind of heroic or national masculinity, and to consider the mountains as a male zone freed from a female presence.

However, these views, as I have been pointing out, can be misleading. Women were not peremptorily disqualified from trespassing on such lofty heights. Rather, they were often admired and encouraged. Articles in the popular press, such as the *Daily Telegraph* ("The Queen of the Alps"), *The Graphic* ("The Scottish Alps"), the *Daily News,* the *Standard*, the *Daily Chronicle*, the *Daily Graphic*, the *Weekly Budget*, and the *Evening News* regularly lauded women's climbing skills. A notice in the 18 July 1892 issue of the *Daily Graphic* praises the ascent "and descent (in a snowstorm) of the Matterhorn by Mrs. Farrar." The reporter remarks that this climb "adds yet another to the long lists of Alpine feats performed by the sex popularly believed to be weaker" and concludes that similarly "stirring achievements of the fair are recorded every year" (Scrapbook, Alpine Club Achives). And "Women as Alpine Climbers," in the 20 August 1898 issue of the *Evening News*, quotes the celebrated climber, Edward Whymper, as announcing his esteem for "the modern race of young women" who "show as much intrepidity, coolness, and skill as men do in most ordinary Alpine climbing." Whymper observes: "As regards caution, women have a long way the advantage of men, and of all the thousands of English and American women who have surmounted the most dangerous Alpine peaks, but few have come to grief as compared with men" ("Women as Alpine Climbers," Scrapbook, Alpine Club Archives).[21]

Indeed, from the mid-century on, female mountaineers were frequently accepted by the very people, including members of the London Alpine Club, who, in historians' and critics' eyes, acted as the apostles of British masculinity, and who, because they refused membership to women, presumably wanted to perpetuate the notion that different sexes belong to separate spheres. I think it telling that in his address to the Alpine Club on 16 December 1889, the Club's fomer president, Clinton Dent, referred to the "Alpine sisterhood" and stated that some of the best winter mountaineering had been accomplished by women: "Indeed, one of the best climbs recorded in the Alps of recent times, the ascent of the rarely visited Aiguille de Bionnassay and the traverse of its entire eastern ridge, was also achieved by a lady." The president goes on to say: "So much the better. It is a good sign that the

---

[21] A year earlier, the *Standard* announced: "A feat of mountain-climbing has been accomplished by Miss Tommasson, an English traveller, while staying at the Dolomites. This intrepid lady ascended four virgin peaks .. She christened two of the peaks in commemoration of the Queen's Diamond Jubilee" (27 August 1897, Scrapbook, Alpine Club Archive).

popularity of mountaineering is not diminishing ... but has really, as the theatrical people say, 'caught on'" ("Presidential Address to the Alpine Club," *The Alpine Journal* 15 [1890]:14). I admit, it would be tempting to dwell on the fact that the only honorary "female" member of the Club before 1976 was Tschingel, the dog with which W.A.B. Coolidge and Meta Brevoort accomplished 66 major climbs and about 100 minor ones.[22] When Tschingel died, Coolidge wrote to the editor of *The Alpine Journal* regretting that he had "to ask space to record the death of a famous mountaineer."[23] However, contrary to what this strange detail suggests, quite a different way of thinking will often be found.

Above the snow line gender mattered less or even ceased to count. As Marion Leslie remarked in 1903, "In no other region of enterprise is a woman placed so completely on an equality with a man as in mountaineering" (310). In spite of their chauvinistic reputation among historians, there is evidence that a more than sufficient number of members in the Alpine Club, as well as the general public, encouraged, applauded, and respected the achievements of British women who showed to the world how "plucky" the English could be: where a French woman might quake, an English woman would bravely persevere. Englishness allowed the transcendence of gender. In 1831, Derwent Conway, recalling his trip to Switzerland, commented:

> I met two parties at the inn preparing to pass the Wengern Alp to Grundelwald; –
> one a party of English; two ladies and a gentleman. The character of the English

---

[22] Tschingel's climbs were duly recorded in *The Alpine Journal*. Under "Alpine Notes," the following climb is noted: "Miss Brevooort, Messrs. S.P. Cockerell, and W.A.B. Coolidge, with Tschingel, a dog, effected the first ascent of the highest point of the Füsshörner which is visible from the Sparrenhorn, but not from the Bell-Alp Hôtel" (5 [1871]: 276).

[23] W.A.B. Coolidge reported to *The Alpine Journal:*
I regret to have to ask space to record the death of a famous mountaineer, the dog Tschingel, which occurred at Dorking on June 16. Tschingel was purchased in the Lötschthal when a puppy by Christian Almer in September 1865. She made her *début* as a climber by an ascent of the Torrenthorn from the Maing glacier, and a few days after crossed her first glacier pass, that from which she derived her name. For several years she lived at Grindelwald as the watch-dog of Almer's house, and in July 1868 passed into the possession of Miss Brevoort and myself. In order to follow us she had perforce to climb peaks and traverse passes, and she acquitted herself so admirably that for nine summers (1868 to 1876) she was our constant companion in our Alpine campaigns ... Among her more remarkable feats were Mont Blanc, Monte Rosa, Finsteraarhorn, Aletschhorn (twice), Nesthorn, Jungfraujoch with *descent* to Wengern Alp, Eiger ... and Col du Glacier Blanc. In no one instance did she ever make a false step, and very rarely required assistance; but on the Diablerets showed a local guide the best way down the precipices of the Creux de Champs. Her Alpine career closed with the death of her mistress. ("Alpine Notes," *The Alpine Journal* 9 [1879]: 310–11)

ladies for enterprise, courage, and perseverance, ranks very high in Switzerland. I have heard some old guides speak in rapturous terms of my countrywomen, or accounts of their contempt of difficulty, and even of danger; while, on the other hand, the reputation of Frenchwomen for these same qualities stands as low as possible in their estimation. (231–32)

Thirty years later, John Tyndall, the distinguished scientist, climber, and member of the Alpine Club, expressed a similar appreciation, even though, as we have seen, he also subscribed to the belief in separate geographical spheres for men and women upon a mountain:

Near to the hotel are two magnificent boulders of green serpentine, which have been lodged there by one of the lateral glaciers; and two of the ladies desiring to ascend one of these rocks, a friend and myself helped them to the top. The thing was accomplished in a very spirited way. Indeed the general contrast, in regard to energy, between the maidens of the British Isles and those of the Continent and of America is extraordinary. Surely those who talk of this country being in its old age overlook the physical vigour of its sons and daughters. (*The Glaciers of the Alps* 101)

In his memoir, Geoffrey W. Young, an avid club member, however, had absolutely no need to qualify his praise when he recalled that in mid-century he had climbed "in the encouraging company of a lady who could play Schumann as he should be played among the mountains" and with whom he had "cut long ladders of steps up the treacherous ice wall of the Col Durand" (51). Young also admitted that some women climbers exceeded his capabilities: "In making the second ascent of the north face [of the Weisshorn], Miss Sanders (Mrs. O'Malley), improved greatly upon our line, crossing from the Weisshorn hut over the east ridge, and direct to the Bies glacier, probably by the route referred to on p. 88" (146). For him, mountains drew together people of diverse ages, interest, as well as sex; the "mountain atmosphere provided a common inspiration" (171).

Sheer Numbers

There is yet more truth to be sought. Histories tend to ignore the enormous number of women climbers. If one looks through the Alpine Club's scrapbooks, journals, and letters, and if one reads through the huge number of climbing narratives written by its members as well as by women mountaineers, one uncovers a complicated picture in which the wives, daughters, cousins, aunts, and female friends of the Club's membership were climbing with the very men who were supposedly holding on to the idea that mountains are male territory. In the mid-nineteenth century, it is not unusual to run across a passage in which a writer quite casually remarks that a young man and his sister are on a climbing holiday or that a climber joins a party in which there is "a London lady of great spirit and vivacity, who, in company with her husband and another gentleman, had climbed the Storr [a mountain in Scotland] on the previous Thursday, encompassed with mist, and in a deluge of rain, and yet she seemed only more determined to brave every difficulty" (Rev. Thomas Grierson 38). In an early 1870s letter home from Switzerland, Havergal, who climbed with Elizabeth Clay and wrote not only a cantata about lady climbers but also poems lauding her alpenstock, writes that she has met Miss Anstey, who "is sister of an Alpine Clubbist, and seems very strong and up to mountaineering" (Crane 145).[24] Moreover, it is not a surprise to learn that Mrs. Freshfield went on expeditions with her husband and son as well as with another woman. As Cicely Williams rightly observes in her *Women on the Rope*: "Husbands and fathers brought their womenfolk to the mountains and frequently encouraged their mountaineering careers" (17).

Photographs in the Alpine Club Film Library often show these mixed climbing parties. One 1860 photo, for instance, displays a group of two men and two women. These pictures also suggest that the presence of women on the mountains was not always thought to spoil the experience. In fact, in *The Alpine Journal*, C.E. Mathews even protested against what he labeled this "preposterous" attitude. He asserted: "The mountain spirit knows nothing of celibacy" ("The Jägerhorn and the Luskamm from Gressonay," *The Alpine Journal* 4 [1868]: 66).

The pages of the *The Alpine Journal* are replete with references to the company of women on mountaineering expeditions. Unless one wanted to highlight the fact that the journal's editor would occasionally refer to these females as simply "ladies" and not acknowledge their actual names, there seems to be no significant attempt to ignore either the presence or the accomplishments of these climbers.[25] Examples are abundant. In the first volume, one member, Robert Spence Watson, reported that he had found a guide who would "be delighted and proud" to "lead his wife to the virgin summit" of the Balferinhorn (12,467') ("Summary of New Expeditions During the Summer of 1863," *The Alpine Journal* 1 [1863]: 135). In

---

[24] Janet Grierson writes that:
> On their climbing excursions, Frances and Elizabeth accompanied by guides, achieved such heights as the 9,649 feet Aeggischhorn, the nearly 10,000 feet Sparrenhorn, the 10,200 feet Gornegrat and the 11,000 feet Col de St Theodule. Only one climb, the 13,000 feet Cerna de Jazi, described as 'the very top of all my Alpine ambition' had to be omitted from schedule, as Elizabeth, who found herself short of breath on long ascents, felt unequal to it and Frances was unable to find another companion. (121)

A few lines from the Havergal's Oratorio entitled "The Mountain Maidens" (Zella, Dora, Lisetta) show how conventionally sentimental it was:
> And you, Lisetta, to the sterner heights,
> Where only foot of Alpine goat may pass,
> Or step of mountain maiden. (103)

[25] One example of this practice is illustrated in the following entry. On 12 August 1864 "Mr. E.N. Buxton and party, comprising two ladies, ascended the Moror from Macugnaga" (*The Alpine Journal* 1 [1864]: 432).

Figure 3.9   Elizabeth Le Blond. "Piz Bernina, Piz Roseg from Piz Corvatsch"

the same issue, yet another Alpine Club man, Stephen Winkworth, complimented J.J. Bennen and J.B. Croz (one of the more famous guides) who had "guided my wife and myself, last July, in an attack on the the Rothorn (9,790') from Zermatt (12.935')" (197).

From the founding of the journal until the end of the century, similar notices are prevalent. Among these announcements, one learns that "a Scotch lady" was required by a storm to spend the night with her guide on the Col de Tête Blanche (12,304'). There is not one word about how indecorous this bivouac was; rather, the emphasis is upon the guide's ingenuity in making a snow-hut to protect them from the elements. And in the "Alpine Notes" section, one reads that a member and "his young wife" made a successful ascent of Hochstetter Dome in the New Zealand Alps; that "On August 16 the ascent of Mont Blanc was made by Miss Flossie Morse, a young lady of twelve or thirteen years of age" (*The Alpine Journal* 14 [1888]:164); and that on July 23 [1888] "Miss Pasteur, Miss Mary Pasteur, Messrs. Charles Pasteur, and Claude Wilson, with August Cupeline, ascended and crossed the southernmost of the three main points on the ridge connecting the Aiguilles 'Verte' and 'du Maine'" (*The Alpine Journal* 15 [1890]: 329).

One can also read about G.S. Barnes, yet another Alpine Club member, who undertook a joint venture to climb the Dents des Bouquetins (12,625') with his friend, Miss Blair Oliphant. Admiring Oliphant's mountaineering skill, Barnes reported: "Miss Oliphant, for whom the unknown has no terrors, desired that the expedition should be an entirely new one" (*The Alpine Journal* 13 [1888]: 529). Roped together with Cecil Slingsby, a prominent member of the Alpine Club, and with Martin Buignier, a porter, Barnes and Oliphant succeeded in reaching the top. The examples proliferate. In the same year (1888–89), *The Alpine Journal* recorded in the "New Expeditions" section, a series of accomplishments by English women in Norway. With well-regarded club members, these women reached peaks that had never "been gained by English ladies" (*The Alpine Journal* 14 [1889]: 508–509). There is pride in this. And there was to be a longing for these moments. At the turn of the century, some of the Alpine Club's founding members looked back upon these expeditions with nostalgia. Rather poignantly, at the annual dinner of the Ladies' Alpine Club in 1909, the Bishop of Bristol, a former President of the London Alpine Club, recalled the pleasure that he and his sister had enjoyed a long time ago when they had climbed together. These pieces of evidence qualify or make one mistrust Ronald Clark's conclusion that "Even as late as 1879, the feeling against women climbers was strong" (176).

Death notices and lists of Alpine accidents in *The Alpine Journal* also offer a vivid sense of the number of women who were climbing alone or accompanying relatives and Club members. The specter of death helps eradicate thoughts of discrimination. As Leslie observes: "crevasses are no respecters of sex" (310). (Only once did I run across a notice that seemed to blame the women for an accident.[26]) Under the heading "Alpine Accidents," one can find references to fatal falls and avalanches: to young girls who have stumbled down rock precipices, and to people such as Mrs. Marks who, with her porter, fell to her death down a crevasse while ascending Mont Blanc. Mrs. Marks' sister, who was behind, was saved through the breaking of the rope. Newspapers also duly recorded these deaths. One article in the *Pall Mall*, 26 November 1897, reported:

> A coffin was landed this morning at Dover from the steamer *Victoria* containing the body of a lady who lost her life on the Alps in 1865. The remains, which are said to have been lain undiscovered for thirty-two years, were identified as those of Miss Arbuthnot, who is believed to have belonged to a county family in Berkshire. (Scrapbook, Alpine Club Archives)

In addition to those lady mountaineers who are familiar to us through mountaineering history books and recent studies, such as Rebecca Brown's *Women on High:*

---

[26] In the *Daily Chronicle* 30 August 1898, there is an article recounting an Alpine fatality in which a father with his two daughters and his son died. The writer states: "the probability was that one of the girls was frightened, and, slipping, lost her presence of mind. The other girl was probably equally disturbed, and the two dragged the Professor and his son (who had recently climbed the Matterhorn) with them" (Scrapbook, Alpine Club Archive).

Pioneers of Mountaineering, and Robinson's *Wayward Women: A Guide to Women Travellers*, I have selected the lost, forgotten, or barely-known Miss Arbuthnots, the Mrs. Marks, and the Miss Oliphants in order to show that there were many more women climbers in the second half of the nineteenth century than most realize. Histories tend to concentrate on the spectacular few and pass by such individuals as Mrs. Blandy, Miss Blanche Blandy, Miss Bridge, Mrs. and Miss Campbell, Mrs. Churchill, Miss Cowan, Miss Dickinson, Mrs. Gilbert, Mrs. Hamilton, Grace Hunt, Anne Lister, Mrs. Millet, Maud Meyer, Marion Sellers Neilson, Mary de la Beche Nicholl (if her granddaughter, Hilary M. Thomas, had not found and published her letters, we would know nothing of her climbs from the 1860s to 1889),[27] Marion Pollock, Frances Maria Richardson, Miss Tomassan, an unidentified "large English party of six ladies" (Mrs, Henry Freshfield 216) and a lady at the *table d'hôte* who, according to Emily Hornby, was going up the Cevdale the next day "with two brothers, a cousin, and another young man" (212).

This is by no means an exhaustive list – a reality that a reviewer for *The Alpine Journal* clearly understood when he admiringly declared: "In endeavouring to keep pace with ladies' ascents an author attempts the impossible, since many ladies are too modest to record their exploits." He concluded: "Thus, where three ladies are named as having climbed the Finsteraarhorn [14,025'], the number ought to our knowledge to be *at least* doubled" ("Reviews and Notices," *The Alpine Journal* 11[1883]: 306).

Recently, I have had the opportunity to go through the application letters of women who wished to join the Ladies' Alpine Club (LAC, referred to earlier as the Lyceum Alpine Club) when it was first founded in 1907. These do not give a sense of women climbing at mid-century but do proffer a glimpse at the numbers of women climbing in the late 1880s and early 1890s. A selection from these applications, with their accompanying credentials, follows: Mrs. A.F. Brown (née Hilda M. Howard) in the year 1888 climbed the Petits Charmoz (9,405'), the Col des Grands Moutets (10,635'), the Col du Géant (10,915'); in 1889, among other accomplishments, she crossed the Ritter Pass (8,832'), ascended Monte Leone (11,670'), the Languinhorn (13,140'), the Alphubel (13,803'), and the Ulrichshorn (12,890'). Brown's list continues into the 1890s and eventually records that in 1898 she climbed to the summit of Monte Rosa (15,217') as well as up other challenging places such as the Dent des Bouquetins (12,625'). Brown's name is followed by a Miss Mary Barber, who in 1897 and 1898, succeeded in doing a number of routes not once, but twice. Then follows Mrs. Jane Inglis Clarke, who actively climbed in Scotland ("6 first ascents on Ben Nevis & others"), and later climbed to the top of Mont Blanc, the Matterhorn, and Monte Rosa. Other names of people climbing between 1888 and 1900 on the list are: Mrs. Morriston Davies of 55 Gordon Square (London), who ascended, among many other peaks,

---

[27]   See Hilary M. Thomas's *Grandmother Extraordinary: Mary De la Beche Nicholl 1839–1922.*

the Matterhorn and the Eiger; Mrs. M.H. Fox from Somerset, who ascended the Col du Géant; Miss. Kate Gardiner, who early in her life climbed the Breithorn (12,400'), the Schwarzhorn (10,512'), and the Schilthorn (10,817'), and Mrs. Hatfield of Tavistock Square (London), who, among other climbs, listed a mountain in Norway. She believed she had been the third woman to climb it. The names continue: Alice Moore Bruce wrote that she had done rock and snow climbing on mountains round Inversnaid and Glencoe with Major C.G. Bruce and Professor Norman Collie [both prominent Alpine Club climbers, lionized for their ascents in the Himalaya]. She added, "I have also done a good deal of climbing in Wales and in Scotland (in winter), much of it with my brother General Bruce, the Himalayan climber." And Marion B. Rooper of 37 Dover Street (London) recorded that in the late eighties, she had succeeded in climbing up the Dent du Midi, the Schilthorn, and three-quarters of the way up the Balmhorn (12,175') (Lyceum Alpine Club Papers, Alpine Club Archives).

Other candidates listing climbs accomplished in the second half of the nineteenth century, some going back to the 1870s and many in the early 1890s, are: Mrs. Rodolph Adlercron, Mrs. Bernard Allen, Miss C.L. Callis, Mrs. Hatfield, E.P. Hughes, Miss Annie Lowson, Mrs. Heron Maxwell, Miss E.E. Mudd, Miss M.T. Meyer, Mrs. Nettleton, Mrs. Anna Onchterlony-Ryman, Mrs. E.F. Ogilvy, Miss M. Osborne, Helen Katharine Smith, Miss Beatrice M. Taylor, Miss Edith Venables, Mrs. A.F. Wedgwood, Mrs. A.E. Willmott, Miss Emily S. Western, and Mrs. Alice Willmott. By no means is the list complete.

Obviously among the candidate letters is a handful of those mountaineers to whom history continues to pay attention.

Among these are Anna Pigeon and her sister, Ellen Abbott (née Pigeon), who accomplished 63 difficult climbs between the years 1869 and 1876 – their candidate letters are impressive. Other names are also familiar. Among these are: Lucy Walker, who, beginning in the 1858, with her father and brother as well as with Emmeline Lewis-Lloyd, completed 98 expeditions, and in 1871 was the first woman to reach the summit of the Matterhorn (the chapter-heading poem honors that accomplishment); Fanny Bullock Workman, the American who, in the 1890s, climbed in the Alps as well as in unexplored areas in the Himalaya, set the women's altitude record with the ascent of Mount Koser Gunge (21,000') and later, as I have already explained, reached the highest altitude ever, for either sex, at 23,300 feet on the Pinnacle Peak; and finally Elizabeth Le Blond who, between the 1880s until the turn of the century, was avidly climbing in the Alps and in Norway. She completed over one hundred expeditions, a number done in winter, many of these were first ascents and without guides. Le Blond acted as the first president of the Ladies' Alpine Club.

None of these individuals was ignored by the all-male Alpine Club. In 1869, when the Pigeons made the extraordinary passage of the Sesia-Joch from Zermatt to Alagna, *The Alpine Journal* did more than carry an announcement of the achievement. The journal also ran a long article praising and describing the climb, even though the title, "The Passage of the Sesai-Joch from Zermatt to Alagna

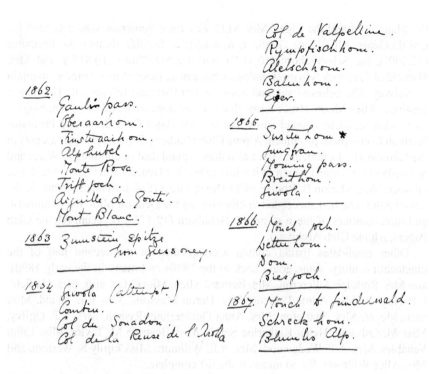

Figure 3.10 Lucy Walker's climbing list

by English Ladies," – but not the article itself – overlooked their names.[28] The opening paragraphs remark on how remarkable their feat was:

> The members of the Alpine Cub heard ... with some astonishment that in the autumn of 1869 two ladies had not only crossed this most redoubtable of glacier

---

28 The article appeared in *The Alpine Journal*. The writer explains:

> Mr. Ball, writing in 1863, referred to the first passage of the Sesia-Joch by Messr. George and Moore, as "amongst the most daring of Alpine exploits," and expressed a doubt whether it was not a *tour de force* which would never be repeated. Mr. Moore, indeed, repeated his exploit with another companion, but he was for many years unsuccessful in inducing anyone else to follow in his footsteps, and both guides and mountaineers seem to have shared the doubts of Mr. Ball as the route being one fit for ordinary use.
>
> The members of the Alpine Club heard, therefore, with some astonishment that in the autumn of 1869 two ladies had not only crossed Alagama, thus descending the wall of rock, the ascent of which had until then been looked on as an extraordinary feat for first-rate climbers.
>
> The details now in our possession leave no room to doubt that Joch should not cease to be considered a *tour de force*, rarely to be attempted, and take its place among the recognised routes into or out of Zermatt. (*The Alpine Journal* 5 [1872]: 367–72)

passes, but crossed it from Zermatt to Alagna, thus descending the wall of rock, the ascent of which had until then been looked on as an extraordinary feat for first-rate climbers. The details now in our possession leave no room to doubt that the Misses Pigeon exactly reversed the steps of their predecessors. (*The Alpine Journal* 5 [1872]: 367–68)

The article then reprints a sensational account of their climb published in an Italian newspaper, and concludes with two pages of notes sent by the Pigeons commenting on their achievement. Their version is straightforward, corrective, and full of self-confidence. A sample paragraph follows:

> The Italian account exaggerates the difficulty we experienced. The rope was never used to "hold up the travelers and let them down one by one." On the contrary, one lady went *last*, preferring to see the awkward porter in front of her rather than behind. At one spot we came to an abrupt wall of rock, and there we gladly availed ourselves of our guide's hand. The sensational sentence about "rolling as shapeless corpses into the crevasses" is absurd, as we were at that juncture rejoicing in the prospect of a happy termination of our dilemma, and of crossing the glacier in full enjoyment of our senses. (371)

Similarly, the journal frequently ran pieces giving accounts of Walker's, Workman's, and Le Blond's successful ascents. *The Alpine Journal* also recognized those accomplished climbers who, for various reasons, did not choose to apply to the Ladies Alpine Club. Among these mountaineers is Katharine Richardson, who climbed nearly two hundred peaks, including the first ascent of the Meije (13,068'), and in record time. She was known for her fast pace and swift movements. The editor of *The Alpine Journal* thought that event to be "the most noteworthy" of the season: "We have recorded above (page 150) the remarkable traverse of the Aiguille de Bionnassay by Miss Katharine Richardson on August 13 last [year]. The same indefatigable lady achieved, on August 24, the ascent of the Meije in Dauphiné, this being the first time the summit has ever been reached by a lady" ("Alpine Notes," *The Alpine Journal* 14 [1888]: 163). There are also many references to other notable women climbers: Jackson (married to an Alpine Club member), who accomplished a number of pioneer climbs during the 1870s and 1880s, Isabella Straton, who beginning in 1861 reached a number of difficult summits (she climbed Mont Blanc four times, and she married her Alpine guide);[29] Meta Brevoort, who with her

---

[29]   C.E. Mathews in his article "The Growth of Mountaineering" recorded that there had been three attempts to ascend Mont Blanc in January 1876.

Mr. Coolidge and Miss Brevoort spent five nights at the Grands Mulets, and succeeded in reaching the Grand Plateau with the two Almers [guides], but were driven back by severe wind. Mr. Eccles and M. Loppé ... too, were driven back from the Grand Plateau ... but Miss Straton succeeded in gaining the summit in spite of all obstacles, the temperature recorded being thirteen degrees below zero (Farenheit). (*The Alpine Journal* 10 [1881]: 259)

nephew W.A.B. Coolidge, made a number of serious Alpine climbs, among which is the first ascent of the Pic Centrale of the Meije (1870) and the first winter ascents of the Wetterhorn and the Jungfrau; Lily Bristow, who, as I have already mentioned, joined premier members of the Alpine Club (Mummery, Cecil Slingsby, Ellis Carr, and J. Norman Collie) in expeditions in the Swiss and French Alps, as well as Mary Mummery.

Part 4: Above the Snow Line

I suggest that the more general assumption that lady climbers *continuously* suffered from "sex antagonism" (as Fanny Bullock Workman reputedly complained) tends to belong to the more facile tongue of retrospect than to a more complete understanding of the actual experience. Although I recognize, as does the first part of this chapter, that prejudice existed, I believe that such charges generally find a stronger voice after climbers have descended from the heights and rejoined the social requirements of life below the snow line. And, as I have already mentioned, examples of sexual bias tend to get replicated in histories that emphasize instances of disrespect at the expense of a fuller picture.

In the second half of the nineteenth century, gender, though often an issue for people climbing in the lower heights, ceased to be as much of a factor when women reached the higher altitudes. Certainly Le Blond, who attempted the first guideless winter ascent of Monte Rosa and traversed the Piz Palü without a guide, was never faulted for her lack of skill or courage. Even one reviewer of her *The High Alps in Winter*, who accused her of writing "a lady's book ... to amuse an idle hour," was forced to admit that her winter expeditions say much for her perseverance – as well as for the judgment and skill of her guides ("Reviews and Notices," *The Alpine Journal* 11 [1883]: 306).

Away from such petty opinions emanating from societal pressures, up high, above the snow line or in distant regions, women climbers could more fully experience equality and power, and be rid of such intrusive nonsense. If they chose, they could be just as sportsmanlike or competitive as the men. They were not bothered by others' opinion about their refusal to be passive. As a result, one reads not only of their taking pleasure in the strength of their bodies but also of their competing with other mountaineers to be the first to set foot on a summit or to reach the highest peak. They could unselfconsciously speak of "a fiendish satisfaction" while scrambling along a high-level route of the Alps (Hornby 17) and of the "delightful sense of security which muscles in first-class condition and complete absence of any sensation of fatigue fully justified" (*Adventures on the Roof of the World* 201). And they could take pleasure in recalling that they had climbed a steep ridge at "an incredible pace" on their way up to a summit (in this case, the Rothhorn) (Hornby 57). These women could readily, if they so chose, also adopt the military metaphors of their male counterparts and speak of "assaulting" a mountain (*Adventures on the Roof of the World* 98), be a leader of many an ascent, and do the ultimate "masculine" thing of going on guideless expeditions.

Throughout the second half of the nineteenth century women pushed into the higher altitudes for competition as well as sport. They felt free to honor an instinct which bade them arrive at a destination before any one else and urged them to record a "first ascent" of a pass or a mountain. It was an impulse of this sort that prompted De la Beche Nicholl (known as "Minnie"), in the 1860s, to tie a white and blue handkerchief to the flagstaff to mark the first time an Englishwoman had reached the summit of the Lomnitz Spitz. And it was a similar inclination that caused Emily Hornby to write: "I have done the Mont Pourri this year [1881], which I believe no female has done, and also crossed the Grand Paradis from Cogne to Val Saranache, which also I don't believe any female has done" (Hornby 15). Such ambition also prompted Elizabeth Le Blond to publish accounts of other women climbers, and probably motivated Frederica Plunket in 1875 to encourage "ladies to pass snow-marked boundaries" (1). The latter was not just interested in urging women to experience the beauties of the higher mountainous landscape; she wanted them to feel the strength of their bodies and the excitement of the climb.

Women could be as competitive as their male counterparts. Some went to extraordinary lengths and were not content, as were the majority, to have their virgin climbs simply noted in the press or in *The Alpine Journal*. One learns, for instance, about Anne Lister who, in 1838, after attaining the 10,820 foot summit of the Vignemale (in the Pyrenees), attempted to make it quite clear to the world that she, rather than the Prince de la Moscowa, had been the first to reach its peak. As soon as she learned that the Prince was making an attempt to climb Vignemale, she speedily set on her way and succeeded in beating him to the top. However, a few days later, she read in the newspaper that the Prince was claiming victory, so Lister, through the services of a lawyer, required the editor to sign a certificate saying that it was she, and not the Prince, who had made the first ascent (Ingham, *The Alpine Journal* 73 (1968): 199–206).[30] Similarly determined, at the turn of the century, Fanny Bullock Workman even hired surveyors to prove that she had exceeded

---

[30] In August, 1838 Anne Lister sent the following information to "Galignani's Messenger":

> Miss Lister will also be much obliged to Messrs. Galignani to insert the following paragraph in the next edition of their *Messenger* after receiving this note:
> "We noticed, some days ago, the ascent of the Prince de la Moscowa and his brother, Mr. Edgar Ney, with five guides, to the summit of the Vignemale, hitherto thought inaccessible. We find that an English lady had, four days before, ascended with three guides to the same summit, which, though inaccessible from the French side, is not more difficult of ascent, from the Spanish side, towards the east, than high mountains in general." (Green 504)

It is interesting to note that the eccentric Count Russell took up residence on the Vignemale and, in a sense, claimed it as his bride. One wonders if he was aware that Lister had claimed it for herself. (Robin Fedden, "Russell and the Vignemale," *The Alpine Journal* 65 [1960]: 80–84).

Figure 3.11   Mrs. Main [Elizabeth Le Blond] after a winter attempt on Piz
Morteratsch

Annie Peck's supposed world record. After great expense, she did indeed prove
that her ascent to the top of Pinnacle Peak in the Western Himalaya surpassed the
American climber's successful 1903 expedition to the top of Huascaran (6,768 m.)
in South America. Due to a snowstorm, Peck had misjudged the altitude and had
calculated it to be 7,300 m. high.

Stepping beyond the regulations and conventions of the world below, both
men and women, once they crossed a certain border (when the skirts more often
than not would come off), left behind what threatened to divide them. As a result,
climbers such as Bell, Bristow, Le Blond, Richardson, and Walker – to name a few
– enjoyed a respectful comradeship with their fellow male mountaineers. Whether
one was ladylike or not was less important; above the snow line, no underlying
sexual nervousness interfered. What mattered more was conquering the mountain
and getting on with it – as Bristow said, in the early 1890s, after climbing with
Mummery, "it was a ripping good climb," "a real snorker" (Mazel 81). Mummery
treated Bristow as a colleague – she was a member of "our party" (Mummery
107): "Our party consisted of Miss Bristow, Mr. Hastings, and myself. Warmly
wrapped in sleeping bags, we sat sipping hot tea … Only when the chill breeze
of night had dried up the rivulets … did we creep into the shelter of our tent"
(Mummery 107). Together, she and Mummery "started up the ice, hewing such
steps as were necessary" (Mummery 108). He admired her rock climbing abilities
and her ceaseless energy for their own sake.

Although Bristow's letters indicate that she never forgot that she was a "lady,"
they speak convincingly of the camaraderie she experienced with her fellow
mountaineers. It is interesting that, after descending from a successful climb to
the summit of the Rothorn, she recalled that when the group "got in about 9 p.m.
it was a great joke, none of the hotel people would believe we had been up the
Rothorn: 'non, Mademoiselle, pas possible!'" But rather than think her audience's
incredulity was referring to her sex – how could a lady do this? – she immediately
accounted for their disbelief by asserting that she and Mummery had executed
a feat beyond the realm of possibility: "They are not used to non-guided parties
here and the idea that Fred and I could calmly track up their most awesome and
revered peak is quite beyond them – they think we must have mistaken some
grassy knoll for the Rothorn" ("An Easy Day for a Lady," *The Alpine Journal* 53
[1942]: 374).

Thirty years earlier, A.W. Moore, in his *The Alps in 1864*, had also treated
his female climbing companion (Lucy Walker) as just another member of the
group. Summoning the inclusive "we," he talked about the climbing party's steady
advance: "we progressed steadily, Melchoir leading, followed by Miss Walker,
Jacob, Mr. Walker, myself, Almer, and Morshead, the latter being consigned to the
rear, in order to check his 'locomotive' propensities and also because he required
less assistance than the other members of the party, – not that any of us called for
very much" (Moore 229). Similar stories could be told of many others, both at
mid-century and toward the turn of the century. Not surprisingly, Le Blond does
not single herself out as a "lady," but includes herself as one of a mixed group of

climbers, and refers to "my brother and sister climbers" (*True Tales of Mountain Adventure* 83).[31] Earlier notes on expeditions published in *The Alpine Journal* quite casually mention that "Miss Katharine Richardson, with Emile Rey and J.B. Birch, left the Montenvers inn at midnight" to start a climb ("New Expeditions," *The Alpine Journal* 14 [1889]: 511).

This sense of inclusiveness punctuates the enthusiasm and self-assurance of Bell's prose when she writes about her mountaineering experiences in the 1890s. Inspired by a German woman who had recently climbed the Meiji and whom she talked to after dinner, Bell determines to have a "shot" at the mountain. One of her lengthy letters home describes the descent after her having successfully reaching the summit:

> Mr. Turner first, then Mathon disappeared, then I felt the tug on the rope, Marius held it tight behind and round I went. Very well done I thought. I did not lose my footing and it was better than I expected. It took us 3 hours up and down the Dents to get to the Pic Central ... At first very pleasant going, then steep and crevassed and we had to cut steps. Coasted along the arête leading to the Pic de L'Homme. At the bottom of the Glacier we unroped and Mr. Turner and I eat chocolate and drank water he was revived [*sic*]. This was about 5, we walked down to the grass together and got in at 6:35. I also was revived by this time.
> (Letter 27 August 1899, The Gertrude Bell Archive)

By the end of the century, women as climbers were more fully established in the popular imagination, and so, by extension, was their commercial value. Burberrys, Singer Sewing Machine, and boot manufacturers featured them in their advertising campaigns. One advertisement for Burberry's displays a self-confident woman standing alone, triumphant upon a peak (dressed, of course, in a Burberry outfit).

Fully trusting their bodies, their authority, and their experience, these mountaineers did not confine their activities to the Alps. Like their male colleagues, they moved beyond these mountains to become part of the reach of empire: to such places as Afghanistan, Africa, the Himalaya, India, New Zealand, Norway, as well as to North and South America. Gender might still play a role in that these climbers were often eager to be "the first lady" up a particular mountain, but gender did not matter in the overwhelmingly debilitating way that commentators have often claimed it did. From the mid-century on, women, in their ascents up high or above the snow line, did not necessarily have to face the crevasse that Mary Taylor's guide had revealed. Mountains were not solely a male sphere. Only in the history of mountaineering has that been made to seem so.

---

[31]   In her *Mountaineering in the Land of the Midnight Sun*, Le Blond is quick to note: "We were a party of four, including Joseph Imboden" (14).

Figure 3.12 Burberry advertisement

Part II

Literary Figures in the Alps

Watercolor sketch with marked route from Georg
Hoffman's 1852 Alpine Sketchbook

Chapter 4
John Ruskin: Climbing and
the Vulnerable Eye

The way to see mountains is to take a knapsack and a walking stick.

(Ruskin, *Works* 26:104)

Part 1: Ruskin the Climber

Most readers either overlook or dismiss Ruskin's climbs in the Alps as being insignificant compared to his avid interest in geology and mountain form. However, I want to suggest that Ruskin's climbing – his physical and kinetic relationship to the mountains – is essential to his understanding of them. His numerous and repeated ascents in the lower Alps were not always easy: in fact, they were often tough and sometimes dangerous. Through a few select examples, in the first part of the chapter, I establish just how difficult many of these scrambles were so that I may proceed, in the second part, to describe how these strenuous experiences influenced his way of seeing the mountain landscape he admired, and how, in turn, they helped shape his concept of imperfect vision.

Although this chapter does not directly address the sinking of the sublime, it does reveal how Ruskin qualified the more popular sublime experience that emphasized terror and force. For him the sublime is not necessarily an intimation of nature's might (what Kant might call the dynamical sublime), but rather introduces the idea of a more limited and rational experience induced by the eye's incapacity to see clearly at great distances. In a sense, the lack of any stable point of reference for the eye as it guides the body's ascent – a source of anxiety, as well as an affective element of perception during his climbs – and his anxious search for the "governing lines" of mountains exemplifies Kant's mathematical sublime. Reason has to fill in what perception cannot grasp as a whole.

Ruskin and Skiddaw

Over forty years ago, while I was visiting the Lake District, I walked up Skiddaw for the first time. Young and careless, I resolved to reach its bare peak. I was not properly equipped: tennis shoes, a light nylon jacket, and no water. The day seemed fine until late afternoon when a storm suddenly blew in. Following cairns that marked the way, I obstinately persisted in reaching the scaly slate of Skiddaw's summit, but, once at the top, I could not find my way down, for I was caught in a dense fog. I saw enough of my surroundings, however, to realize that I was stuck on a narrow ledge; I feared that a miscalculated step would send me hurtling down the mountain's precipitous sides. I had no choice but to wait for the storm to pass. Luckily for me, within an hour, the figure of a hardy, experienced rambler gradually took shape through the mist and broke through the encircling clouds. He gave me water and escorted me down just before darkness fell.

This experience was the beginning of my love affair with Skiddaw. Ever since then I have periodically returned: sometimes the conditions have been clear; at other times, clouds have settled to obliterate the sweeping view. Once or twice, the wind on top has been so strong that I have had to crawl along to prevent myself from being blown over by 70 mile-per-hour blasts. The last time I ascended Skiddaw was the summer of 2005. So many people have now gone up and down its slopes that the paths have eroded, but still Skiddaw beckons me.

In some respects my repeated attraction to Skiddaw reminds me of John Ruskin's own enchantment with this "celebrated mountain" (Richardson and Ruskin, "A Tour to the Lakes in Cumberland" 27). Throughout his life, Ruskin felt the pull of Skiddaw. As a young boy he went up with his parents; in April 1848, while on his honeymoon, he rode up with his wife; and, in his late 40s, he wrote triumphantly of his once more climbing along "the stately ridge towards the summit." Pleased with the rapidity with which he reached the top, he bragged, "I think there may be some life in the old dog yet" (*Works* 36: 534).

Ruskin's repeated references to Skiddaw remind one that he was not only profoundly attracted to the mountain landscape but also lured by the actual physical motion and exertion of clambering over their crags and reaching their heights. As I have mentioned in the introduction to this chapter, this aspect of Ruskin's kinetic relationship to mountains is not one that usually receives much notice. Critics tend to make little of Ruskin's physical accomplishments and, like one of his biographers, reduce his climbs either to "scrambles about the hills" or "to sketching expeditions" (Evans 101, 144). In particular, critics pay minimal attention to his notable feats in the Alps. More to the point, they refuse to see the link between his rigorous climbing and his way of seeing. First, though, I want to give some sense of just how physically demanding these climbs were.

The Thrill of Ascent

Although Ruskin readily admitted that he had "poor climbing powers" because he never learned the most advanced technical skills (*Praeterita* 334), he was a strong walker who could clamber over difficult places and endure long scrambles. His taste for such activity came from his boyhood travels with his family. The Ruskins' frequent trips to the Lake District and to the Continent when he was a young boy whetted his appetite for laborious climbs and precipitous ridges. Reading the earliest accounts of his family's ascents up Skiddaw, to the hills above Chamonix, and up to the top of Mt. Vesuvius, one senses the pleasure and satisfaction he experienced, even when there were difficulties.[1] It was not until Ruskin was in his twenties, however, that his mountain travel became more adventurous. Beginning in 1842, when Ruskin was 23, Switzerland became a second home. For the next forty years or so, he was, with a few exceptions to visit the Alps annually, either with his parents or alone, for months at a time.[2] Here he had more opportunities to clamber over dangerous terrain and ascend into higher regions.

The more serious climbing was initiated when, in 1844, Ruskin's father hired Joseph Marie Couttet as a guide for his son.[3] Fearful that his son's enthusiasm for collecting minerals and making sketches in the Alps might lead to trouble, he told Couttet that Ruskin should be "taken charge of ... and not permitted in any ambitious attempts, or taken into any dangerous places" (*Praeterita* 299). That edict to be careful, however, was not always heeded. Under Couttet's guidance, Ruskin soon learned how to wield an alpenstock, braved many a peak or pass he might not otherwise have attempted, and climbed with a vigor that he had not thought possible. Between 1844 and 1849, when undertaking the bulk of his geological and mountain studies, Ruskin repeatedly went up what many people might consider to be challenging and lengthy climbs, though never, it should be emphasized, up to heights associated with the famous peaks of Mont Blanc (15,781') or the Matterhorn (14,780'). Many of these summits, though, were over seven thousand feet (i.e. Mont Moro at 9,800') and a couple, at least, were over ten thousand. (One should remember that Mt. Washington, which can be a hard and even dangerous climb, is only 6,288'.)

Although it is impossible to list all of Ruskin's numerous ascents, a selection is sufficient to portray their rigorous character. In June 1844, for instance, Ruskin climbed "the Montanvert (6,267') beside a glacier all the way: a thorough scramble, clinging to bushes and swinging from trunks of trees in capital style." On the following day, he describes "a difficult descent to the snow, and then a climb

---

[1]   The diaries of Mary Richardson, Ruskin's cousin, who lived with the Ruskin family, give an excellent idea of the family's travels and climbs. Her 1833 diary of a continental tour, especially, reflects the excitement of the climb: their sliding off recalcitrant mules, their suffering from stones in their shoes, the threatening steepness of the ascent as well as the splendid views. Her 1841 account of their journey to the top of Mt. Vesuvius gives a vivid sense of the family dynamic as well as their delights, difficulties included, during the trip to the crater. These diaries are in the Ruskin Library, University of Lancaster.

[2]   In the 1860s, Ruskin rented houses in Mornex and then bought land in Chamonix so he might build a dwelling for himself. Ruskin visited Switzerland in May–July 1833; July–September 1835; June 1841; June–July 1842; April and September 1845; April and August 1846; May–August 1849; August 1851; July 1852; June–September 1856; May–July 1858; July–September 1859; May–August 1860; May–September 1852; December 1862–May 1863; and periodically in 1866, 1870, 1872, 1874, 1876, 1882, and finally in 1888.

[3]   Joseph Marie Couttet, whose father had been Horace Bénédict de Saussure's guide, was a sagacious and practical person, well versed in herbal medicines as well as cooking and climbing skills. Ruskin called him the "captain of Mont Blanc" for Couttet had climbed that celebrated mountain 11 times.

an hour or more, on steep inclined planes of snow, with formidable loose rocks interspersed." He concluded his climb by clambering over a glacier covered with deep snow, "only one crevice appearing; but the slope was so steep " (*Diaries* 1: 283–84). Later in the month, he and Couttet were off at 8 a.m. "for the Montagne la Côte [8,494'] ... We had a tremendous climb; nothing but *mauvais pas* from beginning to end, and a little too steep to be pleasant; makes the limbs ache." A day later, a restored and pleased Ruskin accomplished "a desperately stiff ascent of a 'couloir' – the hardest thing I have yet done for labour." He attained "a point which I think higher than any I have yet reached" (*Diaries* 1: 289–90).

In July 1844, the climbs continued and so did Ruskin's desire to go "as hard as [he] could" (*Diaries* 1: 295). For instance, he ascended Mont Buet – once referred to as the "Mont Blanc for Ladies" (SummitPost). He reached, for him, a record height of 10,157'. Ruskin's description of this ascent, written a day later in his diary, reflects his involvement in the climb for its own sake. Only peripherally does he attend to the painterly perspective offered by the early morning light and shadow gliding across the distant view of Mont Blanc. The going up Mont Buet was tough. He scrambled "up a slope of loose, black, ugly calcareous slate" and found his breath and strength "very much taxed." Then he went up to the summit and discovered himself to be in a position "which I did not altogether like – a ledge of snow overhanging a cliff of three thousand feet down." He complained of feeling a "great weakness in the middle of my thighs," and not being able "to work hard enough to warm myself." Once he began his descent, his courage failed when he was unexpectedly confronted by another long climb. Having managed this obstacle, he and Couttet temporarily lost their way, and consequently, "plunged down among heaps of slippery mud and slime." After a "most uncomfortable hour of exhaustion and dread of fatigue-fever ... things began to improve." Ruskin closes his account with a rare excursion into the vernacular: "It was a desperate day – a regular choker " (*Diaries* 1: 307–308).

Back among the Alps in the summer of 1845, he continued these rigorous expeditions: for instance, buffeted by icy winds, he ascended places "about Buet-height, 10,000 ft." and later climbed to the top of the Riffelhorn (9,603'), an ascent that is now considered to be moderately difficult and somewhat technical.[4] Throughout the subsequent decades and into the 1870s, Ruskin persisted in

---

[4]   In a note following his description of the climb, Ruskin reveals just how attentive he could be to the business of climbing:

> Independent travelers may perhaps be glad to know the way to the top of the Riffelhorn. I believe there is only one path; which ascends ... until, near the summit, the low, but perfectly smooth cliff ... seems ... to bar all farther advance. The cliff may, however, by a good climber, be mastered even at the southern extremity; but it is dangerous there: at the opposite, or northern side of it, just at its base, is a little cornice, about a foot broad, which does not look promising at first, but widens presently; and when once it is past [*sic*], there is no more difficulty in reaching the summit. (*Works* 6: 285–86)

returning periodically to his higher climbs, at 7,000' and above. He seems to have gone up to the Riffelhorn again, for on the inside of the back cover of a later diary, is an unpublished sketch that Ruskin dashed off of Couttet clinging to overhanging rocks of the "Riffel."

Figure 4.1   John Ruskin. "A try to draw? Coutet going up angle of Riffel"

He also made a strenuous *tour de Mont Blanc*, and then climbed with his friend Richard Fall – on one expedition, they descended two thousand feet by means of a glissade (a rather daring and fast way down).[5] In his thirties and forties, among many other climbs, Ruskin repeatedly went up the Grand Salève (4,290'), back up to Montanvert, and, in his late fifties, ascended the Wengen Alp (6,160').

There is no doubt that Ruskin took his climbing seriously. In 1847, when he was courting Effie Gray, he wrote her a humorous and self-conscious description of himself "coming down from the high snows." Ruskin's words offer a rare picture of his climbing mode. In the letter, he wonders if she would care to see his

> face *burned*, literally scarlet … Then the costume: Fancy – first – me with a huge pair of dark blue – double glassed – spectacles. Over these – over the whole face, a green gauze veil – doubled, and fastened down in the waistcoat – Then a broad straw hat on the top of all – tied tight down with its flaps *over the ears* – by a handkerchief over the crown of it – tied under the chin! Many a hard days walk have I had – so accoutred – enough to frighten anything in the world but Alpine Sheep – whom nothing frightens. (James 65)

Eventually Ruskin gave up his residence in Switzerland. Sadly, his last trip to Switzerland, when he was 69, ended in physical and mental breakdown. He retreated to Brantwood, where he could occasionally and more modestly walk up the hills of the Lake District. Memories of Switzerland remained, and Ruskin designed a zig-zaggy path on a steep slope in his garden that is said to represent Dante's Purgatorial Mount, but which more convincingly seems to abstract the numerous ascents of his previous years that brought him in physical proximity to the mountain landscape.

Part 2: Ruskin Sees

In this section I want to suggest that Ruskin's strenuous experiences not only influenced the way in which he regarded and represented the mountains he studied, but also made him more aware of a disturbing chronic weakness in his eyes – an impediment that contributed to his thinking about the nature of interruption or obstruction, as well as about the privileges of imperfection.

---

[5]   In his autobiography, Ruskin remembered this descent: "Couttet and I … showed him [Richard Fall] how to use foot and pole, to check himself if he went too fast, or got head-foremost; and we slid down the two thousand feet to the source of the Arveron, in some seven or eight minutes; Richard vouchsafing his entire approval of that manner of progression by the single epithet, 'Pernicious!'" Ruskin's note at the bottom of the text adds: "including ecstatic or contemplative rests: of course one goes much faster than 200 feet a minute, on good snow at an angle of 30 [degrees]" (*Praeterita* 409).

Ruskin and the Art of the Climber

Ruskin's climbing could not help but influence the way he beheld the mountains he admired and studied. The relation of Ruskin as a traveler to the character of his perception has already caught the attention of critics such as Jay Fellows, Elizabeth K. Helsinger and Lindsay Smith, who recognize that his eyes were those of an itinerant viewer; as Smith notes, "to see is to travel" (21). They suggest that, for him, seeing, reading, and traveling were partially interchangeable (20). Helsinger, in particular, speaks of Ruskin's "excursive sight" – a progressive mode of perception that follows the traveler's motions as he moves "leisurely" through a scene or a subject (13–14). In this manner, Ruskin is said to move from detail to detail and from view to view, through a gradual unfolding of the landscape. Helsinger's emphasis on the words "leisurely" and "gradual," however, distort the picture and soften the physical roughness and anxiety that often accompanied his rambles on the mountains.

As I hope I have proved, Ruskin was by no means exclusively a leisurely hill climber. To typify his efforts in this way almost runs the risk of linking him with the tourists he despised. Ruskin did see with the eyes of a traveler, but as one who, time after time, month after month, and year after year, scrambled, slid on treacherous slate, perched on precipitous ledges, swung on branches, exhausted himself, clambered over difficult spots, felt the brutal wind, and suffered either from the burning sun or altitude headaches. There was little relaxation in Ruskin's attempts to ascend as hard as he could. "Rigor," not "leisure," is the more appropriate word. Such a shift in vocabulary affects one's understanding concerning not only the character of his climbs, but also the nature of his perception. Among the mountains, his was not necessarily an "excursive sight" but rather one that was tutored by loose footing, aching limbs, and, of course, exhilaration. Ruskin's remarks after making his way down from the upper glacier of Blaitière capture these more rugged encounters. He comments that the "direction and manner of progression" were "so awkward that I had no *leisure* for looking at the rocks ..." (*Diaries* 2: 430; emphasis mine).

Ruskin's knowledge of the mountains reflects this more potent and bruised experience. His numerous on-the-spot study sketches of the peaks, the rocks, and the clouds, or what he preferred to call his "memoranda," are executed at the utmost speed. They recognize the inescapable temporality that accompanies an ascent, and they acknowledge the roughness of the surroundings. Ruskin's quick brush strokes, rapid pencil lines, and washes reflect the strain of the instant. Fragments of summits, hasty studies of clouds, outlines of precipices, and cataracts fill his diaries. Blotches of daring color splashed on whatever paper is at hand seize a passing moment in which he penetrates the composition of a cloud formation, a rock, or a precipice. Nothing is gradual. Each image is unframed, for here there is no time to think of a boundary.

He is, in his words, made "half mad" by his attempts to "fix one trait" of the "glorious skies" before they fly away (*Diaries* 2: March 1844).

Figure 4.2   Sketch from the Diary of John Ruskin, 1844

Figure 4.3   Sketch from the Diary of John Ruskin, 1845

In a sense, the study sketches Ruskin executed while climbing are as breathless as he was. Occasionally resting on a single detail, his drawings and watercolors follow and attempt to replicate the various foci of the eye's attention as it guides the body's ascent. They reflect the anxiety that emanates from there being no stable point of reference, and hurriedly catch a view or a particular just before it disappears. In a letter to his father, Ruskin describes such an experience when he talks about journeying over the Col de la Seigne to Courmayer, one of the most rugged parts of the Alps. He describes how, on the way, he quickly tried to capture a view of Mont Blanc before the mists would again obliterate its contours:

> When we got up, the last cloud – except a small group on the Monts Combin and Velan far away – had melted; Mont Blanc and his whole company of hills were clear, and after again consulting my feelings and pulse, I unpacked my sketch-book, sat down under a stone, and made a memorandum which I do not intend to touch hereafter – as I fancy few artists can show a careful sketch in colour, made at 8000 feet above the sea when suffering under violent sore throat. (as quoted in Wildman n.p.)

Climbing a mountain, one maneuvers one's body through a landscape, parts of which are elusive and threaten to disappear. In *The Elements of Drawing* (1856–57), Ruskin speaks of this reality when he reminds his student readers that when drawing from nature:

> The clouds will not wait while we copy their heaps or clefts; the shadows will
> escape from us as we try to shape them, each, in its stealthy minute march, still
> leaving light where its tremulous edge had rested that moment before, and involving
> in eclipse objects that had seemed safe from its influence. (*Works* 15: 90)

He advises: "You must try therefore to help what memory you have, by sketching
at the utmost possible speed the whole range of the clouds; marking, by any
shorthand or symbolic work you can hit upon, the peculiar character of each"
(*Works* 15: 129).

Within the context of such a fugitive landscape, Ruskin's rage to discover the
"governing lines" of a mountain's form becomes pressing and understandable.
Surrounded by a vista that does not hold still, and subjected to the elements that
can turn upon one and wipe out a perspective, a person needs to identify some mark
of orientation, some stability, in order to find the way and not slip into error. For
Ruskin, the answer was in tracing the defining lines that distinguish one mountain
from another and that represent a mountain's particular shape. It was by seizing
these leading or governing lines that "likeness and expression are given" (*Works*
15: 91) to a drawing – no matter what details escape the eye. These lines anchor
a continuously moving world and help shield the observer, as both climber and
painter, from its fluctuations.

Climbing and its Visual Consequences

Ruskin was well aware that his moving up among the mountains and grasping the
boulders to get to the next step were essential to his way of seeing and knowing.
Given his rage to see the particular and to get up as close as possible – to look
down into – what he was describing, Ruskin had little choice but to move bodily
among the rocks and passages of these crags or peaks. His aesthetic demanded
it, no matter what the subject under his perusal, whether a tile on a floor or a
geological specimen lodged just below a mountain crest. It is interesting to note
that this impulse to see and "read" what was before him also prompted him to
scramble over the roofs and climb up to measure the windows of Venice so that he
might meticulously examine their ornamentation and structure. It is no accident
that when he was studying Venetian architecture in preparation for writing *The
Stones of Venice*, he had Couttet at his side, as if they were both still clambering
among the Alps and determining the angles of their slopes. The orientation and the
motivation were similar.

Ruskin's need to examine things closely, though often hurriedly, placed him in a
position to think about the ways in which the movements of the body influence the
ways in which one sees. Climbing was among the most explicit expressions of this
link between seeing and doing. For instance, when Ruskin introduced *Deucalion*,
his geological study, he made the significant point that "many and many such a
day of foot and hand labour" have "been needed to build that book" (*Works* 26:
222). There could be no more telling phrase. Ruskin understood that the haptic and

optic are not autonomous but work together. To touch, to observe, and to move one's feet over stones were all part of the act of seeing and comprehending. His connecting the visual moment to motion was affiliated with the ideas of a number of contemporary theorists, such as Alexander Bain. In *The Senses and the Intellect* (1855), Bain accorded a special place to the movement of the eye as it scans, treks a landscape, and from time to time, rests upon a single point or a fraction of the field of view. In particular, Bain speaks about looking at a mountain, and about how the eye, just as the body, migrates, shifts from one perspective to another, lingers occasionally on a single point or narrowly inspects the parts:

> If I look at a mountain, there are many trains that I may be led into by taking this as
> a point to start from. By contiguity, I may pass to the other mountains of the chain,
> to valleys and villages beyond, to the mineral composition of the mass, to the
> botany, to the geological structure, to the historical events happening there. (562)

I do not want to develop or repeat what others, such as Jay Fellows, who in his *The Failing Distance: The Autobiographical Impulse in John Ruskin* (1975), and Lindsay Smith, in *Victorian Photography, Painting and Poetry* (1995), have so acutely and carefully researched concerning optical theory in the nineteenth century. Rather, I want to suggest another way of regarding Ruskin's connection to the visual experience, by dwelling upon the ways in which his years of climbing in the Alps contributed to a pressing awareness of his own vulnerable vision, and how this consciousness led him to a more complete understanding of the importance, and even the privilege, of imperfection.

The Vulnerable Eye

Among many subtle observations in his study of the nature of vision in the nineteenth century, Jonathan Crary suggests that from the beginning of that century there was a significant shift in people's notion of what an observer was and what constituted vision. No longer was the observer perceived as being shielded by a mechanical apparatus such as the camera obscura that guaranteed access to an objective or pre-given truth about the world and, hence, removed the observer from the site of the optical experience ("Modernizing Vision" 31). Crary proposes that, released from this prescriptive and rigid enclosure, the nineteenth-century observer experienced a new perceptual autonomy, and, necessarily, had to contend with a direct viewing of the prospect – like Turner in his late work, who was compelled to confront "the dangerous brilliance of the sun" (*Techniques of the Observer* 138) – as well as manage a vista that is no longer fixed in a timeless order. With this alteration, there emerges an understanding that, by extension, the viewer's sensory organs and their activity not only are "lodged within the unstable physiology and temporality of the human body" (70) but also are "inextricably mixed with whatever object they behold" (72). The individual is no longer detached from any active relation to the exterior world. "The symbolic confines of the camera obscura have crumbled" ("Modernizing Vision" 35).

Although Crary's remarks about such a shift shed light upon Ruskin's attempts to modernize the idea of vision – a development that Crary explores fully (see *Techniques of the Observer* 94) – I want rather to isolate part of Crary's argument in order to illustrate the nature of Ruskin's work in the mountains. At the risk of oversimplifying Crary's discussion, I propose that his assertion that the nineteenth-century observer is seen to be no longer detached from an active relation to the exterior helps situate Ruskin's mountain studies. As I have noted, a majority of Ruskin's sketches bear the full brunt of the elements; they originate in "disagreeable windy bleak days" that spoil his drawing (*Diaries* 1: 294). They are not the issue of a protected environment. With the exception of his occasional drawing through the window of his hostel, his memoranda reveal an observer who functions without an obstacle between him and the scene, even when he seeks shelter so he can draw more comfortably.[6] As we have seen through his climbing experiences and drawings done under difficult conditions, Ruskin was entirely willing to face the instability and temporality of what surrounded him. What is more, he exhibited an extraordinary sensitivity to the interaction of his own body and eyes with what lay directly before him. His practice suggests that Crary's model of the crumbling camera obscura and the consequent autonomy of the eye implied a new risk, exposure, and vulnerability for the vision and the person of the observer.

What needs to be noted is that when Ruskin immersed himself in a "real [mountain] landscape" (*Works*: 20: 185) and bared his body to the vagaries of the mountain terrain, he registered the consequences of this exposure, almost physically, in his eyes. That Ruskin would pay attention to the effect on his eyes is not surprising. As many critics and readers have often recognized, Ruskin was "eye-driven" (Rosenberg 4). He firmly believed that "the greatest thing a human soul ever does in the world is to *see* something." He added, "Hundreds of people can talk for one who can think, but thousands can think for one who can see" (*Works* 5: 333). Throughout his life, he expressed his gratitude for occasionally having eyes strong enough to see the mountains clearly and not just stout limbs to carry him up the steep hillsides (*Works* 37: 409). Eyes were the source of knowledge, even, as I shall discuss, when they were flawed.

Tutored by the example of Saussure's close attention to the glaciers he was studying (*Praeterita* 79) as well as by his own proclivity for "rapturous and riveted

---

[6]   As those familiar with Ruskin's mountain paintings know, not all were done while he was actively climbing. Before or after a day's ramble, he would also periodically set up his paints at the window of his hostel. Away from the stress and liabilities of ascent, these pictures fall under the immediate control of a more static eye. Nevertheless, they are ultimately neither rigid nor lifeless, for they carry with them traces (or memories) of the scenery as experienced by the moving eye. The knowledge he has gained from his hastily executed sketches during his ascents informs his hand and introduces movement.

observation" (50), Ruskin strongly maintained that one must work with one's own eyes.[7] Like Saussure, who went to the Alps "only to *look* at them, and describe them as they were" (*Works* 6: 476), one must not conform to the vision of others or become blinded by acquired notions of how things ought to appear. When Ruskin recalled his first attempts to describe mountain scenery, he admitted "scarcely any single fact was rightly known by anybody, about either the snow or ice of the Alps." He continued,

> Chiefly the snows had been neglected: very few eyes had ever seen the higher snows near; no foot had trodden the greater number of Alpine summits; and I had to glean what I needed for my pictorial purposes as best I could, – and my best in this case was a blunder.

A page later, he confessed, "If I had only *looked* at the snow carefully, I should have seen that it wasn't anywhere as thick as it could stand or lie" (*Works* 26: 129–30).

Given the importance of sight, it is not surprising that Ruskin was acutely aware of its vulnerability. He understood that even the vision of the person who observes with the educated eye can suffer from imperfections. His diary entries frequently speak of his own frustration in not being able to get things right as well as his dissatisfaction in his inability to catch the sweep of a mountain curve. The eye cannot always be relied upon; it has its limitations. In *Modern Painters*, thinking of how difficult it is to determine the actual peak of the Matterhorn, he despairs "how little the eye is to be trusted for the verification of peaked outlines" (*Works* 6: 227); he notes how the pyramidal form of the aiguille, as seen from a certain point, is entirely deceptive, and worries that after a certain point, the eye is not cognizant of proportion. Sight is not always reliable; it can mislead and deceive.

The Vulnerable Eye and its Impediments

For Ruskin, the quandary was that the eye could not only deceive the beholder, but also that it could, paradoxically, block or impede vision. Ruskin knew his own vision was literally vulnerable. Even when he was not climbing, there were times when he suffered from a weakness in his eyes affecting the clarity of his sight. Indeed, once when Ruskin was examining a painting by Tintoretto, Couttet noticed a little blue vein standing out beneath Ruskin's eye and put an end to their viewing for that day (Hunt 157). The anxiety remained with him through most of his adult life. In July 1869, for instance, he wrote to his mother to explain why he was staying longer in Venice than she hoped he would. He justified his decision by telling her that he must remain in order to complete his studies: "But I am fifty, and

---

[7]   Horace-Bénédict de Saussure's *Voyages dans les Alpes* was published in the late eighteenth century. Ruskin and his cousin, Mary, read Saussure on their first continental tour in the 1830s.

my sight *may* fail soon of its present power" (*Works* 36: 574). To understand this dilemma and to better comprehend the importance of this anxiety for his studies of the mountains and of Venice, it is necessary to trace the nature of interference, both in Ruskin's specific case and in principle.

Ruskin was aware that there were often interruptions to his vision that hindered and frustrated his attempts to observe as accurately as possible. This interference seemed to affect him most acutely when he was studying the mountain landscape, especially when his eyes were compromised by snow blindness, or when drifting clouds obscured the panorama and aggravated the intrusions created by the motes that floated in his eyes. When Ruskin first started going to the Alps, he was having problems with his vision. His letters and diary entries from the months he was spending on the Continent offer a glimpse into his preoccupation with this predicament. In October 1841, he wrote,

> Well, I think my eyes are very little worse since I was walking last year down that steep hill on the road to St Étienne – rough-work both for wheels and horses – and watching the motes in my eyes as they danced about the granite cliffs and over the chalkey road. They were very troublesome during that walk, and it has been a kind of date ever since – as the sketching at Nice. (*Diaries* 1: 217)[8]

Two days later he interrupted his diary to remark, "I really think my eyes are so much better than they were that day at Valence. I remember when I was watching the distant mountains I could not get the circles out of my eyes at all – would interfere wherever I looked, vexed me very much" (*Diaries* 1: 218). He was frustrated by the small particles that floated in his eyes and compromised his efforts: "The things [the specks before his eyes] are large in my eyes today" (*Diaries* 1: 169).

A few months earlier, a worried Ruskin had written to a friend that "My sight caused me at first more anxiety than anything else, but as that is not, on the whole, worse, though much tried by glaring sun and a good deal of sketching, I do not trouble myself more about it" (*Works* 1: 390). Ruskin did, though, continue to trouble himself about his eyes: they became the subject of anxious correspondence between him and his father. In August 1841, John James advised his son not to read *The Times* or, at least, to dry the newspaper every morning before looking at it or have the valet read "choice subjects" from it out loud: "The Times is printed by steam & hurts the eyes" (Burd 2: 681). Worrying about the motes floating in his son's eyes, he also consulted a physician. From London, he wrote to Ruskin:

---

[8]   In October 1840, Ruskin had been in Nice and had written in his diary that "I walked out yesterday afternoon, just to see the sunset: a strange burst of glowing light over the sea from behind blue thundery cloud, the waves sobbing heavily along the shore. Yet it was fine again this morning, and I climbed and sketched; got two general view, but my eyes were weak and worse" (*Diaries* 1: 95).

I was uneasy about your Eyes & went to Alexander [a doctor whose name appears in the father's accounts for 1842]. He says the danger to them would be *high* Living – no fear of this under Jephson [Ruskin's doctor at the Leamington Spa]. He says there is nothing to apprehend but that these [illegible] long in the Eyes establish themselves & never depart. Call on your coming to Town on Alexander. (Burd 2: 686)

For the next two years Ruskin continued to fret about the intrusion of these specks in his eyes. Back in England, in May, 1843, he complained, "If my eyes only would let me alone I should do capitally, but they don't get better" (*Diaries* 1: 246). And in Switzerland the next year, he protested that the motes interfered with his attempts to draw, a condition made worse by the glare of the Alpine snow: "My eyes were desperately bad too in an attempt to draw, and farther hurt by the immense quantities of snow" (*Diaries* 1: 279). To alleviate this snow blindness Ruskin had sunglasses made, not only for himself but also for his valet and guide – a practice he had actually already begun when he was a student at Oxford and wore tinted spectacles to protect his eyes from the sun. This practice earned him the nickname of "Giglamps."[9]

Ruskin's concern about his vision might seem somewhat trivial to readers who think that suffering from motes in the eyes is not only a common but also a harmless and transient problem.[10] However, if one looks at current literature about "floaters," optometrists and ophthalmologists are not as sanguine as, perhaps, the general

---

[9]   Dearden in *John Ruskin: A Life in Pictures*, points out that many people paid attention to Ruskin's eyes and spoke of their being "wonderful" and being "the bluest eyes in all England ... They could express anything." Dearden also states that Ruskin "at certain periods of his life," seems "to have taken a quite neurotic interest in his eyes, their function, and their protection." He goes on to remark that as an undergraduate, Ruskin wore blue spectacles that earned him the nickname "Giglamps" (5).

[10]   Large specks that resemble insects and circles in the field of vision are caused by a posterior vitreous detachment (PVD):

The vitreous body loses support as lacunae accumulate [pockets of liquefied vitreous], and the vitreous framework contracts. Liquified vitreous escapes to the retrohyaloid space, and the vitreous separates completely from the sensory retina. You'll observe an annular ring where the posterior vitreous attaches to the optic nerve head; this ring floats over the posterior pole. The large floater the patient describes is really the shadow from the annulus. (Sowka and Kabat 67–68)

A layman's definition is easier to follow:

Flashes and floaters result from changes in the vitreous. The vitreous is gel that fills most of the eyeball. Clumps may form in the vitreous. These clumps appear as floaters across the vision ... As a normal part of aging, the vitreous gets more watery and begins to separate from the back of the eye (the retina). After separating, the vitreous sometimes moves forward and floats in the middle of the eyeball. Then you see a large floater. This process is called vitreous detachment. It is most common after age 55. (*Adult Health Advisor* 2005:4)

Figure 4.4   John Ruskin, c. 1864, by
                  an unknown silhouettist

public might think, for the phenomenon can bring about a loss of side vision and also have the effect of causing blurred and distorted sight. They are quick to suggest that any doctor who learns that a patient has multiple floaters should take the symptom seriously, for, as Dr. Joseph W. Sowka and Dr. Alan G. Kabat write, "flashes and floaters may indicate a serious, vision-threatening problem" and can indicate retinal-related damage (72). In an article in the *Review of Optometry*, "How to Make Sense of Flashes and Floaters," these doctors describe various symptoms and the likely causes for them. It is interesting to note that in one part of their article, they isolate a group of specific symptoms that the young Ruskin speaks of in his letters: the combination of the circles in his eyes, the multiple floaters that dance over his field of vision, some of them large, as well as decreased vision. This set of symptoms, they suggest, is "the typical cause of PVD [posterior vitreous detachment – the technical term for floater] in *young* [italics mine] patients" and is a condition that is "due to cystoid macular edema" (68).

The emphasis on "young" is important. Articles on the subject all suggest that floaters are usually associated with aging – for the 55-year old and up. However, what is significant about Ruskin's problems is that they were already acute and consistent when he was in his twenties and thirties. The circumstance suggests retinal damage. It is little wonder that both Ruskin and his father took these troubles seriously; that Ruskin felt despondent about them, and wrote of the recurrence in terms of an evil "black serpent" (*Letters from Venice* 169). Moreover, and much to the point, recent medical opinion suggests that they would have interfered with his sight not only for the reasons given above but also because these floaters and circles are "most noticeable in bright light," and are "more obvious when looking at a light background like a white wall" (Eye Advisor 2007.2) – hence, Ruskin's particular difficulties in seeing within the context of the bright snow covering the mountain landscape or at the moment when the brilliant sun would strike his eyes as he looked up at the details ornamenting the buildings of Venice.

Motes in the Eyes and Clouds in the Skies

Without pressing the correspondence too far, I want to suggest that the motes floating before and impeding his field of vision have some relation to Ruskin's sense of the way clouds frequently obstructed, barred, and shadowed his view of the mountain peaks and precipices he was studying. I am certainly not implying that these troublesome motes were the reason why Ruskin paid so much attention to the clouds in the landscape. He was, obviously, indebted to a tradition of landscape painting and Romantic poetry that drew the eye and the artist's or poet's concentration to clouds. Indeed, Ruskin's careful study of clouds is obliged to Constable's watercolor studies (with annotations about the precise time and wind direction) that caught the fleeting nature of clouds, and, of course, is also beholden to Turner's work that renders the swirling clouds as an effectual part of a painting's composition. I am, rather, proposing that these motes sometimes contributed to the frustration he experienced when clouds obliterated a mountainous landscape so that he could not adequately catch a peak's governing lines, and could not, for the moment, accurately measure the angle of a mountain's sides. In his diaries from his mountain climbing years, Ruskin occasionally hinted at a parallel between these motes and the interrupting clouds. For instance, as if externalizing these particles (these motes) that hampered his sight, Ruskin wrote of the clouds that enveloped him on his way up a mountain near Chamonix by summoning a vocabulary typically associated with descriptions of motes in the eyes: "The cloud was very thick and floated before the eyes in *visible particles, like dust*" (*Diaries* 2: 428; emphasis mine). A day later, because his view was still blocked by the clouds, Ruskin had to content himself with "watching the lines of pine" (*Diaries* 2: 429). In another entry, he noted that he was "waiting ... constantly on account of clouds" (*Diaries* 2: 435). Like the circles and motes in his eyes, these clouds compromised his view of his intended subject. It is interesting to note here that Ruskin knew of the theory that particles of dust, referred to as *motes* in the air, helped to form the clouds, the rain, and snow on the mountains (see *Works* 37: 524–25). And, in addition, that these motes created the wonderful blue of the sky. Although he was well aware that there never could be "perfectly *moteless* air," he did write, in 1885, to Professor Oliver Lodge, wondering whether such a pure condition could be possible – a query that reflects his lasting frustration with his compromised vision and his discomfort with the notion that such a beautiful color depended upon something as mundane as a speck of dust.

Clouds, of course, were not the only source of interference. Reading through Ruskin's descriptions and diary entries, one becomes increasingly aware of his observations concerning the cleavages, the shadows, and the horizontal strata that cut across and often hinder or obliterate a view of a mountain's curves and precipices as well as of its whole anatomy.

Angles and Daguerreotypes

Compensating for the imperfections of the eye and its susceptibility to deception, Ruskin spent a great deal of his time scrambling among the rocks measuring the angles at which the side of a mountain or a precipice slanted and stood in relation to others. He filled his diaries with extensive lists of these calculations and diagrammatic drawings. It is as if he were realizing his youthful resolve to "make himself master of trigonometry." In an early letter to his father, he had bragged: "I'll measure em [the mountains], I'll know the height in feet inches and lines, of every crag in the united [*sic*] Kingdom, ... see if I don't" (Burd 1: 280). Later, of course, a more mature Ruskin was to do just this in the Swiss and Italian Alps where, on the basis of what he measured, he drew abstract diagrams of mountain forms.

His diaries from those years are packed with data and recorded moments when he stopped "to take the angle of the right hand precipice, which had for some half mile back shown its profile in the most magnificent way, overhanging in the blue sky" (*Diaries* 2: 422).

As part of this impulse to counteract his somewhat compromised sight and to get things right, Ruskin, beginning in the 1840s, also occasionally resorted to making Daguerreotypes to correct the details and proportions of his paintings or drawings – Ruskin claims to have made the first image of the Matterhorn as well as the aiguilles of Chamonix "ever drawn by the sun" (Birchell 8).[11] In 1845, Ruskin commented:

> It [the daguerreotype] is a noble invention ... and any one who has worked and blundered and stammered as I have done for four days, and then seen the things he has been trying to do so long in vain, done perfectly and faultlessly in half a minute, won't abuse it afterwards. (Rabb 110–15)

Later, in 1849, he wrote of it as being a corrective to the inadequacy of the eyes:

> After this I drew at my beautiful place near Les Tines and worked hard for two hours, and did everything wrong; nearly the same in the evening, when I could not draw the aiguilles from my window, and got nervous and uncomfortable. I have this morning put all to rights from Daguerreotype. (*Diaries* 3: 394)

The technique corrected deception: "For fear of being deceived ... I daguerreotyped the Cervin from the edge of the little lake under the crag of the Riffelhorn" (*Works* 6: 287). As Lindsay Smith points out in her study of the complex relationship between Victorian discourse and photography, Ruskin often turned to the photographic medium as an additional referent to counteract "perceptual aberration, for vision

---

[11]   On many of his travels, Ruskin's two servants, Frederick Crawley and George Hobbs, carried the daguerreotyping equipment and helped Ruskin take and develop the prints.

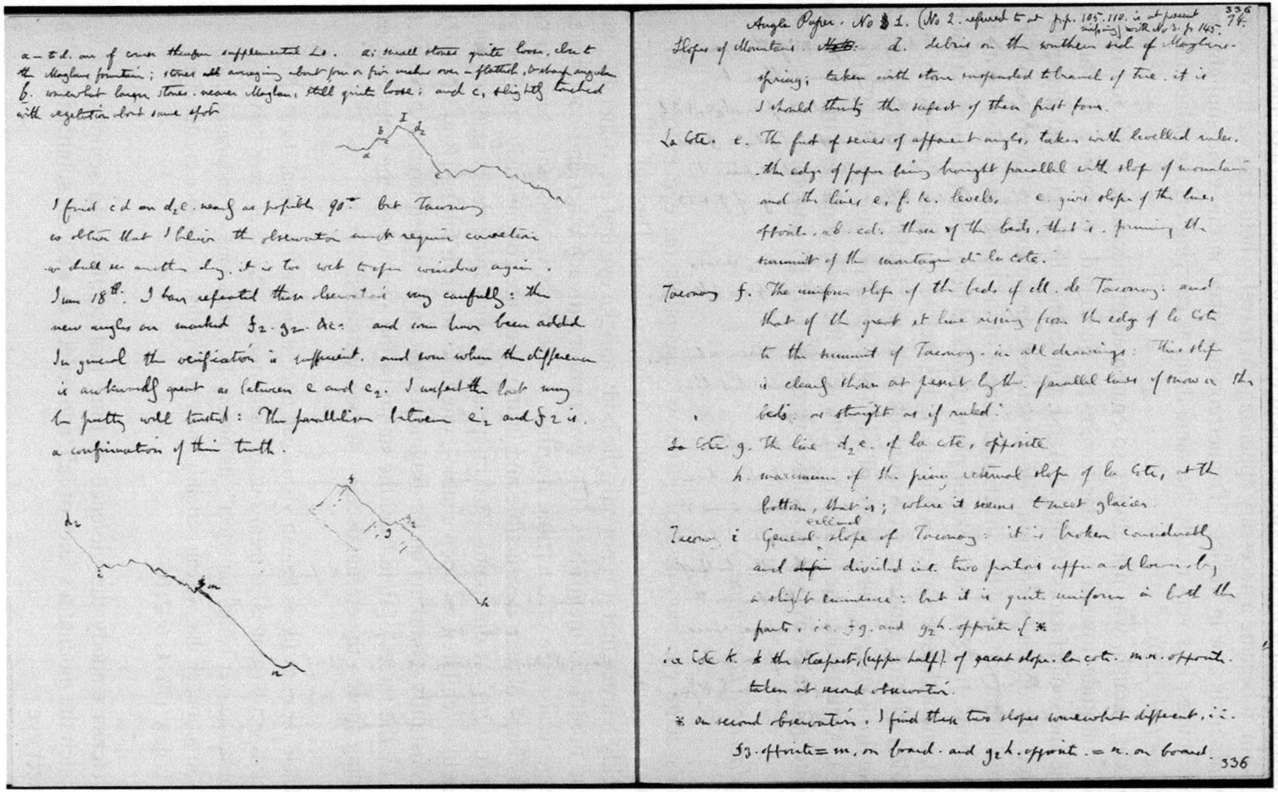

Figure 4.5 The Diary of John Ruskin, 1848–49

gone awry" (Smith 5). The daguerreotype called into question the concept of a faithful transcription of the external world as seen by the imperfect naked eye. For Ruskin, it became a necessary appendage of travel, whether, as we have seen, in the mountains, or in Venice: "Daguerreotypes taken in this vivid sunlight are glorious things. It is very nearly the same thing as carrying off the palace itself" (*Ruskin in Italy* 220).

Ruskin, though, was not always so enamored of mechanical aids to vision. Ruskin's attitude toward the daguerreotype fluctuated "according to various aesthetic and social factors" (Smith 10) and, at moments, he rejected and adamantly distrusted its optical mediation. He developed an antipathy toward anything mechanical that replaced the direct engagement of the human eye – even with its imperfections. In 1881, he spoke of photographs as being "horrid things" (Rabb 110–15), and a decade earlier, when giving his lectures as Slade Professor of Art, he pleaded with his audience: "Go and look at the real landscape, and take care of it: do not think you can get the good of it in a black stain portable in a folio" (*Works* 20: 165). At this point, he had come to think of the photograph as a mechanistic substitute, rather as cast iron is an inferior replacement for sculpture.

The Vulnerable Landscape

Ruskin's acute consciousness of just how susceptible the eye is to weakness found an accomplice in the very mountains he explored. Through his climbing, he quickly learned that it is not only the body and the eye that are vulnerable, but also the mountains themselves. The two reinforced each other and contributed to the general sense of a terrible fragility. These massive structures seem to be "everlasting," but are destructible and brittle; they are continuously "perishing" (*Works* 6: 176). At one point, Ruskin speaks of the Alpine peaks standing on a plateau like "children set upon a table"; one fears for their falling (*Works* 6: 207). He is constantly remarking on the fragments that have slipped from or have been hurled by the forces of time from the summits, the avalanches, the watercourses, the sliding snow – the eternal decay – of the mountains:

> Their form, as far as human vision can trace it, is one of eternal decay. No retrospection can raise them out of their ruins ... No eyes ever "saw its substance, yet being imperfect"; its history is a monotone of endurance and destruction: all that we can certainly know of it, is that it was once greater than it is now. (*Works* 6: 210)

His sketches embody the violence of time that continues to sculpt the Alps. They catch the mountain's lines of fall, and reflect, as well, his submission to the imperfect eye.

Fragments, Omission, and the Nature of Seeing

Knowing that it was impossible to see purely (without impediment) or completely, Ruskin eventually came to understand that "nothing is ever seen perfectly, but only by fragments, and under various conditions of obscurity" (*Works* 15: 120), and that "WE NEVER SEE ANYTHING CLEARLY" (*Works* 6: 75). The latter quotation from "Of Turnerian Mystery" is very much about Ruskin's more general belief that seeing is as much a spiritual act as a physical one; that to see completely is to reflect a knowledge of what lies beyond outward, visible details. To see completely is to possess imaginative insight into the mysterious infinity of things, a gift few artists have: one of these few was, of course, Turner. It is important to note, however, that embedded in the statement that "WE NEVER SEE ANYTHING CLEARLY" is the raw experience of physical sight which Ruskin uses, as a foundation, to explicate this principle. In an earlier version of the passage in "Of Turnerian Mystery," Ruskin remarks:

> Whatever we look at is full of mystery. Everything we look at, be it large or small, near or distant, has an infinite quantity of details still too small to be seen; and the only question is not how much mystery there is, but at what point the mystery begins. For instance, I suppose most people think they can see their own hand clearly. If they do, let them try to count the small furrows, or the lines of the light down which give its texture to the skin, and to trace the course of the fine veins through the shadows of the fingers. You suppose you see the ground under your feet clearly; but if you try to number its grains of dust, you will find that it is as full of confusion and difficulty as the distance; only the confusion on the horizon is of trees and houses, here, of pebbles and dust. (*Works* 6: 75–76)

It should be emphasized, however, that even though he could continue to wish to see "an infinity quantity of details" and hope for a "perfectly *moteless*" sky, this reality was not necessarily disheartening, for Ruskin also found pleasure in "seeing only part of things rather than the whole" (*Works* 6: 73). Frustration dissolves when he marvels at the summits that push through "the rolling clouds" (*Diaries* 1: 19) and are "bathed in light clouds" (Hayman 141). He is ecstatic when he sees the Dents de Morcles coming "through the solid distant flakes of cumulus clouds" (*Diaries* 2: 432), and exhilarated when, through a rent in the grey rain, he seizes a glimpse of the Bernese Alps burning "like hot coals" (MS diary 2 July 1866). In these instances, there is no attempt on Ruskin's part either to unveil the mists and clouds or to rage against these exaggerated motes in the sky. Such a fragmented display enhances or reveals the nobility and the mystery of his subject.

Significantly, through these incomplete experiences, Ruskin came to understand that "What we call seeing a thing clearly, is only seeing enough of it to *make out what it is*" (*Works* 6: 76). Omission is part of seeing; it is a necessary part of the truth – a circumstance that he also recognized in Turner's representation of mountain scenery, when the painter would obliterate certain details in order to capture the veracity of the landscape. In *Modern Painters*, Ruskin comments that "every one of his [Turner's] compositions [is] evidently dictated by a delight in seeing only part of things rather than the whole, and in casting clouds and mist around them rather than unveiling them" (*Works* 6: 73).

Ruskin understood that the gatherings of clouds, rather than obscuring his sense of the mountain form, could also paradoxically reveal it. The clouds, clinging to each promontory, expose its outline. In another instance, Ruskin talks about a beautiful morning view of the mountains when the clouds, that had broken into fragments about the Chamonix aiguilles, showed "the whole form [of the crags] through" them, by means of a sort of transparent interruption: "the tops of the crags were all clear; freshly and deeply laden with snow, and dark against the pale morning blue; but each had, blowing from its peaks northward, a fringe of sunny cloud of intense brightness; that on the Charmoz was unbroken, and appeared like a glory" (*Diaries* 1: 287).

Ruskin realized that too much clarity was unnatural – that it is not possible to draw the whole of nature. To see too clearly is to absorb the viewer in the deadening effect of excess. The more intense the perception, the more things, which one normally would partly see, multiply and baffle the viewer. At one point, while looking at the aiguilles through a cloudless sky – when not a single atom of a cloud was to be found out by the most telescopic eye – he gave up all hope of analysis of the mountains' form. In despair, he "watched the inextricable confusion of the fractures" (*Diaries* 2: 433). Such seemingly unimpeded sight caught him in too much detail and confused his capacity to see the larger, more abstract pattern. The lack of interruption deterred his ability to find the law.

Ruskin's resistance to absolute clarity is linked to his antipathy to mechanical reproduction – such as the Daguerreotype discussed above. He understood that a mere transcript of a scene has little to do with art and its representation of emotion, impression, mystery, and memory. Ruskin was adamant that although it was important to have a scientific knowledge of a mountain and its anatomy, the act of investigating strata and structure by itself "reduces all mountain sublimity to mere detritus and wall building, so that one looks on a great mountain only as a 'group of beds'" (*Diaries* 3: 416). The facts within a transcript do not make Art. There is, obviously, a difference between a topographical representation of a scene and an artistic one. In a topographical picture, "not a line is to be altered, not a stick nor stone removed, not a colour deepened, not a form improved"; it is merely a reflection of a place "in a mirror" (*Works* 4: 31). Ruskin's two drawings of "The Pass of Faido" illustrate this principle. The first is simply a topographically correct drawing; the second is an on-the-spot sketch. In the first, all is unnaturally clear; the lines are clean and definitive. No shadow crosses the paper; no cloud blocks the view, no mote interferes. All is stationary, and what Ruskin would call "bad." ("You will soon begin to understand under what a universal law of obscurity we live, and perceive that all *distinct* drawing must be *bad* drawing" [*Works* 4: 79].) The second sketch, based upon Turner's drawing, admits clouds, mists, patches of obscurity, and it replicates the violent force of the mountain's falling lines as well as the swirls and the toss of the crests in the raging water. Here the eye that understands the anatomy of the scene works with the imperfect, on-the-spot vision that must engage the mists and clouds as they move across the Pass and sculpt the motion of the moment. The topography is brought to life and allowed to admit the frail elements of human sight as well as the vulnerability of landscape itself.

Ruskin seems to have understood that one needs these clouds or exaggerated motes in the sky – these interferences – to function as elements of mediation. These obstacles lead to and leave room for mystery, and they summon memories of similar moments. (Ruskin always thought of Turner's paintings as being a collection of memories, especially those mountain scenes that recalled the mountain scenery of his youth in Yorkshire.) If Ruskin had not moved among the mountains, had not ascended through rough and dangerous territory, and had not exposed his body as well as his eyes to the elements, he would not have understood as thoroughly the necessity of leaving some things out, nor would he have appreciated as much the fragility of the mountains he clambered over and preserved with his fleeting sketches.

Venice and the Mountains

As I have already mentioned in passing, Ruskin's climbing in the Alps seems to have its corollary in his clambering over some of the grand buildings in Venice. In the 1840s and early 1850s, with tape measure in hand, daguerreotype equipment in tow, and with his plaster cast molds, he got himself into danger by recording their dimensions and by carefully studying their architectural details, no matter how high from the ground – awkward maneuvers that caused a stir among some spectators, who followed him around, watched, and then dusted off the powder from his clothes once he had descended.

This correlation between Ruskin's mountain climbing and his ascending ladders and scampering on the roofs of St. Mark's or the Ducal Palace extends significantly beyond the similarity in the physical exertion and skill. The parallel also suggests a corresponding viewpoint – that is to say, the observations Ruskin made while on his climbs in the Alps set a precedent for the way in which he compared, for instance, the tracery of French Gothic buildings to the winding paths and varied slopes in the Alps (*Works* 8: 89), and, a few months later, affected the way in which he approached Venice.

In the letters written to his father while he was living and studying in Venice from 1851 to 1852, Ruskin often registers his nostalgia for the Alps. Through these passages, one recognizes that, even within the context of this splendid and engrossing city, Ruskin still continued to be moved by the "magnificent," ennobling mountainous landscape he had either just left behind or was about to enter. The mountains are rarely out of view, physically or emotionally. With a painful pleasure, he looks upon the broad expanse of the Bernese Alps that border the horizon as he stands on "the low quay opposite Murano" (*Letters from Venice* 182) and that, within the wider and deeper perspective, unite with the immediate and compelling sight of the architecture in the foreground. Sometimes the view of these mountains reminds Ruskin of his harder climbing days when he was more vigorous. At these moments his fear that his strength was declining bothers him, especially as he anticipates a trip to Switzerland with his parents:

> I do not think I shall ever be able to be a strong climber on the hills – and without that power, the sight of them would sometimes be less pleasure than pain ... I do not intend to take any more hard climbs for several years – and when a man is 33, and likely to lie by for several years – it is very possible he many not care to scramble much more. (*Letters from Venice* 144–45)

It is no accident, then, that, in *The Stones of Venice* (1851–53), among the passages from Volume I that he claimed to think most highly of are "the little bits about the Matterhorn" (*Letters from Venice* 141). It is also not surprising that, when he first introduced the great city to his reading public, Ruskin, with his excursive eye, positions both himself and his readers at a location from which the distant hills and mountains are visible – as if acknowledging their importance as overseers or guides of his work and his temperament. The Alps circle the horizon and, from afar, help direct his understanding of the structures that rise directly before him. He writes:

> at what seemed its northern extremity, the hills of Arqua rose in a dark cluster of purple pyramids, balanced on the bright mirage of the lagoon; two or three smooth surges of inferior hill extended themselves about their roots, and beyond these, beginning with the craggy peaks above Vicenza, the chain of Alps girded the whole horizon to the north – a wall of jagged blue, here and there showing through its clefts a wilderness of misty precipices, fading far back into the recesses of Cadore, and itself rising and breaking away eastward, where the sun struck opposite upon its snow, into mighty fragments of peaked light, standing up behind the barred clouds of evening, one after another, countless, the crown of the Adrian Sea, until the eye turned back from pursuing them, to rest upon the nearer burning of the campaniles of Murano, and on the great city, where it magnified itself along the waves, as the quick silent pacing of the gondola drew nearer and nearer. (*Letters from Venice* 124–25)

The eye turns toward Venice after first gazing upon the Alps: the mountains looming on the horizon preface his sight and prefix his understanding of the city. The "chain of Alps," with their jagged roughness and vulnerability, with their frailty as well as their power, heighten his sensibility to loss and fragmentation in Venice. The view of them intensifies his distress at seeing a once mighty city deteriorate, crumble, or fall prey to misdirected renovations. Consequently, as was his practice while climbing, he responds by hurriedly sketching as many of the remaining fragments as possible over two long winters – before they elude the eye or disappear altogether. He was sketching from one side of the building while the restorers were wrecking the other side. These drawings of the buildings' details and remnants exude the same breathless quality as his mountain "memoranda" – a feature that disturbed Ruskin's father who complained to a friend that in Venice his son was "drawing perpetually fragments of everything from a Cupola to a Cart-Wheel, but in such bits that it is to the common eye a mass of Hieroglyphics" (*Works* 8: xviii).

To repeat: the eye that looks at the Alps before it regards Venice discovers an analogue between the two landscapes. The geological specimens Ruskin has collected in Chamonix seem to be the very stones that compose the magnificent city and turn St. Mark's into "one precious mineralogical cabinet" (31 July 1869 MS letter to Mother); the sight of St. Mark's "entangled among the rainclouds" becomes a "Venetian aiguille Dru [a peak in the Swiss Alps]" (*Letters from Venice* 54); a fragment of a building in the Alps illustrates a principle of architectural structure (*The Stones of Venice* 51); the curve or movement of the glaciers he has followed among the Alps sympathizes with and allows Ruskin to mark the abstract lines of ornamentation; and the precipitous, frozen summits of the Alps furnish a vocabulary for describing the structure of roofs or details of windows: a roof is raised into "all manner of peaks, and points, and ridges" (*The Stones of Venice* 81).

But, most notable of all, the savageness of the mountains and his memories of his sojourns amid their rugged terrain allow him more fully to comprehend the nature of the Gothic. Here is where the Alps most significantly preface his work in Venice and his thoughts about the historical Gothic, especially that emanating from the North and based upon English and French examples. When describing the architecture of the North, Ruskin is conscious of the analogy, and notes that there is a fraternal relationship between the wild mountains and the Gothic edifices. He remarks on:

> this wildness of thought, and roughness of work; this look of mountain
> brotherhood between the cathedral and the Alp, this magnificence of sturdy
> power, put forth only the more energetically because the fine finger-touch was
> chilled away by the frosty wind, and the eye dimmed by the moor-mist, or
> blinded by hail. (*The Stones of Venice* 164)

I want to suggest that Ruskin surveyed these structures from the perspective of a climber who had experienced the "roughness of work," and who had suffered severe headaches in the high air – a memory that Ruskin recalls vividly in a February 1852 letter written to his father while working in Venice and worrying about his health and physical exhaustion (*Letters from Venice* 168). He looked upon these buildings with the memory of his own vulnerable body: with recollections of his hands that during his climbs had fumbled in the frost, and of his sight that had been blinded by mist and sun. It is interesting to note that when Ruskin was still in the process of writing *The Stones of Venice*, the eye trouble that had often interfered with his mountain studies continued to frustrate his efforts. For instance, in a 24 April 1852 letter to his father, Ruskin complained again of the motes before his eyes: "I was drawing, in the morning, from a high subject at St Marks which made me raise my eyes and let them fall very often – and the black specks tormented me excessively, and I fancied there were more of them coming and was getting despondent about them" (*Letters from Venice* 258–59). The same month, he worried that he could not look "long enough at anything to fix it in my mind – not even read an inscription of the front of Sta M. Formosa, for want of which" a chapter was difficult to complete (*Letters from Venice* 253). Both are part of a larger and more universal sense, mentioned earlier, that it is never possible to experience a visual whole, that the act of seeing is necessarily partial and fragmented.

Although there are several other pressing concerns and sources that were of great importance to Ruskin in his vindication of the Gothic in his *The Stones of Venice*, his own vulnerable body and weak eyes also seem to have played a role in his defense of the workman's achievements, with its imperfections and irregularities. Indeed, Ruskin's condemnation of the English taste for mechanical perfection, his efforts to restore the moral and imaginative to the consciousness of English culture, and his understanding that imperfection is a value recognized and tolerated by Christianity, all assemble and shape his justification of the Gothic. His larger understanding that irregularity is a sign of life as well as a source of beauty, though, is also to some degree indebted to the physical experiences of climbing and living with the interferences chronically impeding his sight. As a result, when he speaks of the irregularities and imperfection in the achievement of the workmen who built the Gothic cathedrals, he is doing so partially within the context of his own vulnerable body, especially his eyes, dimmed by clouds, and interrupted by motes, wind, or shadows. While in the Alps, his blundering efforts to look directly at and represent what surrounded him allow him to empathize with and recognize the value in the workmen's prickly independence and their on-the-spot vision that result in the irregularities of Gothic ornamentation. Their flaws are also Ruskin's. And so is their refusal to mimic convention, their preference for "the true leaves," and their ability to make fire as real as if it were bursting out of Hades' gate (*The Stones of Venice* 170).[12] His celebration of – his relief in seeing – the workmen's imperfections recalls his rejection of purely mechanical, enslaving renditions of mountain landscapes as well as his preference for a painting that admits error as well as its own limitation; he values most those works that are devoted not simply to accuracy but also to the individual imaginative soul that engages the mystery of what lies beyond the visual: "On the whole, very accurate workmanship is to be esteemed a bad sign; and if there is nothing remarkable about the building but its precision, it may be passed at once with contempt" (*The Stones of Venice* 189). In a 6 June 1852 letter to his father, Ruskin, despite his devotion to accuracy and

---

12   Ruskin remarked that:
     the Gothic inventor does not leave the sign in need of interpretation. He makes the fire as real as he can; and in the porch of St. Maclou at Rouen the sculptured flames burst out of the Hades gate, and flicker up, in writhing tongues of stone, through the interstices of the niches, as if the church itself were on fire. (*The Stones of Venice* 170)

to getting things "*perfectly* right," admits: "But yet, I am happy to say that a fine drawing, made with feeling – is always worth a great many casts or daguerreotypes – and a first rate one ... is worth any quantity of them. There is something in it besides the facts ... a human soul" (*Letters fron Venice* 297).

I suggest that not only the rugged, irregular topography of the mountains themselves but also Ruskin's climbing and his sketching in the Alps did much to impress upon his consciousness the vulnerability of the eye, a circumstance that offered him yet another context for his celebration of the Gothic and his larger defense of irregularity. It seems that Ruskin climbed not only for the thrill of exertion and the rage to collect his geological specimens, but also for a perspective that reveals more than a panorama – one that also exposes, in spite of the accompanying annoyances and frustrations, the privilege of the imperfect vision, which opens up a space for the imagination and leads one into the spiritual mystery of the landscape.

Chapter 5
Toothpowder and Breadcrumbs:
Gerard Manley Hopkins in the Alps

The Monte Rosa range are dragged over with snow like cream ... Above the
Breithorn Antares sparkled like a bright crab-apple tingling in the wind.

(Hopkins, *Journals* 181)

Introduction

On 3 July 1868, Gerard Manley Hopkins, then in his middle twenties, started for
Switzerland with Edward Bond, a university friend. This was to be Hopkins's last
holiday before he entered Manresa House and Stonyhurst as a Jesuit novitiate. He
and Bond remained in the Alps until the end of the month.[1] During those several
weeks,the two of them, with a Baedeker in hand, followed the familiar routes,
and, like many other visitors, went up to such places as the Rigi to see the rising
sun. They hired Swiss guides; visited the glaciers at Grindelwald; walked up the
Gornegrat (10,289') to get a view of the Monte Rosa range; admired the three falls
of the Reichenbach; paid the almost mandatory visits to the Baths of Rosenlaui
and to the St. Bernard Hospice, but, because of poor weather, failed to get a
"completely clear view of the Matterhorn" (*Journals* 182). The two also made a
few modest ascents, and completed a fairly ambitious climb to the summit of the
Breithorn (13,685'), a seven-and-a-half hour journey from the Riffel Inn. Although
Hopkins did not go into many details about the social context of the tour, the two
seemed to have endured the requirements of the *table d'hôte*. Moreover, as did so
many tourists, Hopkins, once in a while, indulged in some chauvinistic feelings by
remarking on how "repulsive" a French face could be and how "strange" a party
of Americans was (*Journals* 179, 177).[2]

---

[1] For a full description of Hopkins's itinerary in Switzerland, see Tom Zaniello's
"Alpine Art and Science: Hopkins' Swiss Adventure," 3–17.

[2] On 20 July, Hopkins wrote in his journal:

At the *table d'hote* of the inn there I first saw that repulsive type of French face. It
is hard to seize what it is. The outline is oval but cut away at the jaws; the eyes are
big, shallow-set, close to the eyebrows, and near, the upper lid straight and long,
the lower brought it down to a marked corner in the middle, the pupils large and
clear; the nostrils prominent; the lips fleshy, long, and unwaved, with a vertical

By following such an itinerary, Hopkins seems to have joined his fellow tourists and slipped into the conventional mold of those who tramped around the familiar spots and attempted a few climbs. However, as anyone familiar with Hopkins's verse as well as with the inventive language of his notebooks might easily anticipate, these similarities were merely superficial. One cursory glance at the journal entries he made during his travels reveals that Hopkins's remarkably unconventional way of seeing set his observations in an entirely different class from the clichés uttered by the usual tourist. When, for instance, he noted that the mountains, in particular the Silberhorn, "are shaped and nippled like the sand in an hourglass" (*Journals* 174) or that the trees, colored by the red, green, and purple of a rainbow, "looked like a slice of melon" (*Journals* 171), he stepped outside the boundaries of the expected. In particular, to someone schooled in the Romantic tradition, these images would have been almost alien. And when Hopkins compared a mountain pass to a "billiard board" (*Journals* 171), he uncompromisingly parted company with both the Cook's tourists and the Alpine Club men who celebrated the grandeur of the mountains that promised to release them from the ordinary and the trivia of their everyday surroundings. The following passage from his Swiss diary gives a vivid idea of his distance from these fellow travelers:

> The Monte Rosa range are dragged over with snow like cream. As we looked
> at them the sky behind them became dead purple, the effect unique; and then
> the snow according to its lie and its faces differenced itself, the upward-looking
> faces taking shade, the vertical light, like lovely damask. Above the Breithorn
> Antares sparkled like a bright crab-apple tingling in the wind. (*Journals* 181)

When Hopkins traveled to Switzerland, he was on a different kind of journey to that which most visitors to the Alps had made. Rather than succumbing to the more general cultural or traditional pressures that would have invited him to regard its mountains in the context of popular notions of the sublime, Hopkins chose, instead, to honor his own idiosyncratic voice and vision so that he could spiritualize the ordinary and articulate his sense of the energy of creation in the small as well as the large. To understand these preferences, it is helpful to consider Hopkins's reaction not only to the more traditional ways of representing a mountainous landscape but also to contemporary scientific debates about glacial movement. This chapter opens with an examination of Hopkins's descriptions of the Alps within the context of the sublime and closes by comparing his descriptions of its glaciers to those written by John Tyndall, the famous climber and scientist, whom Hopkins met while on his Swiss holiday. What emerges is a more complete

---

curling at the end (in one case at any rate); the nose curved hollow or so tending;
the head large; the skin fair – white and scarlet colour. (*Journals* 179)
A few days earlier Hopkins had remarked that he had seen a "strange party of Americans" (*Journals* 177).

understanding of his sense of the spiritual power imbedded within the ordinary as well as within the scientific.

The Context of the Sublime

As we have seen in previous chapters, popular notions of the sublime were still a force with which to reckon. Even though the sublime's presence was diminishing, its influence was still apparent, and, therefore, had to be accommodated. The question, therefore, arises: Did Hopkins, who was steeped in eighteenth- and early nineteenth-century continental and English literature and philosophy, succumb to its authority? It seems that when in Switzerland he did not – although, at one point, he did remark upon the seductiveness of the mountains when he wrote: "How fond of and warped to the mountains it would be easy to become!" (*Journals* 172). Unlike many others who traveled to that region in the mid-nineteenth century, Hopkins was not as predisposed to lug with him the more popular conceptions of the Romantic sublime that were accessories to most tours. Hopkins's goal was not necessarily to stand in awe, as so many had done, before the monarch of the mountains (Mont Blanc) or to gaze at the glaciers so that he might summon lines from Schiller, Byron, or Coleridge and speak of the landscape's "overpowering sublimity" (*A Budget of Letters* 19).

It is an appropriate coincidence that not long before Hopkins departed for Switzerland, he called upon Ernest Hartley Coleridge, the grandson of the poet – the two had initially become friends at Sir Robert Cholmeley's Grammar School in Highgate. In a way, Hopkins was for the moment saying farewell not only to an acquaintance, but also to a reminder of a sensibility belonging to an earlier generation. When Hopkins left for the Alps, he set aside aspects of the inherited tradition with which he was intimately and studiously familiar. At this point he was choosing no longer to rely upon that sense of the stupendous sublime found in Coleridge, nor was he desiring to repeat the raptures of that poet's "Hymn before Sun-Rise in the Vale of Chamouni," based upon Frederika Brun's "Ode to Chamony." In Coleridge's poem, the choice of images reflects the sense of grandeur and awe that attended the sublime at the turn of the century; its description evokes the wild strength associated with the Alps that guidebooks and pictures of the region celebrated and propagated. Coleridge's lines are traditionally majestic:

> Ye Ice-falls! Ye that from the mountain's brow
> Adown enormous ravines slope again –
> Torrents, methinks, that heard a mighty voice,
> And stopped at once amid their maddest plunge!
> Motionless torrents! silent cataracts!
> Who made you glorious as the Gates of Heaven
> Beneath the keen full moon? (ll. 49–55)

The anonymously-written explanatory note, probably composed by the paper's editor, that preceded the first publication of Coleridge's poem in the *Morning Post* on 11 September 1802, resonates with the same popular notion of the sublime, including its acoustical grandeur:

> Chamouni is one of the highest mountain valleys of the Barony of Faucigny
> in the Savoy Alps; and exhibits a kind of fairy world, in which the wildest
> appearances (I had almost said horrors) of Nature alternate with the softest
> and most beautiful. The chain of Mont Blanc is its boundary; and besides the
> Arve it is filled with sounds from the Arveiron, which rushes from the melted
> glaciers, like a giant, mad with Joy, from a dungeon, and forms other torrents of
> snow-water, having their rise in the glaciers which slope down into the valley.
> (Coleridge, *Coleridge's Verse* 377)

Both the poem's and the passage's exaggerated portrayals of the ice-falls are far removed from Hopkins's diminutive or less-than-grand metaphor to describe an Alpine cascade: "We walked by the Brünig pass to Brienz. In the pass first noticed the way in which clusters of water like the moistened end of a pocket handkerchief wave and fall, down the cascade" (*Journals* 173).

On his 1868 trip to the Alps, Hopkins was not attempting to replicate Coleridge's voice nor was he interested in imitating the awe-inspiring episodes that William Wordsworth had experienced crossing the Alps (or climbing Snowdon). Hopkins might later write about the world being charged by the grandeur of God or of the Windhover's ecstatic brilliance, but while in Switzerland, he was not intent on being suddenly overwhelmed by flashes of insight into the grand, universal presence of a larger being. From the top of a mountain, he paid little attention to Wordsworth's "blue chasm … A deep and gloomy breathing-place, through which/ Mounted the roar of waters, torrents, streams/ Innumerable, roaring with one voice" (*Prelude* 1805 13: ll. 57–59); instead, he chose to look conscientiously at mere "clusters of water" (*Journals* 173) and at "little brows of grass between the shale landslips" (*Journals* 174). In the Alps, Hopkins consciously replaced the grand image with a more intimate one. Influenced by what his own sketching had taught him and by a desire to break up outworn conventions, as well as craving to be innovative, he left home intending, in his own idiosyncratic way, to discover, with fresh eyes, what he called either the "law" or the "inscape" and the "instress" of the particulars in the landscape – to see what essentially individualizes something or distinguishes it from anything else, and to determine the energy that upholds that distinctiveness.[3] In this respect, Hopkins was not completely turning away from Wordsworth, for,

---

[3]   W.H. Gardner offers definitions of "inscape" and "instress":
      As a name for that "individually-distinctive" form (made up of various sense-
      data) which constitutes the rich and revealing "oneness" of the natural object,
      he [Hopkins] coined the word *inscape*, and for that energy of being by which
      all things are upheld, for that natural (but ultimately supernatural) stress which

in his own way, he was still honoring Wordsworth's sense of the "spots of time." As Catherine Phillips points out, these selected moments did help to support Hopkins's desire to capture the essence of what he gazed at. Intensely aware of his Romantic heritage, Hopkins had copied out a passage from an essay by J.C. Shairp on Wordsworth's "spots of time" printed in the *North British Review* in 1864. Shairp's thoughts seem to have helped Hopkins find a relationship between Wordsworth's ideas and the notions of "inscape" and "instress":

> Each scene in nature has in it a power of awakening, in every beholder of sensibility, an impression peculiar to itself, such as no other scene can exactly call up. This may be called the 'heart' or 'character' of that scene. It is quite analogous to, if somewhat vaguer than, the particular impression produced upon as by the presence of each individual man. Now the aggregate of the impressions produced by many scenes in nature, or rather the power in nature on a large scale of producing such impressions; is what, for want of another name, I have called the "heart" of nature. (Phillips 60–61)

It is important, however, to note that Hopkins's fresh way of seeing was initially encouraged in his childhood and adolescence. Hopkins had been raised among family members who were unusually attentive to the patterns of color and shape in their world.[4] For instance, on their holidays, carrying on a family tradition, he and his brother Arthur had frequently sketched studies of trees and rock formations,

---

determines an *inscape* and keeps its being – for that he coined the name *instress*. (Gardner xx)

[4]   Catherine Phillips in her study *Gerard Manley Hopkins and the Victorian Visual World* writes at some length about the Hopkins family's interest in the arts. In addition to mentioning his father's and his brothers' (Arthur's and Everad's) professional engagement in the arts, Phillips talks about the cousins', the aunts', and the uncles' interest in painting, graphic design, and photography. Phillips quotes from Manley Hopkins's (the father's) travel diaries. These diaries often display an interest in form and pattern. Phillips prints an example from his 1875 journals, written during a trip to France. The passage reads:

> On our way back to *Le Pay*, we alighted at the Village of *Espailly* or *Expailly*, and walked to the remarkable basaltic Cliff called from its parallel prisms *Les Orgues*. They certainly resemble organ-pipes in being regular, close, and detached. In the centre they are perpendicular, whilst at one end they curve forward or rather to one side, like those lateral pipes seen in some modern organs which produce very percussive and trumpet-like notes. (Phillips 1–2)

Jerome Bump, in his essay "Hopkins' Drawings" also discusses in detail the art education and interests of the Hopkins family. He points out that of the many aunts and uncles who taught drawing to the Hopkins children, three were particularly important. Ann Eleanor Hopkins, a portrait painter and musician, who "lived with them and tutored Gerard in drawing until he was twelve. Maria (Smith) Giberne also taught him how to draw from nature and George Giberne encouraged him to draw from photographs as well" (Bump 71).

and had drawn images of breaking waves and falling water.[5] When at the seaside, they had been invariably intrigued with the patterns of waves. Although there are differences in their sketches, there are also striking parallels that indicate just how intent the Hopkins family was upon capturing patterns of particulars and, moreover, how they relished playing with language. A note accompanying a drawing of the sea at Whitby, from Arthur's 1875 sketchbook, is a verbal example of this shared sensitivity. As R.K.R. Thornton observes, Arthur's description of his Whitby drawing could easily be mistaken for a passage composed by his brother. In the entry quoted below, Arthur's attention to the edging of the waves and to the motion or dynamic of the surf closely corresponds to Gerard Manley Hopkins's lasting eagerness to identify patterns visible within the details of a landscape.[6] Furthermore, Arthur's unusual comparison of the wave to a "cauliflower" forecasts the unusual metaphors in Hopkins's Swiss notes – where trees might be compared to a slice of melon and a mountain pass to a billiard board. The passage reads:

> The "Cauliflower" forms of the water just broken, have for the most part dark green centres, clouding into white at their edges. The water behind them rushes underneath the lip of each of them, so that to some extent each "Cauliflower" is like a little wave running towards one. (Thornton 36)

Another note in Arthur's 1875 sketchbook reflects the similarities in their perspective:

> The foam of waves is very white & wrinkled, but the "soapsuds" it leaves on the sheen, are hardly perceptible in parts, so much do they lose their whiteness. Sometimes, as when the soapsuds lie underneath an approaching breaker they actually tell darker than their sheen, because there the sheen is a yellowish white, under the reflection of the breaker. (Phillips 70)

Hopkins's earlier drawing and painting trained his eye so that in Switzerland he was sensitive to the ways in which the light struck the trees or illuminated the glistening water. In the Alps, Hopkins was able to stare at a "long streak of cloud in the blue sky" and, with a painterly eye, wonder if there possibly could be "a rose hue suppressed in the white" (*Journals* 171). Moreover, his youthful sketching experiences increased his awareness of the patterns or "the law" in the leaves, the glaciers, and the water running off the cascades and the crags. Touring among the Alps, Hopkins was eager to catch the "straight quains and planing" of the mountains (*Journals* 171), the scaping of the muddy river, the spraying of the trees, and the inscape of the glaciers. In Sketchbook C, containing his Swiss drawings, Hopkins, utilizing sketches where words failed, attempts to capture, for instance, the motion

---

[5]   Arthur Hopkins was to provide illustrations for a number of novels; he also worked for *The Illustrated London News*, the *Graphic*, and *Punch*. He was a member of the Royal Society of Painters in Water-Colour.

[6]   For a full discussion of Hopkins's impulse to map the landscape, see Colley's "Gerard Manley Hopkins and the Idea of Mapping."

and the outline of the "Huddling and precipitation of the fir-woods down the cleft" as seen from the "Side of the Rossberg, fr. The Rigi."

Figure 5.1   Gerard Manley Hopkins. "Side of the Rossberg fr. the Rigi, July 8"

The book also includes his rough sketches, showing sections of various mountains and glaciers. These simply trace the selected fragment's defining lines.

Figure 5.2   Gerard Manley Hopkins. "July 15 Little Scheidegg"

I should add that before Hopkins traveled to Switzerland, the observant eye of his youth was strengthened and developed as a student at Oxford, where he wrote essays that reveal a concern for pattern and composition. This orientation was encouraged by the aestheticism of mentors such as Walter Pater (Pater tutored Hopkins in 1866), who was sensitive to the subtle gradations among the details of the visible and the audible world, and John Ruskin, who with his drawings captured fleeting details of particulars in the landscape and architecture around him.[7] Indeed, such was Ruskin's influence that, as Norman White suggests, not only did Hopkins sketch, as Hopkins admitted in an 1863 letter to John Baillie, "in a Ruskinese point of view" but also based the form of his observations in Switzerland on "the natural sights that Ruskin had seen and commented on *his* diaries on his tour in 1835" ("The Context of Hopkins' Drawings" 64).[8] As Patricia Ball remarks, "Hopkins's Journals in particular reveal the affinities between them. The influence of Ruskin is profound and goes far beyond the imitation of a style of drawing or the prompting of alertness of the eye" (104).

As a result of these various factors, Hopkins left for the Alps on a quest that was, as I have already suggested, hardly indebted to preconceived notions of a wild, terrifying, and grand Alpine panoramic perspective that elevated the soul; instead, he was on a tour partially devoted to a patient study of details and patterns visible in the various minute and seemingly insignificant fragments in the landscape before his naked eye. Hopkins did not feel obliged to fill his Alpine journal with hackneyed declarations of the landscape's sublimity. Other travelers might unfold their panoramic maps from the pages of the guidebooks so that they might grasp and name all the mountains within and beyond their range of vision (as many did from the top of the Rigi), but Hopkins, in his 16 July 1868 entry, for instance, summarily rejects an inclination to scan a grand Alpine vista behind the glaciers at Grindelwald. Finding the view unsatisfying, he interrupts the naming of the mountains in his journal entry with a curt and dismissive "etc:" "Behind them lies the Vierscherhörner, on the left the Schreckhörner and the Wetterhörner, on the right the Eiger etc." (*Journals* 175).

This abrupt abbreviation conclusively halted the kind of prospect his Baedeker encouraged. Hopkins preferred to stare at just one corner of that panorama or to look down at a detail visible in a leaf or in a nearby waterfall. When he walked up to the Wylerhorn, he noted that there was a clear view of the neighboring mountain. But rather than concentrate upon that larger perspective, Hopkins chose to gaze at a more interesting and isolated detail in the snow that revealed the spot's inscape: "The snow is often cross-harrowed and lies too in the straightest paths as though artificial, which again comes from the planing. In the sheet it glistens yellow to the sun" (*Journals* 172). In this respect, Hopkins's Swiss notes bear little resemblance to the usual tourist's diaries that document a traveler's search for "stupendous scenes of desolate magnificence" (Cole 130). Rather, as Mary Ellen Bellanca rightly suggests, Hopkins's notebooks are closer to the tradition of British nature diaries that, with curiosity and wonder, record daily fragments of a landscape, concentrate upon their details, and glorify the singularity of particulars (Bellanca 205). In his

---

[7] In his "Preface" and "Conclusion" to his *Studies in the History of the Renaissance*, Walter Pater, of course, insisted that aesthetic criticism be based upon seeing the object as it really is, and that the critic should aspire to realize it distinctly.

[8] See also *Further Letters of Gerard Manley Hopkins*, 202.

Alpine notebook, Hopkins collected bits of the natural world and remarked on their characteristics in much the same fashion as had Gilbert White, Dorothy Wordsworth, Phillip Gosse, Emily Shore, and George Eliot – though, of course, projecting his own intense stylistic idiom in an attempt to capture the complexity and patterns of the object before his eyes. The precedent was there, for, as a child, Hopkins had gathered specimens from tidal pools and had read such books as Ann Pratt's *Chapters on the Common Things of the Sea-Coast* and George Johnston's *History of the British Zoophytes* (Mackenzie "Hopkins and Science" 86). Hopkins had been raised among family members who belonged to a nineteenth-century culture that cherished natural history studies. He had lived in a household in which, as Norman H. Mackenzie and Joseph J. Feeney, S.J. point out, both father and son not only delighted in playing with language, but also took pleasure in closely observing natural phenomena.[9] Feeney remarks on the fact that both Manley Hopkins and his son liked "to stare closely as some familiar thing and observe its details." While Manley examined the grains of common dust through his microscope, his son looked carefully at "the hexagonal prisms … produced in the drying of smooth mud by the sun" and crouched down "to gaze at the crushed quartz glittering and sparkling like millions of diamonds" (Feeney 280).

For most mid-century tourists, partially enthralled by the sublime tradition, and therefore still wishing to be subjected to the power of all-encompassing vistas, Hopkins's reverence for a mere fragment of that landscape would have been alien, even unsuitable. His attention to such details would have seemed especially incongruous for those who subscribed to Burke's requirement that a scene needed a "Greatness of Dimension." As a result, these travelers would not have appreciated Hopkins's more leisurely, and sometimes hasty, attention to mapping bits of that larger prospect and gazing at a jagged edge of a glacier, the cross-harrowing of the fallen snow, creases in the rushing water, skeined patterns in the waterfalls, a spike of a flower, or the fretted leaves of the fir tree. For Hopkins, these were the details that disclosed the object's nobility, but for those attached to a more popular sense of the sublime, these pieces of the landscape were not equal to grand mountainous prospects.[10] Moreover, the objects of Hopkins's attention not only lacked the vastness of a prospect but they also failed to threaten or elicit fear in the beholder. Because they were contained and small, these particulars were not terrifying. Yet another source of the sublime was lacking. Few of Hopkins's descriptions, if any, exuded the tension of danger and death that haunted the Romantic vision. As Phillips suggests, many of the entries

---

[9]   Norman H. Mackenzie talks about Hopkins's father's interest in collecting fossils and an essay "Essex Elephants" that the father contributed to *Once a Week* in 1860 ("Hopkins and Science" 87). Similarly in "His Father's Son: Common Traits in the Writing of Manley Hopkins and Gerard Manley Hopkins," Joseph J. Feeney, S.J. discusses their mutual interest in looking closely at the landscape around them (Feeney 280–84).

[10]   In his Swiss notebook, Hopkins remarked that "every cliff and limb and edge and jutty has its own nobility" (*Journals* 172).

are deficient in "the sense of horror or the sublime of many Romantic reactions to the Alps" (81). By finding "nobility" in the smallest detail, Hopkins was turning the sublime upside down and reversing the concept's traditional dependency upon the elevated. Hopkins's was distributing the sublime and romanticizing the particular.

Contrary to the inclination of someone viewing the Alpine landscape in the Romantic mode, his eye was not always turned upwards, but was just as devoted to or intrigued by what was beneath the heights and was sliding or falling from a mountain crag. As if wanting to emphasize the fluidity of a mountain rather than its rugged or solid presence, Hopkins concentrates upon the water that cascades from it. If one leafs through the pages dedicated to the weeks in Switzerland, one cannot help but notice the frequency with which Hopkins sees how the water from a glacier can be seen descending and vanishing: how "clusters" of water catch the fall of a cascade; how, at a distance, they drop "like wax gutterings on a candle" or "like rockets when they dissolve," and head downwards (*Journals* 173). Rather than raise his eyes in reverential awe, more regularly, he gazes down into valleys and into "the foam-cuffs in the river" (*Journals* 177). One description of a waterfall captures the drama or the stages of the water's motion as it descends:

> Across the valley too we saw the fall of the Gelmer – like milk chasing round blocks of coal; or a girdle or long purse of white weighted with irregular black rubies, carelessly thrown aside and lying in jutty bends, with a black clasp of the same stone at the top – for those were the biggest blocks squared, and built up, as it happened, in lessening stories, and the cascade enclosed them on the right and left hand with its foam; or once more like the skin of a white snake square-pied with black. (*Journals* 178)

The passage recalls an early entry into his 1863 notes, when he had written:

> a mass of yellowish boiling foam wh. Runs down between [the] fans, and meeting covers [the] whole space of [the] lock-entrance. Being heaped up in globes [with] bosses [with] round masses [the] fans disappear under it. This turpid mass smooths itself as [the] distance increases fr. [the] lock, But [the] current is strong and if [the] basin into which it runs had curving banks it strikes them and [the] confusion of the already folded and doubled lines of foam is worse confounded. (*The Early Poetic Manuscripts and Note-Books* 86)

This downward attention contributed to his understanding of the Alpine landscape. On 9 July 1868, after Hopkins had looked out of his window and had seen "a scape of stars" in the early morning sky, he cast his eyes down to the highlands below and comfortably and respectfully compared the atmospheric light of the mountains to familiar gestures belonging to the life below – to a person's affect and to the experience of being interrupted:

The sun lit up the bright acres of the snows at first with pink but afterwards clear white: the snow of the Bernese Highland remained from its distance pinkish all day. – The mountain ranges, as any series or body of inanimate like things not often seen, have the air of person and of interrupted activity; they are multitudinous too, and also they express a second level with an upper world or shires of snow. – In going down between Pilatus and a long streak of cloud the blue sky was greenish … (*Journals* 171)

Hopkins concentrated on what is "down": "Down the Rigi, entering the mist soon, to Wäggis, where we lunched under thick low plane trees. By steamer to Flüelen and then to Lucerne again. On the way back rain fell and then a very low rainbow against the sides of the lake colouring the trees …" (*Journals* 171). In the quoted passage, the scaping of the sky has allowed him to understand the patterns of what rests beneath such heights. What is small and what is below also reflect the grandeur and beauty of "Christ our Lord." Contrary to the tradition of the sublime, Hopkins sees the spiritual from below, as well as within the meek and the humble.[11]

Toothpowder and Breadcrumbs

Hopkins' attention to an autonomous and seemingly-insignificant detail rather than to a panoramic prospect, as well as his propensity to look down or below, was obviously not all that separated him from others looking through the Romantic lens. He also distinguished himself from popular notions of the sublime when he compulsively and playfully, if not anxiously, searched for unusual metaphors that would catch the distinctiveness of what particular lay before his eyes. These unusual figures of speech broke through clichéd representations of the sublime. To this end, Hopkins repeatedly and daringly defied custom by associating striking segments of the mountain landscape with – amazing to say – "toothpowder" or a "breadcrumb," identified a magnificent glacier with "rows of dogteeth," compared the blue color of the upper Grindelwald glacier to "starch in ruffs," and the Rhône glacier to a box of plaster of Paris (*Journals* 171, 175, 177, 178) – these remind one of his brother's use of "cauliflower" to describe the wave. Once more, through these images, Hopkins discovers or reveals the spiritual power of the trivial and the ordinary.[12]

---

[11]   Part of this practice could be due to what Phillips and others recognize as a tenuous balance between the beautiful and the sensual. Phillips writes: "the balance was precarious; his response to beauty was intense and sensual. On several occasions his Journal shows him punishing himself by keeping his eyes downcast or willing himself to give up beauty until he felt he had God's leave for it (6 November 1865)" (Phillips vii).

[12]   Norman White in his *Hopkins: A Literary Biography*, recognizes that "Hopkins's imagery was peculiarly inventive" on his Swiss holiday (165).

Throughout his Alpine entries, Hopkins's metaphors frequently take their tenor from such seemingly unremarkable and ignoble details that threaten to contradict the grandeur and vastness of what they supposedly help portray. Going against the popularly established Romantic idiom, he habitually compared a turn in the brook, a muddied way, a waterfall, the surface of a glacier, the snow, a cloud, a ledge, a crag, or a gorge to insignificant fragments of daily life that, more often than not, tend to get discarded or brushed away. Instead of associating the dramatic Alpine scene with something grander than itself – as was the habit – he did quite the opposite and made an unexpected turn toward the familiar and the domestic: to slices of melon, rags of drying cambric cloth, coffee foam, pieces of glue, crisp celery, endive, milk, wet pocket handkerchiefs, pleats, shining rice, and upturned troughs. Hopkins relied on such images, when, for instance, he compared a mountain's shape to crisp celery and the snow upon it to a freshly cut lawn. His description of the view of the Silberhorn (12,156'), one of the peaks of the Jungfrau, is an example. In the following entry, which I have already partially quoted, his only bow to the romantic convention is his mentioning the "pyramid peak" – a predictable comparison often used by writers wanting to give a sense not only of the shape of its peak but also of its mysterious nobility:

> The mountains and in particular the Silberhorn are shaped and nippled like the
> sand in an hourglass and the Silberhorn has a subsidiary pyramid peak napped
> sharply down the sides. Then one of their beauties is nearly vertical places the
> fine pleatings of the snow running to or from one another, like the newness of
> lawn in an alb and sometimes cut off short as crisp as celery. (*Journals* 174)

For those familiar with Hopkins's idiosyncratic perspective and style, these metaphors are not shocking.[13] As we have seen, Hopkins often coupled the grand with what is usually thought of as being mundane. The practice was to continue – and not only in his poetry. A few years after he visited the Alps, Hopkins preached from what Father Joseph Feeney identifies as a "very proper pulpit in London's Mayfair." Before what would have been a group of horrified parishioners, Hopkins compared the Church to a milk-cow and the seven sacraments to its teats (Feeney 285). But even for those alert to Hopkins's "ways," his Swiss notebooks read in the context of other nineteenth-century aesthetic narratives, which describe mountains

---

[13]   Various critics have noted that Hopkins turned to domestic items when he composed his metaphors. For instance, Norman White, in his literary biography of Hopkins, mentions that there are a "large number of domestic images which give this journal a homely, happy, and human quality" (*Hopkins: A Literary Biography* 165). As I suggest in this chapter, though, these more familiar metaphors do not lend a "homely" tone to Hopkins's prose; rather, they are part of a more spiritual sense of the world. Furthermore, when critics speak of these domestic metaphors, none considers them in the context of mid-nineteenth century satires on the sublime.

rising above the trifling matter of ordinary lives, these unexpected comparisons can be surprising.

To add to this sense of disorientation, there is the realization that these seemingly odd associations were – strange to say – of a kind often to be found in the numerous satires on traveling in the Alps, discussed in Chapter 1, that were intent on mocking or leveling the sublime in the second half of the nineteenth century. As we have seen in that opening chapter, these incongruous comparisons were supposed to be uttered by characters who did not know any better and whose vulgar, stupid taste destroyed anything lofty. How can one forget Charles Lever's satirical *The Dodd Family Abroad* (1854) in which the bumbling and stout Mrs. Dodd inappropriately compares the mountain snow to an egg-pudding? Her ridiculous figure, exaggerated by her preposterous metaphor, sends the sublime tumbling down to the lowlands of Parnassus. Other texts are replete with unfortunate figures of speech that compromise the sublime, such as when an avalanche is compared to the "bursting of a champagne bottle" (*Cook's Tourist's Handbook* 83) and the mist of Mont Blanc to the smoke of a cigar (115). Moreover, one cannot help but recall the *Haps and Mishaps of the Simpleton Family Abroad* (1863) in which the floundering Mrs. Simpleton is compared to a "great porpoise" ("Bell" 6). How does one, then, distinguish between these comparisons and Hopkins's description of the feeder-glacier from Monte Rosa as a "turbot tail" (*Journals* 181) and the Rhône Glacier as a "fan-fin of a dolphin" (*Journals* 178)? How does one not confuse his domestic metaphors to describe the Alpine scenery – such as the coffee-foam waterfalls – with Mrs. Dodd's exclaiming that Mont Blanc resembled an egg-pudding? And, in this context, what about Hopkins's habit of comparing segments of the Alpine landscape to shining rice, celery, crisp endive, starch, rags of cambric, sponges, and cream?

Mrs. Dodd and her companions were obviously not created to reach beyond the limits of their domiciles and their unwieldy bodies. Bounded by the narrowness of their lives, they were not meant to find, as did Hopkins, a kinship among the particulars visible before their eyes. Nor were they supposed to recognize any subtle interplay between realms that the sublime traditionally separated. The Mrs. Dodds and the Mr. and Mrs. Simpletons were not created to discern a parallel that Hopkins detected between the evaporation of moisture in clouds and the steam of hot chocolate (Banfield 177).

These figures were, of course, completely devoid of Hopkins's religious perspective, which prompted him to infuse divinity into the domestic. Hopkins's domestic metaphors are a reminder of his understanding that everything – including rice, celery, and toothpowder – carries within it a trace or an imprint of the grandeur and beauty of "our Lord."[14] Two years after he visited the Alps, Hopkins made this conviction explicit when he noted in his journal: "One day when the bluebells

---

[14] According to Phillips, this perspective could have been partially encouraged by Father Peter Gallwey's *Exhortations to Novices* – given to Hopkins as a novitiate – in which the priest urges the novitiate to understand:

were in bloom I wrote the following. I do not think I have ever seen anything more beautiful than the bluebell I have been looking at. I know the beauty of our Lord by it" (*Journals* 199). Those familiar with Hopkins's poetry will recall a similar sentiment in "Pied Beauty," in which he celebrates the glory of God in smaller, less elevated things:

> Glory be to God for dappled things –
>   For skies of couple-colour as a brinded cow;
>   For rose-moles all in stipple upon trout that swim;
> Fresh-firecoal chestnut-falls; finches' wings;
>   Landscape plotted and pieced – fold, fallow, and plough;
>   And áll trades, their gear and tackle and trim.
> All things counter, original, spare, strange;
>   Whatever is fickle, freckled (who knows how?)
>   With swift, slow; sweet, sour; adazzle, dim;
> He fathers-forth whose beauty is past change:
>   Praise him.

Hopkins and Science

To understand why Hopkins chose to honor his own idiosyncratic voice rather than fall into the more traditional ways of representing a mountainous landscape, it is helpful to consider the influence of contemporary scientific debates upon his description of the Alps. Hopkins's Swiss notes not only remind us of his ability and desire to see the glory of God in smaller, less elevated things but also of his ability to fuse the scientific and the spiritual. Hopkins was, as Gillian Beer points out, forming his ideas at a time when scientific thought was "openly available" and "transforming Victorian perceptions" (118, 123). (In the 1870s, for instance, Stonyhurst, where Hopkins did part of his training for the Jesuit priesthood, enjoyed a scientific prominence. There Hopkins could continue his studies of natural science and learn about meteorological phenomena at the nearby observatory headed by Stephen Joseph Perry, a leading Victorian astronomer.)[15]

One manifestation of Hopkins's long-standing interest in science is that when he looked at the Swiss landscape, he sometimes transferred the vocabulary usually reserved for music to the visual – a parallel advanced not only by aesthetic theory

---

One necessary effect of chastity is a positive hatred of all the pleasures of the Senses – a loathing of all that gratifies the body. Custody of the eyes is actually custody of the mind – we should keep remembrance of Christ crucified in our hearts. Everything around us should recall Him ... the hills should recall Calvary, the trees the tree of the Cross, the stream Jordan." (Phillips vi)

[15] For another essay on this subject see "Black Rain in Lancashire" in Tom Zaniello's *Hopkins in the Age of Darwin*, 58–84.

but also by historical and contemporary scientific theories. In strolling in an Alpine valley, for instance, Hopkins noticed "the Melodious lines of a cow's dewlap" (*Journals* 171), and on the way to the Rigi, he became aware that the colors of the lakes blend as do the notes of a "chord"; and that the blues and purples "modulate" by way of their "sharps" and "flats" (*Journals* 170). Current scientific thought would have encouraged Hopkins's sensitivity to this relationship between music and color. Hopkins would have probably known Isaac Newton's study of the analogous relationship between the seven colors of light and the seven tones of the diatonic scale (Zaniello, *Hopkins in the Age of Darwin* 64). And from his own century, Hopkins would have absorbed the various discussions responding to H.L.F. Helmholtz's *On the Sensations of Tone as a Physiological Basis for the Theory of Music* (English edition 1877), a text that, among other things, examines in what ways "the phenomena of mixed colours present considerable analogy to those of compound musical tones" (Zaniello, *Hopkins in the Age of Darwin* 68–69). In addition, he might have read the correspondence concerning that analogy in the first volumes of *Nature* that appeared in November 1869 (see Beer 128). And, as Tom Zaniello suggests, he might also have been familiar with George Field's popularization of the correlation between music and color.

In his 1820 study of aesthetics, Field, a chemist, paint maker, and inventor, superimposed his "chromatic" scale of colors on a diatonic scale of tone, and tried to prove that "the distance on the scale from sound to sound, and that from color, are equally *intervals* ..." (Zaniello, *Hopkins in the Age of Darwin* 65). In his discussion of this theory, Field demonstrates how the analogy between colors and musical tones works. He explains:

> [when] one of the semitones of the octave falls between the notes B and C, or blue and green, [these] colors are discordant, and require the intermediate *demitint* opposed to the semitone to satisfy the eye, to connect the octaves in series, and to complete the harmony of the scale. (Zaniello, *Hopkins in the Age of Darwin* 65)

For Field, this equivalence was an imitation of God's "perfect system" – an observation that would have appealed to Hopkins.

Which of these specific theories influenced him we can never know. However, we do know that these scientific discussions contributed to his understanding and combined with the sensuous experiences attached to his aesthetic sensibility, so that, during his Swiss holiday, Hopkins, in a fashion, scored as well as painted the phrases of his notebook. The consequent blending of color and tone often found expression in his notebooks and contributed to the unusual flavor of its entries. The following passage from an 8 July 1868 entry extends the analogy current in scientific thought and echoes a synaesthetic orientation:

> From Lucerne by steamer to Küssnacht, thence walk across to Immensee, thence by steamer over lake of Zug to Arth, whence up the Rigi – The normal colour of

the lake water, from near at least, bottle blue; from some way up we saw it with the sea shoaling colours, purple and blue, the purple expressing the rose of the chord to the eye (– in the same way as the same colour in a rose fading expresses the blue of the chord – the converse case: in fact, it may perhaps be generalized that when this happens the modulation in question is the flat of the next term and not the sharp of the former one). From the top the lakes egg-blue, blue strongly modulated to green. (*Journals* 170)

Later, in an 1879 letter to Robert Bridges, Hopkins was to comment upon, and thus confirm, a more general relationship between his way of seeing and his interest in science, art, and music: "No doubt, my poetry errs on the side of oddness ... But as air, melody, is what strikes me most of all in music and design in painting, so design, pattern or what I am in the habit of calling *inscape* is what I above all aim at in poetry" (*Letters* 66).[16]

Far more significant for Hopkins's various responses to the Alps, though, is his interest in thermodynamics. Because he recognized the energy of creation in the small as well as in the large, he was attracted to contemporary theories of thermodynamics, which claimed that various fields of energy were manifestations of a single and constant force that was being continually transferred and transformed. Critics such as Marie Banfield, Gillian Beer, Jason H. Lindquist, Norman Mackenzie, Julie V. Nixon, and Tom Zaniello have within the last ten or so years recognized and have, in various degrees, explored Hopkins's dialogue with this problem in physics. They, consequently, have firmly established the scientific context of Hopkins's work. To Hopkins, the energy that continuously imprinted itself on and organized the various individuated objects around him (and created the phenomena of "inscape" and "instress") were but manifestations of the grandeur of God, "the matrix of nature's energy, ceaselessly holding all creation in being" (Banfield 185) – a conviction or understanding that shapes his well-known poem "God's Grandeur." (Nixon has an excellent discussion of how nineteenth-century energetics shaped the poem.)

In his Swiss journal, Hopkins displays his awareness of this sort of dynamic and interrelation between matter and energy when he notes how the movements of the water shape its patterns and metaphors: "Rushing streams may be described as inscaped ordinarily in pillows – and upturned troughs" (*Journals* 176). His sense of an organizing charged energy as well as his attentiveness to a kinship between the grand and the ordinary are also noticeable when he describes the movement and patterns of the falls of the Reichenbach: "At the take-off it falls in discharges of rice or meal but each cluster as it descends sharpens and tapers, and from halfway down the whole cascade is inscaped in fretted falling, vandykes in each of which the frets or points, just like the startings of a just-lit lucifer match,

---

[16]   It is interesting to note that when the scientist and climber John Tyndall watched crystals of frost floating in the air, he thought of them as "arranging themselves as if they moved to music, and ended by rendering that music" (*The Glaciers of the Alps* 130).

keep shooting in races, one beyond the other, to the bottom" (*Journals* 177). Later in the entry he notices that the water in the second fall is "fretted like open sponge or light bread-crumb where the yeast has supped in the texture in big and little holes" (*Journals* 177).

Tyndall and Hopkins

Of all the Swiss entries, however, those describing the various glaciers he visited are most notably indebted to his knowledge of thermodynamics. Some of his most vivid and inventive entries are those describing the glaciers reaching down from the Jungfrau, the upper and lower glaciers at Grindelwald, and the three stages of the Rhône Glacier (*Journals* 174, 175, 178). His fascination with glaciers was part of a general attraction shared by most visitors to the Alps who made it a point to cross at least one of these ice fields – usually, the Mer de Glace near Chamonix.

Innumerable mid- and late-nineteenth-century photographs show strings of men, women, and children, with their alpenstocks, determinedly, yet gingerly, walking over the ice and clambering over the awkward moraine. Hopkins was part of this pilgrimage. In the mode of other tourists, he had, as he wrote, "a trudge" over at least the Rhône Glacier and even tumbled over its side (*Journals* 179).

Hopkins's attraction to these glaciers, however, was not just because it was the thing to do. He was also intrigued because theories about their movements were an active part of the scientific debate – a conversation that involved theories about thermodynamics. For someone interested in the fluidity of the landscape, these theories were essential. It is a remarkable coincidence that Hopkins happened to be in Zermatt at the very time when John Tyndall (1820–93), one of the main figures in the controversy, was about to set off on an ascent of the Matterhorn. Tyndall was not only well known as a scientist but also as an Alpine Club man – he was an outstanding mountaineer. Hopkins went to see Tyndall to get medicine for Bond, his traveling companion, who was ill (one only wishes Hopkins had recorded their conversation), and, on 26 July, he arose at two o'clock in the morning so that he could attend a mass held in a little chapel for the guides accompanying Tyndall up the Matterhorn. Hopkins writes: "It was an odd scene; two guides or porters served; the noise of a torrent outside accompanied the priest. Then to bed again" (*Journals* 182). Tyndall was to make a successful climb.

Following the lead of figures such as Horace Bénédict de Saussure (*Travels in the Alps*) [*Voyages dans les Alpes* 1796], scientists were now questioning the traditional explanations concerning glacial composition and movement. When Hopkins visited the Alps, arguments concerning the validity of these various theories were still current and sometimes antagonistic or heated. Among the most prominent of the mid-nineteenth-century scientists interested in the nature of glacial movement was Tyndall, who, in 1857, explored the glacial tributaries feeding the Mer de Glace.

Figure 5.3 Tourists on the Mer de Glace

Tyndall's studies of glacial motion created an enduring controversy with people such as James David Forbes and James Thomson, as well as with Ruskin. Tyndall, who like Hopkins was interested in the fluidity of the landscape, insisted that the glaciers do not, as Tom Zaniello explains: "flow in their beds like rivers but crack under pressure and then freeze again" ("Alpine Art and Science: Hopkins' Swiss Adventure" 8). Tyndall strongly disagreed with Forbes, who subscribed to the theory that rather than being shaped by pressure, glaciers often follow the "laws of the river" and flowed like viscous fluids. Forbes maintained that varying stresses caused by different velocities of the flow created the fissures in the ice. Tyndall vigorously and doggedly fought this theory and insisted that it was the pressure on the ice that squeezed the lower portions out and down, and, subsequently, created such fissures as well as blue veining in the glacier. Paul L. Sawyer explains that Tyndall was adamant that "glaciers do not conform to their beds, as rivers do, but melt or fracture under pressure and then freeze again at the point of contact – a phenomenon called 'regelation' by his great mentor Faraday" (218).

When Tyndall was carrying out his experimental work on glaciers, he sometimes used models made of wax and other substances that develop fissures under pressure to test his hypothesis. And when Ruskin tested his theories about glacial movement, he used piecrust and treacle (Sawyer 221). The use of these household items to carry out such experiments suggests the interesting possibility that Hopkins's comparison of the Rhône Glacier to "bright-plucked water swaying in a pail" and to "a box of plaster of Paris … a little moist" (*Journals* 178) is not as far-fetched as most perceive it to be. These kitchen metaphors are, perhaps, not just a product of Hopkins's inventiveness and willingness to link the microscopic and macroscopic, but are also reflections of a common scientific approach to learning more about the behavior of the natural world. When Hopkins observed that the second stage of the Rhône Glacier "appeared like … starch or toothpowder" (*Journals* 178), he appears to be adopting the very idiom of the scientists thinking about glacial movement; he might be imagining Tyndall's and Ruskin's experiments with wax, piecrust, and treacle.

The coincidence of Hopkins and Tyndall being on the glaciers at the same time, however, suggests more than a borrowing of an idiom or a shared sense of a dynamic, fluid landscape. It also proffers an opportunity to take a look at the ways in which each regarded the glaciers and, thereby, to gain a better sense of what Hopkins was doing when he was writing his journal. Even though one was a priest/ poet and the other a scientist/climber, in certain ways, Hopkins's and Tyndall's approaches to their surroundings were not foreign to one another. To begin with, they were both committed to finding the law of the glaciers. Independently the two were patiently sorting through the chaos of their surroundings to reach a better understanding of the glaciers' shape and structure. Hopkins sketched the outline of glaciers and gazed at their forms until a pattern emerged. A sketch simply dated "July 23" is an example.

In *The Glaciers of the Alps* (1861), Tyndall recorded a similar impulse when he explains how he must work himself through the "utter confusions" of details

Figure 5.4   Gerard Manley Hopkins. "July 23"

to find order and law. He admits that at first "the ice presented an appearance of utter confusion, but we soon reached a position where the mechanical conditions of the glacier revealed themselves." What stands before his eyes "becomes order and beauty" (13). And, just as Hopkins was ecstatic when he was able finally to see the defining edges of a detail so that he could catch its pattern or its inscape, so too was Tyndall thrilled when he was able to distinguish the illuminated outline of the clouds in a storm. Although the style is distinctly different, the following passage from Tyndall's *Mountaineering in 1861* records the analogous moment:

> The darkness is intense, and the intermittent glare correspondingly impressive. Now it is the east which is suddenly illuminated, now the west, now the heavens in front; now the visible light is evidently the fringe of an illuminated cloud which has caught the blaze of a discharge far down behind the mountains. Sometimes the lightning seems to burst, like a fireball, midway between the horizon and the zenith, spreading as a vast glory behind the clouds and revealing all their outlines. (8)

Tyndall's enthusiasm for the "discharge" and burst of light in the quoted passage recalls yet another similarity in perspective. Their mutual alertness to the physical theories of thermodynamics made them, in their own way, keen to catch or represent the fields of energy that ran beneath the surface and shaped the glaciers' movements and form – what, of course, Hopkins referred to as their "inscape" and "instress." Hopkins's active verbs and participles when he was describing a glacier reflect or represent, in another key, the very pressures and stresses that Tyndall was measuring with his instruments. Hopkins notes, for instance, that in the first of the Rhône Glacier's three stages he can see "swells of ice rising through the snow-sheet and the snow itself tossing and fretting into the sides of the rock walls in spray-like points" (*Journals* 178). Below the Gornergrat, "It was easy to see the cross-hatched lines of flow in the glaciers ... they make a table or stage from which the mountains spring" (*Journals* 181). Tyndall's descriptions of these same glaciers are not that far removed from Hopkins's efforts to map these forces:

> Right and left from these longitudinal bands finer curves sweep across the glacier ... They mark the direction in which the subjacent ice is laminated. The glacier lies in a curved valley, the side towards which its convex curvature is turned, is thrown into a state of strain, the ice breaks across the lines of tension, and a curious system of oblique glacier ravines is thus produced. (*Mountaineering in 1861* 24)

Though there are differences, especially because Tyndall relies on passive constructions and slightly technical words like "subjacent," their attention to the stress lines that mark a glacier reverberate with one another.

When Tyndall studied a glacier, he, like other scientists, took measurements with various instruments and dug six-foot holes into the ice in order to track the glacier's movement. The description Tyndall gives of this latter action is a remarkable piece of prose that, at times, reverberates with Hopkins's sense of the lovely and the dangerous "fire that breaks" from the windhover ("Windhover" l.10) or the "shining" grandeur of God ("God's Grandeur"). Tyndall writes:

> When a staff was driven into the snow low down the mountain, the colour of the light in the orifice was scarcely sensibly blue, but higher up this increased

in a wonderful degree, and at the summit the effect was marvellous. I struck my
staff into the snow, and turned it round and round; the surrounding snow cracked
repeatedly, and flashes of blue light issued from the fissures. The fragments of
snow that adhered to the staff were, by contrast, of a beautiful pink yellow, so
that, on moving the staff with such fragments attached to it up and down, it was
difficult to resist the impression that a pink flame was ascending and descending
in the hole. (*The Glaciers of the Alps* 29–30)

In spite of the temptation to attend to the echoes between Tyndall's and Hopkins's
sensitivity to the drama – and even to the ecstasy – of such moments, it is also
important to notice a significant disparity between the two: Tyndall is more
physically engaged with the landscape than is Hopkins. Tyndall digs into the
glacier; he turns the ice and his staff round and round, and he registers the crackling
of the snow beneath his feet. Tyndall also places his ear close to the ice, and passes
his frozen fingers to and fro over the cracks (*The Glaciers of the Alps* 87) – as
Sawyer remarks, "Tyndall's thinking was 'physical'" (225). He wants not only
to engage the glacier or the mountain with his athletic body but also to discover
what is underneath it – its inner workings. At one point, Tyndall wishes he had a
microscopic eye so that he could view what lies out of sight.

Hopkins, however, is content with what the surface reveals. Just a few weeks
before becoming a novitiate and increasingly careful or anxious about the pleasure
of the sense and the body, Hopkins chooses to engage and touch his surroundings
through his eyes.[17] The ecstasy that reverberates throughout his body originates
in the act of seeing, not in running his fingers across the ice. The material "I"
is invisible, so as to permit the seeing eye to comprehend what is visible on the
surface. The living, breathing body belongs to the landscape and not to Hopkins,
who rarely registers his own presence. Standing on a glacier, Hopkins sees the
clouds as if they are "fine shapeless skins of fretted make, full of eyebrows"
(*Journals* 179), gazing at the three parts of the Rhône glacier, he thinks of them
as "the heel, instep, and ball of toes of a foot" (*Journals* 178), and looking at the
Grindelwald glaciers, he sees them as two descending limbs (*Journals* 175). These
perceptive moments replace touch and penetration. There is a space between him
and what he views. His description of the Grindelwald glaciers portrays this
absence. One feels his distance from the scene – though one does not feel the lack
of the sensuous eye, especially when he introduces the startling metaphor of blood
rising to the surface of wounded flesh:

Above where the mountains make hollows they [the glaciers] lie saddle-wise in
them and then shouldering through the gorges are broken up – but the question is
whether by the pressure or the slope. In slanted brooks the bias keeps falling from

---

[17]   For further thoughts on the subject of Hopkins's anxiety about the pleasure of the
sense and the body, see Julia Saville's *A Queer Chivalry: The Homoerotic Asceticism of
Gerard Manley Hopkins*.

bank to bank across and so knits the stream and glaciers also are cross-hatched with their crevasses but they form waves which lie regularly and in horizontals across the current ... In the gut these glaciers are hollowed in the middle, not rounded up. Below this they open out and part lengthwise. These Grindelwald glaciers are remarkable for their ruggedness, I believe: the upper one looks like rows of dogteeth. The blue colour (which compared by a glance with the sky is greener) retiring into these clefts looks like starch in ruffs. Becoming deep within it looks like deep flesh-cuts where one sees the blood flush and welling up. (*Journals* 175)

Of all the differences between them, Tyndall's unwillingness to let go of the conventional Romantic vocabulary is, perhaps, the most striking. It exposes a wide gap between the two and confirms the novelty of Hopkins's response to the Alps. Although the two shared a sensitivity to the way light fell upon the mountain landscape and both had an active and enthusiastic understanding of thermodynamic forces shaping its glaciers, they parted company once they stepped upon a mountain. At once Tyndall, reverting to the boundaries of convention, responds to the scenery with a vocabulary and metaphors inherited from popular conceptions of the sublime. It is not unusual, therefore, in Tyndall's description to find the well-used references to the glacier as a sea ("the glacier here has the appearance of a sea, which, after it had been tossed by a storm, had sufficiently stiffened into rest") and to a serpent ("the glaciers issuing from the hollow of the eternal hills, and stretching like frozen serpents through the sinuous valley") (*The Glaciers of the Alps* 37, 114).

After reading his magnificent description of the flashes of blue light issuing from the glacier's fissure (quoted above), it is disappointing to discover this limitation, especially since Tyndall's style, with its intermittent vivid phrases and breathless rhythms, can otherwise be distinctive, if not haunting. One wonders what might have been the result if Tyndall had left out the conventional references to an Alpine landscape's savage magnificence as well as to the mountains' grandeur and gloom. Typical is a passage from Tyndall's account of an expedition in Oberland, which, in the midst of frightening images, such as "the weird rattle of the [glacier's] debris," falls back on the familiar terminology. In spite of its homage to tradition, though, the passage is, nevertheless, convincing and strangely exquisite:

We halted in the night of the 16th at the Jungfrau Hotel, and next morning we saw the beams of the rising sun fall upon the peaked snow of the Silberhorn. Slowly and solemnly the pure white one appeared to rise higher and higher into the sunlight, being afterwards mottled with gold and gloom, as clouds drifted between it and the sun ... I finally reached the end of a glacier, formed by snow and shattered ice which fall from the shoulders of the Jungfrau. The view from the place had a savage magnificence such as I had not previously beheld, and it was not without some slight feeling of awe that I clambered up the end of the glacier. It was the first I had actually stood upon. The loneliness of the place was very impressive, the silence being only broken by fitful gusts of wind, or by the weird rattle of the debris which fell at intervals from the melting ice. (*The Glaciers of the Alps* 11)

In this passage, Tyndall draws attention to his subjective reaction to the experience of actually placing his feet upon a glacier. One sees the landscape through his tactile relationship to it. In Hopkins's description of the very same glacier, however, the emphasis is different, for his own physical interaction with the landscape is secondary. When Hopkins describes the glacier, he instead places the burden of the experience on his metaphors, and he stands at a distance. It is they, not his physical being, which are primary. They bear the whole load. The 15 July 1868 entry, describing the identical glacier falling from the shoulders of the Jungfrau, vividly demonstrates how Hopkins throws the whole weight of the moment into his metaphors – away from his own physical presence. The passage immediately heeds the glacier's likeness to a tiger-skin rug (one he might have seen in houses he visited) and the wild motion of the skin being flung before it falls and settles so that its defining lines map the glacier's marks of stress. One of Hopkins's sketches of this scene, "This is a glacier, though you wd. not think it," verifies the metaphor (see Fig. 5.5 overleaf).

This image captures the glacier's movement and pattern:

> They are round one of the heights of the Jungfrau two ends or falls of a glacier. If you took the skin of a white tiger or the deep fell of some other animal and swung it tossing high in the air and then cast it out before you it would fall and so clasp and lap round anything in its way just as this glacier does and the fleece would part in the same rifts: you must suppose a lazuli under-flix to appear. The spraying out of one end I tried to catch but it would have taken hours: it was this which first made me think of a tiger-skin, and it ends in tongues and points like the tail and claws; indeed the ends of the glaciers are knotted or knuckled like talons. Above in a plane nearly parallel to the eye, becoming thus foreshortened, it forms saddle-curves with dips and swells. (*Journals* 174)

A Divine Way of Seeing

The surprise of the comparison and the strength of its movement capture the idiosyncratic vision that had been a part of his earlier experiences and was to continue in the poetry he was to write between 1876 and 1889. The metaphor of the flung tiger-skin represents the essence of that odd distinctiveness Hopkins himself referred to when he wrote to Bridges on 15 February 1879 that "No doubt my poetry errs on the side of oddness ... it is the vice of distinctiveness to become queer. This vice I cannot have escaped" (*Letters* 66). Freed from the commands of the popular sublime, Hopkins embraced the grandeur of the glaciers by recoiling from trite images and reaching for those that captured the landscape's

This is a glacier think it July 15, 68. though you wd. not

Figure 5.5   Gerard Manley Hopkins. "This is a glacier, though you wd. not
think it"

overpowering presence. Without reverting to the tired metaphors of the sea
and the serpent that Tyndall had recalled, he replicated the power of the scene
through unexploited and, at once, familiar objects. In a sense, Hopkins did not
leave the sublime behind when he traveled to the Alps. Rather, through his fresh
metaphors, he reintroduced the idea of grandeur and astonishment in a new key.
At the end of the passage quoted above, the image of the tiger's claws and talons

leaves one sensing the strength, the threat, and, perhaps, even the sublime terror of the glacier. Throughout his Swiss notes, Hopkins continuously turns what the scientists measure into living things. He breathes life into what is either a cliché or is reserved for what Tyndall entitled, in part 2 of his *The Glaciers of the Alps*, the "Chiefly Scientific." Through his metaphors and his verbs that carry the energy of the landscape, Hopkins not only recasts the sublime but also turns facts into being. He fuses the scientific and the spiritual, and shows how the empirical eye can be a divine way of seeing.

Chapter 6
Snowbound with Robert Louis Stevenson

My consciousness of my body immediately signifies a certain landscape about me.
(Maurice Merleau-Ponty, see Fisher, *The Essential Writings of Merleau-Ponty* 219)

A wooded ridge shuts in the [Davos] valley at the northern end where it rises above the lake. Mountains of nearly ten thousand feet flank the sides and protect it from biting winds, leaving it like a basin into which the sun pours its concentrated light and warmth.

(Lockett, *Robert Louis Stevenson at Davos* 29)

Introduction

Given the reverential and enthusiastic regard most people had for the Alpine landscape, it is interesting to note that Robert Louis Stevenson chose not to partake in the popular regard for its grandeur. Particularly during his first months in the Alps, an ailing Stevenson found the snow-covered mountains to be dispiriting and uninspiring.[1] In the winter of 1880 until the spring of 1881, confined to what the guidebooks described as the "lofty Alpine valley" (Baedeker 450) of Davos and sheltered by mountains that protected him and the other patients from the North and East winds, he was miserable and wrote little, even though "his mind was full of literary enterprises" (Colvin 2: 4).[2] Stevenson characterized his attempts to write

---

[1]   In his thirtieth year, Stevenson was happily back in Scotland, but soon his chronic health problems began to be more than usually threatening. The hemorrhaging from his lungs had returned and prompted his physician to recommend that he spend the winter in the mountain valley of Davos in Switzerland. He traveled to Davos in October, 1880 and remained there until the end of April, 1881. In 1880, one approached Davos "by an eight hours' laborious drive up the valley of the Prätigau" (Lockett 32). During those months he and his family lived at the Hôtel Belvedere, an invalid hotel. While he was in Davos, Stevenson became friendly with John Addington Symonds who lived in a house nearby. Symonds, who suffered from tuberculosis, had made his home in Davos.

[2]   Sidney Colvin recalls:

For the Highland history he read much, but composed little or nothing, and eventually this history went to swell the long list of his unwritten books. He saw through the press his first volume of collected essays, *Virginibus Puerisque*, which came out early in 1881; wrote the essays *Samuel Pepys* and *The Morality of the Profession of Letters*, for the Cornhill and the Fortnightly Review respectively,

as "dissipated" (Colvin 2: 20) and admitted to his friend Sidney Colvin that his progress on his proposed history of modern Scotland was in abeyance: "three out of five parts remain hitherto entirely unwritten. Smack!" (Colvin 2: 23–24) Indeed Stevenson's inertia so alarmed John Addington Symonds that he contacted Leslie Stephen and proposed that Stevenson review books for the *Cornhill Magazine*, an assignment he hoped would invigorate Stevenson and prompt his friend to put pen to paper more often. As Stevenson explained in a letter to Colvin, Symonds and Stephen wanted "to save my brain" (Colvin 2: 29).

Stevenson's lack of productivity, though, was not, as many have suggested, simply the consequence of his feeling unwell and discouraged by the company of others suffering from tuberculosis or delicate health. If one reads through Stevenson's essays, travelogues, and letters, one begins to understand that Stevenson's negative reaction to the Alps also originated in the landscape itself. Although his poor health interfered with his appreciation of his surroundings, there was far more at play. Stevenson's response to Davos as well as to other natural settings suggests just how beholden his imagination was to the character of the immediate scenery as well as to the movement of his body through that landscape. As we shall see, the topography of his surroundings played an essential role in the mapping of his texts. Stevenson's reaction to the Swiss valley and its adjacent mountains offers the reader an insight into the ways he created the style and rhythms of his prose. In a sense, the immediate landscape functioned as a kind of mirror, the reflections from which inscribed his text.

Leslie Stephen and Robert Louis Stevenson

It seems appropriate to begin this discussion of the importance of landscape in the shaping of his prose by recalling Stevenson's acquaintance with Leslie Stephen. A few years before Stevenson, in dangerously bad health, was sent to Davos, he met Stephen, who at that time was not only known as the editor of the *Cornhill Magazine* (Stephen edited the journal from 1871 to 1882) but was also widely lionized for his remarkable mountaineering feats in the high Alps. In fact, Stephen visited Stevenson in Edinburgh when the climber came in February, 1875 to give a "couple of lectures on the Alps" (Maitland 249).[3] Stephen was among the most eminent of English mountaineers. By the 1880s he had ascended most

---

and sent to the Pall Mall Gazette the papers on the life and climate of Davos, posthumously reprinted in *Essays on Travel*. Beyond this, he only amused himself with verses, some of them afterwards published in *Underwoods*.(Colvin 2: 4)

[3]   Stephen seems to have regretted having to give these lectures. In a 8 February 1875 letter to Charles Eliot Norton, he complained: "How I came to be such an infernal fool as to say that I would go surpasses my present comprehension" (Maitland 249). During this visit, Stephen seems to have introduced Stevenson to W.E. Henley. In a letter to his wife, Stephen wrote: "I went to see Stevenson this morning, Colvin's friend, and told him all about the

of the prominent mountains in the Alps (including ten "virgin" peaks), and had published detailed accounts of his expeditions. His *The Playground of Europe* (1871), describing his many climbs, had caught the public's attention, and so had his account of being the first ever to reach the peak of the Schreckhorn (13,385'). Moreover, he had served as one of the earliest presidents of the Alpine Club (1865–68).

When the two had first talked in London and then again in Edinburgh, Stephen regarded the 25-year-old Stevenson as "a youth of some literary promise" (Maitland 246) and had begun publishing several of his essays in issues of the *Cornhill Magazine*.[4] The two shared many similar literary tastes, but they did have at least one significant point of difference. That is, Stevenson simply did not participate in Stephen's enthusiasm for Alpine scenery. During their acquaintance in the 1870s and 1880s Stevenson never once seems to have mentioned the editor's adventures in the Alps. There is no evidence of these bold activities' making any impression upon him. The celebrated mountaineer's extraordinary tales of narrow escapes on mountain ledges and his shivering progress across profound crevasses slipped by – an odd circumstance if one reminds oneself that the individual whom they eluded was himself repeatedly attracted to danger and to the narrow scrapes of his fictional protagonists, as well as choosing to take considerable risks in his own right. In a sense, Stevenson's daring and persistence with regard to his own survival was not unrelated to Stephen's persona holding on to a rock for dear life after he had lost his footing and was left dangling over a precipice (described in "A Bad Five Minutes in the Alps," published in 1873). Both took chances and clung to life. Yet, the reality is that Stevenson did not share Stephen's admiration for the Alps or for Davos.

Unlike Stephen, who took immense pleasure in the Alpine winter landscape where the snow lays a "kind hand ... softly on a sick man's brows" (*The Playground of Europe*, 286), and who found that the love of mountains is "intimately connected with all that is noblest in human nature" (66), Stevenson, in Davos, felt himself degraded, cursed, and confined to an invalid and trite world.[5] The enclosing mountains trapped him in the monotony of snow, and he lost the perspective of contrast and change that are necessary for perception, recollection, and narrative. Stephen's sense of ardor upon visiting Davos was not to be his.[6] Stevenson who,

---

poor creature [Henley had been in the infirmary for eighteen months after losing his foot to tuberculosis of the bone], and am going to take him there this afternoon" (250).

[4] Leslie Stephen revealed in a later essay, "A Critical Essay on Robert Louis Stevenson" that he thought Stevenson "a man of genius" (2). In that review he also shows his awareness of the importance of style for Stevenson and suggests that the most pressing question for Stevenson at that time was "not what to say but how to say it" (5).

[5] For Stevenson's description of this monotonous landscape see his essay "Davos in Winter" (*Essays on Literature, on Nature; Juvenilia* 165–68).

[6] In 1889, Stephen wrote to Charles Eliot Norton and reported that he was in Davos and could "feel fragments of my old Alpine ardour reviving" (Bicknell 2: 367).

perhaps under Stephen's tutelage, had expected to admire the place, once there exhibited little inclination to embrace his editor's zeal.

Stevenson's Unresponsiveness to the Alps

This lack of keenness on Stevenson's part is quite astonishing if one recalls that by the 1880s the Alps were a well-established part of the British imagination. His refusal to accept or participate in Stephen's fervor goes beyond the boundaries of his reaction to his editor and extends to a rejection of a far-reaching and popular enthusiasm.

From the mid-century on, as I have already noted, the Alps had become an "English preserve" (Bernard 25). Indeed, 1850, the year of Stevenson's birth, was the heyday of Alpinism. Attempting to leave behind the fashion and pressures of the world, the British came either to climb, to walk on the glaciers, to participate in winter sports, or to enjoy a few weeks away from the business of their lives at home. Holiday-makers flocked to the Alps in both summer and winter; new summits and routes continued to be "conquered"; and writers extolled the liberation as well as the moral and intellectual benefits of their presence. British climbers and tourists chose to spend as many summers in the midst of these natural wonders as possible, and some celebrated their honeymoons among the glorious views of the mountains.

In addition, of course, the mountains were admired because of their health-giving properties. By the time Stevenson was at Davos, there were already numerous high-altitude sanatoria, filled with tubercular and asthmatic patients, in the European Alps. Davos, in particular, was a center, and one that continued to grow, so that by 1911, Baedeker's guide to Switzerland listed as many as ten sanatoria, some large with 110 beds and some designed only for female patients. Baedeker also identified schools for "delicate boys" (*Fridericanum*) and girls (*Frau Steinbeck's School*) (Baedeker 449).

Stevenson's unresponsiveness to his surroundings in Davos not only went against the grain of the popular imagination, it also ran counter to and separated him from a long literary tradition in which writers readily exposed themselves to the sublime scenery of a mountain landscape. During that first winter, however, Stevenson did not share Shelley's exquisite belief in the ethereal beauty of the towering mountains. Nor was he inclined to mention Nature's transcendent glory. Even the sublimity expressed by Wordsworth and Byron hovered at a significant distance. In fact, Stevenson was generally not attracted to grand scenery. Before going to the Alps, he repeatedly remarked that a "little hot sunshine over lowland parks and woodlands" was far superior to "the war of elements round the summit of Mont Blanc" (*Essays on Literature, on Nature; Juvenilia* 96). Already in his 1874 review of Basil Champney's *A Quiet Corner of England*, Stevenson seconded the author's irritation with the undiscriminating enthusiasm and thoughtless preference that tourists displayed for the Alpine ranges; he even suggested that mountains are nothing but just "very big hill[s] of no particular shape with some white snow upon the top" ("A Quiet Corner of England" 253). Later, in a sketch composed in the 1880s, he asserted "Bold rocks near at hand are more inspiriting than distant Alps" (*Essays* 295).

Once in Davos, though, contributing to his reluctance to sit "awe-stricken" before a grand mountain (*Essays* 187) was the oppressive reality of the unrelieved winter snow that covered the neighboring peaks as well as the bounded nature of the valley landscape. Such surroundings overwhelmed him and did little to endear the Alps to him. The invariable sameness of the landscape had a sterile, prison-like effect upon his imagination. It polluted his thought, as did the warm air from Italy that settled, from time to time, like "a load of sins" (*Essays* 164) upon the valley and sent the invalid world into its private chambers.[7]

The Body in the Landscape

Given Stevenson's friendship with Stephen as well as the public pressures and cultural traditions pressing upon him, several questions arise: Why was Stevenson so unwilling to participate in the popular reverence for the Alps; moreover, why did he write so little that winter?

One obvious answer is that Stevenson associated the mountains with sickness and his imprisoned body. Unlike people who regarded the Alps as a place of refuge where they could escape from themselves and their commodified lives, Stevenson could neither flee his ailing physical being nor avoid reminders of it. Even when he walked away from the hotel where he was living, one sufferer would be either behind or ahead of him on the path. They, his vulnerable body, and the landscape conspired to enclose him; worse, the surrounding oppressive mountains vitiated rather than released his energy. Stevenson sensed an "underlying languor" (*Essays*

---

[7] Perhaps in Stevenson's defense, one should mention that he was not always alone in finding Davos to be monotonous. Employing a similar vocabulary, his acquaintance and soon-to-be friend John Addington Symonds, who had settled in Davos because of his own tuberculosis, occasionally remarked:

> Those who are obliged, as I have been, to live for their health's sake in an Alpine Valley, escape from it with alacrity from time to time [he would go to Venice]. There is a sense of being imprisoned, a feeling of physical and mental stifling, owing to the narrow limits of the landscape & the monotony of *everlasting* pine woods. (*Our Life in the Swiss Highlands* 124)

Especially when he was feeling unwell, Symonds would write to his friends and complain – in this instance to Swinburne: "I lead a difficult life, condemned by a slow disease ... to exile in a monotonous valley of the Alps, where I freeze, where the pulses of enjoyment slacken & energy fails" (*The Letters of John Addington Symonds* 2: 762–63). Nevertheless, Symonds could also recognize that the Alps "in their winter robe of snow" offer "a spectacle which for novelty and splendour is not surpassed by anything the fancy can imagine" (*Our Life in the Swiss Highlands* 11); when away in Venice, he often longed to return to "the tranquil never-changing scene" in Davos (*Our Life in the Swiss Highlands* 125).

174). He was obviously not able, as could Stephen and climbers like him, to measure and appreciate just how massive and glorious the Alps could be through the muscular exertion of his physical being. He could not, as had Stephen, translate their glory through the medium of his body nor feel the peaks' stimulating influence in the very marrow of his bones. His circumstances remind one of Maurice Merleau-Ponty's understanding that the body is a mediator between the world and perception; and that a subject perceives in conformity with his body. In Merleau-Ponty's words: "The body must be the necessary intermediary between the real world and perception ... Perception can no longer be a taking-possession of things which finds them in their proper place; it must be an event internal to the body and one which results from their action on it" (Fisher 143). Stevenson's situation is an example of this relation between the body and sight.

In Davos, perhaps the only dramatic exception to Stevenson's sense of weakness and imprisonment occurred when he would occasionally go tobogganing at night. Then, the excitement of racing like the wind down the icy slopes and the feeling of having his heart in his mouth would slice the sameness of the snows and cut through the monotony of his static life. His imagination would momentarily revive. During these thrilling seconds, the night would be "made luminous with stars and snow," and the landscape would be "girt with strange white mountains" (*Essays* 172). Briefly, for these moments, there was something approaching the sublime, and Stevenson, in the context of the Alpine scene, would sense "an accustomed tune" (172) that temporarily removed him from the limits of his body so that he could feel the rhythms of the universe and observe the stars reeling and flashing above. In the spirit of Edmund Burke's understanding of the sublime, Stevenson could speak of the "joyful horror" when "the head goes, the world vanishes; your blind steed bounds below your weight" (171). What these interludes tell us is that not only was the body the mediating agent between the external world and the perception of it, but, even more significantly, it was the *moving* body that was essential to Stevenson's sense of his surroundings. He needed to move through a landscape in order to see and represent it. By examining Stevenson's responses to the Alps, one realizes how dependent his imagination and style were upon the repositioning of his body in a landscape as well as upon the character of the scenery about him. For Stevenson, physical movement is an act of perception. In this respect, Stevenson's experience illustrates what several contemporary psychologists, other than Merleau-Ponty, have recently noted: that consciousness is closely allied to physical motion.[8]

Stevenson was a traveler who loved the open roads and turbulent seas where one moves from place to place and cruises from island to island – hence, his pleasures when, a few years earlier in 1878, he had rambled through central-southern France with his donkey Modestine. Stevenson would have identified with Stephen's pleasure in walking tours that elicit a "delightful sensation of

---

[8]   See, for instance, R.F. Port and T. Van Gelder's *Mind as Motion: Exploration in the Dynamics of Cognition* and Alvin Noë's *Action in Perception*.

independence and detachment" (*Studies of a Biographer* 3: 241), and he would have recognized the truth in Stephen's observation that during such an activity, "you trust your own legs, stop when you please, diverge into any track that takes your fancy, and drop in upon some quaint variety of human life at every inn when you put up for the night" (3: 241–42). Among the Alps, an enclosed Stevenson did not feel such freedom; the surrounding mountains were all about him "like a trap" (*Essays* 167). There was no route to cut over the field and walk at will. The paths at Davos were prescribed by others; there were no unexpected nooks or crannies and no outlook. The enclosing mountains cut off what lay behind them. The layout of the landscape simply did not match what he called his "old gipsy nature" (Colvin 2:27). Two years earlier when he had been walking in the Cévennes, he had, more or less, determined his own route and moved through the landscape: followed a steep slope, ascended a pass, reached a summit, descended, and continued his journey, each time finding a new prospect and a slightly different landscape or solving the mystery of what lies beyond. As he asserted in his account of the trip: "the great affair is to move" (*Travels with a Donkey* 35). Moreover, while traveling in the Cévennes, Stevenson had not been subjected to the invariable and trite sameness of the winter snow that eradicated the infinite variety and subtleties of his surroundings. Walking in the south of France, he could think of advancing beyond his own limits and raising his eyes "above the summit" and seeing, like Cortez, "a new quarter of the world" (*Travels with a Donkey* 62). Trapped in Davos, that prospect was impossible.

Writing and the Moving Body

As these sentiments and the tobogganing example imply, the act of moving the body through a landscape was necessary to the way Stevenson related to his surroundings, and, hence, as I am proposing, fundamental to his writing. Often when he became animated, he rose and walked about as he spoke, a phenomenon that John Singer Sargent's familiar painting of him and Fanny captures. Words and language emerged from the mobility and gestures of his physical being. In a sense, I am suggesting that his texts should be regarded as the space between the landscape and the body. If the physical being is the mediator of our relation to what lies beyond it, then, when the body is shut off from such stimulation (as was Stevenson's during that first winter), neither language nor meaning can materialize. Davos, where there was no freedom of passage, offered no motivation and no resources with which to fashion a sentence on a page. For Stevenson to pass through a landscape and, hence, to engage change was to find his way through a text. As Stevenson wrote in his 1875 essay "An Autumn Effect," "Clear vision goes with the quick foot" (*Essays* 103).

Stevenson's prose written before he first went to Davos registers the footprints of a writer who wanders, crosses, or saunters through the countryside. One feels the body stirring and simultaneously composing. As one can see in the quotation that follows, sentences emerge: thoughts and words move along their winding roads, and present participles push the essays forward. Active verbs bring the texts as well as the landscape to life as if they were moving, swelling, and rising. The difference, for instance, between the styles of his 1876 fragment, "A Winter's Walk in Carrick and Galloway" and his 1880 "Davos in Winter" is striking. In the earlier piece, an unhindered Stevenson, journeying through the lowlands of Scotland, responds to the shifting and variable scene. The sentences briefly rest in qualifying details that momentarily arrest the motion and let the reader see shadows in the dells and farms scattered here and there among the contours of the rising hill. The resulting irregular spaces invite metaphors that open up his consciousness and take him beyond what is directly before the eye. Notice how the blanket of snow, contrary to what Stevenson was to experience in Davos, is consequently a positive and comforting image. In the following passage from "A Winter's Walk," one can sense just how the movement associated with the hilly landscape, as it "rises," "swells out, and "loses itself," parallels in some way the onward movement of the observer and the accumulative, onward motion of the prose itself:

> At the famous bridge of Doon, Kyle, the central district of the shire of Ayr, marches with Carrick, the most southerly. On the Carrick side of the river rises a hill of somewhat gentle conformation, cleft with shallow dells, and sown here and there with farms and tufts of wood. Inland, it loses itself, joining, I suppose, the great herd of similar hills that occupies the centre of the Lowlands. Towards the sea, it swells out the coastline into protuberance, like a bay-window in a plan, and is fortified against the surf behind bold crags...
>
> It had snowed overnight. The fields were all sheeted up; they were tucked in among the snow, and their shape was modeled through the pliant counterpane, like children tucked in by a fond mother. The wind had made ripples and folds upon the surface, like what the sea, in quiet weather, leaves upon the sand ...
>
> Over the white shoulders of the headlands or in the opening of bays, there was nothing but a great vacancy and blackness; and the road as it drew near the edge of the cliff seemed to skirt the shores of creation and void space. (*Essays* 124)

In contrast, the style and content of "Davos in Winter," written during his first stay in the Alpine valley, fail to move beyond the static tedium of what is in front of him. Although Stevenson attempts to slide away from the bleak, repetitious monotony of the dull, blank snow, he is compelled to return to where he began and stare at "fields of white and blots of crude black forest" that are anything but nurturing to his imagination:

> Snow, it is true, is not merely white. The sun touches it with roseate and golden lights. Its own crushed infinity of crystals, its own richness of tiny sculpture, fills it, when regarded near at hand, with wonderful depths of coloured shadow, and, though wintrily transformed, it is still water, and has watery tones of blue.

But, when all is said, these fields of white and blots of crude black forest are but a trite and staring substitute for the infinite variety and pleasantness of the earth's face. (*Essays* 165)

Subjected to the Davos landscape, the feeling of exciting anticipation that had pervaded Stevenson's prose in his *Travels with a Donkey* disappears. When the author had earlier wound his way through the Cévennes and through the upper Gevaudan, the movement of his body had elicited perception: "Hill and valley followed valley and hill" and "the little green and stony cattle-tracks [had] wandered in and out of one another, [had] split into three or four, died away in marshy hollows, and [had begun] again sporadically on hillsides or at the borders of a wood" (*Travels with a Donkey* 25). Here, there had been the pleasure of a prolonged expectancy – the kind of delight Stevenson mentioned in another of his 1870s essays, "Roads" (1873), that offers, through a route's "subtle windings and change of level ... a continuous interest that keeps the attention ever alert and cheerful" (*Essays* 188).

Pools in the River

During the first winter in Davos, in addition to being affected by the snow-covered landscape and the restricting mountains, Stevenson was also distressed by the continuous, unalterable roar of the river (*Davoser Landwasser*) that falls down the Davos valley: "A certain furious river runs curving down the valley; its pace never varies, it has not a pool for as far as you can follow it; and the unchanging senseless hurry is strangely tedious to witness. It is a river that a man could grow to hate" (*Essays* 162). The unceasing noise of the water was as debilitating to his writing as were the blankets of snow that eradicated any subtlety of experience and blocked any sense of change.

When Stevenson wrote to a friend, A.G. Dew-Smith, who had sent him a present of a box of cigarettes – Stevenson smoked throughout his sickness – he enclosed a poem in which he revealed his utter impatience with this river. In the first few verses, he especially emphasizes that the river does not ever pause. It does not know "the comfort of a pool":

A river that from morn to night
　　Down all the valley plays the fool;
Not once she pauses in her flight
　　Nor knows the comfort of a pool;

But still she keeps up, by straight or bend,
　　The selfsame pace she hath begun –,
Still hurry, hurry, to the end –
　　Good God, is that the way to run?

> If I a river were, I hope
>   That I should better realize
> The opportunities and scope
>   Of that romantic enterprise.
>
> I should not ape the merely strange,
>   But aim besides at the divine;
> And continuity and change
>   I still could labour to combine.
>
> Here should I gallop down the race,
>   Here charge the sterling like a bull;
> There, as a man might wipe his face,
>   Lie, pleased and panting, in a pool. (Colvin 2: 11–12)

Embracing change and movement, Stevenson longed for interruption and shifts in the rhythm of its flow, especially for those pools where all settles for a moment before carrying on. The playful poem says something about Stevenson's style and demonstrates, once more, how important the landscape was to the way he wrote. I surmise that the tedious river, reflected in the regular iambic tetrameters of the first stanzas: "Good God, is that the way to run?" contradicts what he attempted to replicate in his style of writing, where the sentences not only move in delicate gradations and pause in pools of meaning but also progress through brusque juxtapositions, irregularities, or even through outlandish uses of words. In any case, there is a break in the tedium or regularity that continuously revives his prose. Just as when he traveled in the Cévennes, and Modestine had "refreshed her feet" (*Travels with a Donkey* 64) in a pool formed from a stream that had crossed the track, so do his sentences break their continuity for a moment by submerging themselves in reviving figures of speech or by dipping into images that invigorate meaning. Sentences emerge as the footpath meanders. One is free to look one way toward the beaten path and then shift one's gaze toward the hedge. The "continuity and change" Stevenson so desired in his poem to his friend becomes possible. A few lines from his essay "Roads" illustrate the point:

> The road rolls upon the easy slopes of the country, like a long ship in the hollows of the sea. The very margins of waste ground, as they trench a little farther on the beaten way, or recede again to the shelter of the hedge, have something of the same free delicacy of line – of the same swing and willfulness. You might think for a whole summer's day (and not have thought it any nearer an end by evening) what concourse and succession of circumstances has produced the least of these deflections; and it is, perhaps, just in this that we should look for the secret of their interest. (*Essays* 188–89)

Here there is the typical Stevenson mixture of irregularity combined with restful moments: for instance, the unexpected word "trench" and the forced pause between the unusual sequence "this that" stand close to the more relaxed alliteration of "The road rolls" and the interlocking alliteration and assonance of "same swing and willfulness." The combination of this irregularity with these restful moments in this description of the landscape do as much to empower Stevenson's prose as did the pockets of water that break the flow of the changeful and delicate river in which Stevenson had longed to immerse his tired body on a hot day while traveling through the Cévennes (*Travels with a Donkey* 65). These alterations and interruptions are like what Stevenson once identified in his essay "On Some Technical Elements of Style in Literature" (1885) when he remarked that each sentence moves through successive phrases that come into a "kind of knot" (marked by a pause) that suspends meaning and brings the pleasure of expectation before they reach their conclusion: "In every properly constructed sentence there should be observed this knot or hitch; so that (however delicately) we are led to foresee, to expect, and then to welcome the successive phrases" (*Essays* 38).

From time to time, Stevenson constructed his essays by prefacing his subject with a vivid reminder of a watercourse's irregular path that occasionally drifts into soothing pools of meaning – an opening that reflects the irregular and unpredictable flow of ideas in the essay itself. For instance, he opens "The Manse" by recalling the pools and eddies within the dammed Leith River (*Memories and Portraits* 106–107). The water's motions, to and fro upon the surface, help him find his way back to memories of his grandfather, as well as to the revered crannies of his own childhood. Stevenson's recollections of his grandfather flow in and out of the river's interrupted streams. Similarly in "Pastoral," the current and hesitations of the lowland waters preface and lead Stevenson to his portrait of John Todd, "the oldest herd on the Pentlands" (*Memories and Portraits* 93). Dependent upon these watercourses to "inspire [his] pen" (93), Stevenson returns through his imagination to

> Tummel, or Manor, or the talking Airdle, or Dee swirling in its Lynn; on the bright burn of Kinnaird or the golden burn that pours and sulks in the den behind Kingussie! ... I may not forget Allan Water, nor birch-wetting Rogie, nor yet Almond; nor, for all its pollutions, that Water of Leith of the many and well-named mills – Bell's Mills, and Canon Mills, and Silver Mills; nor Redford Burn of pleasant memories; nor yet, for all its smallness, the nameless trickle that springs in the green bosom of Allermuir, and is fed from Halkerside with a perennial teacupful, and threads the moss under the Shearer's Know, and makes one pool there, overhung by a rock, where I loved to sit and make bad verses, and is then kidnapped in its infamy by subterranean pipes for the service of the sea-beholding city in the plain. (91–92)

The irregular list of names, the variety of activities ("talking," "swirling," "pours," "sulks"), the repetition and variation ("the bright burn ... the golden burn") – all imitate the chaotic assortment of the rivers' flow. The chain of clauses devoted to "the nameless trickle" imitates the slow and interrupted course of the water it describes, and a syntactic pause coincides with the description of a lull in the river's flow and moments of pause in the life of the writer. The essay takes its shape or voice from these moments.

The monotonous pace of the *Davos Landwasser* lacked the sweet and quickening effect associated with the rivers of home. Its unrelenting swiftness found no correspondence in the rhythms of Stevenson's writing. No wonder that Stevenson complained in a letter to Colvin (spring, 1881): "like a violin hung up, I begin to lose what music there was in me" (Colvin 2: 27). Without variety and pauses in the Alpine world surrounding him, there was no melody within. A few years after leaving Davos, Stevenson published his thoughts about the sympathy between music and literature in which he suggested that one writes in groups or phrases that are divided by gaps between continuous sound. Literature and music contrive their patterns through designs of "sounds and pauses" (*Essays* 38). As Stevenson recognized, the thundering roar of the falling water at Davos silenced such patterns of sound in his writing. Once more the landscape was involved in inscribing and shaping the text – this time in a negative way.

As I have suggested, only within a changing and unfolding topography of contrast could Stevenson find pleasure in the mountain landscape. Therefore, previously in August, 1879 as an amateur and suffering emigrant to America, riding mile after mile on the train that crosses "a deadly" and paralyzed land (*The Amateur Emigrant* 212), the relief of seeing the mountain ranges and watching a cascade somewhere near at hand as well as noticing the trout pools among the mountain rivers had been immense and wonderful.[9] Here the mountains had represented hope and opportunity of a new life, unlike the sterility that Stevenson was to experience a couple of years later in the Alps. As long as he could know the mountains in the context of a changing landscape, he was able to admire them – perhaps sense their sublimity. Earlier, when Stevenson had walked through the vales and mountains of the Cévennes, he had recognized the power of the mountains with "cliffy battlements and here and there a pointed summit" (*Travels with a Donkey* 77). He had even been prompted to think of Byron and marvel at "the monstrous ribs and gullies of the mountain" that are illuminated by the moon (*Travels with a Donkey* 89).

---

[9]   Soon after *Travels with a Donkey* was published (July, 1879), Stevenson left home to join Fanny Osbourne, who was living in California. He had met her about a year earlier at an artists' colony in France. The journey across the Atlantic Ocean and then across America by train was arduous. Stevenson fell dangerously ill. With help he recovered, and eventually married Fanny.

After Davos

After Stevenson left Davos in the spring of 1881 – he departed against doctor's orders – he gradually felt better, moved to Pitlochry, in the Highlands of Scotland, and started writing. Now he was surrounded by a landscape that stimulated his imagination and moved his pen. In a June, 1881 letter to Colvin, Stevenson wrote: "My health improves. We have a lovely spot here: a little green glen with a burn, a wonderful burn, gold and green and snow-white, singing loud and low in different steps of its career, now pouring over miniature crags, now fretting itself to death in a maze of rocky stairs and pots; never was so sweet a little river ... Sweet spot, sweet spot" (Colvin 2: 36–37). Again in July, he wrote to Edmund Gosse that he was "enjoying his first decently competent and peaceful weeks for close upon two years; happy in a big brown moor behind him, and an incomparable burn by his side; happy, above all, in some work – for at last I am at work with that appetite and confidence that alone makes work supportable" (Colvin 2: 43). Removed from the unvaried topography of Davos in winter, he could regain his impulse to compose and could once more hear the melody that had been lacking in the uninterrupted roar of the *Davoser Landwasser*. The irregular flow of the rivers and streams ran through his pages and set the rhythm of his prose in motion.

Unfortunately, in August 1881, the hemorrhaging that had first sent Stevenson to Davos returned; he had no choice but to go back the following winter.[10] Persuaded that the mountain air would be beneficial – if not lifesaving – he stayed seven months. This time, though, he was less discontented. He became more prolific, actually writing forty thousand words. He composed the latter half of *Treasure Island* and, among other things, the entire rough draft of *The Silverado Squatters*, a book that describes his and his wife's life in the California mountains shortly after their wedding in May 1880. Now, a second time in Davos, he knew what to expect; he understood that he could leave; he no longer lived at the invalid hotel, but at a rented chalet on a hillside near the Symonds – their "society is my great stand-by" (Colvin 2:71). But most important of all, as W.G. Lockett points out, the winter was considerably milder – indeed, Stevenson complained that, at times, it was too hot. In November 1881 he wrote to W.E. Henley that the "weather has been hot and heartless and un-Davosy" (Colvin 2: 70). The monotonous snow that had obliterated his words and enclosed him physically and imaginatively now sat lightly on the surrounding mountains that were as accessible as in the warmer seasons. That winter, the Schiahorn (8,900') which reared up immediately behind the resort, was, at midwinter, as easy to ascend as in summer (Lockett 95). Now the sameness of the blankets of snow had gone. There were only pockets of snow in the occasional gully, and with that liberation. Stevenson could hear the music within him; the rhythms of change and contrast returned; they beat out the

---

[10]   Stevenson returned to Davos in the autumn of 1881 and remained there until mid-spring 1882.

fluctuating fortunes of the characters in *Treasure Island* and let the ambivalence hailing from and surrounding Long John Silver's person resonate.

Such was the difference in Stevenson's point of view during the second winter that when he composed his rough draft of *The Silverado Squatters*, he was free to recall how he had gazed upon Mount Saint Helena, the "Mont Blanc of one section of the Californian Coast Range" (*The Silverado Squatters* 7), and admit that he had found the sight to be satisfying. Although that mountain had stayed the progress of the railroad, in his mind, it no longer obstructed the passage of his prose. Though enclosing, the mountain (on looking back) was seen as part of a variable landscape:

> And there was something satisfactory in the sight of the great mountain that enclosed us to the north: whether it stood, robed in sunshine, quaking to its topmost pinnacle with the heat and brightness of the day; or whether it set itself to waving vapors, wisp after wisp growing, trembling, fleeting, and fading in the blue. (*The Silverado Squatters* 14)

From this perspective, the looming stature of Mount Saint Helena never obliterated the varying plains of fog and light. Nor did it eradicate, within its sphere of influence, the contented, quiet image of a "cow stretched by the roadside, her bell slowly beating time to the movement of her ruminating jaw" (*The Silverado Squatters* 15). Furthermore, even if the mountain's surroundings had become a place for consumptives, "a kind of small Davos" (*The Silverado Squatters* 66), the landscape's hilltops did not imprison Stevenson, but rather functioned as crossing places through which people journeyed. During his second winter at Davos, Stevenson could refresh himself by recalling that, in Silverado, he had dipped a "gray metal pail into the clean, colorless, cool water" and carried the spring water back while watching "a broken sunbeam quivering" in its midst (*The Silverado Squatters* 86). Stevenson was able once more to find, if only in memory, those pools that rejuvenated and reflected the topography of his prose.

Part III
Coda

Geoffrey Hastings. "Nanga Parabat, 8,125m. Punjab Himalaya" (1895)

Part III

Coda

Geoffrey Hastings, *A Vision of Parbate, c.12,5??, Punjab Himalaya* (1895)

Coda: The Himalaya and the Persistence of the Sublime

My wanderings cover a period of nineteen years, during which I have not been able to do more than pierce these vast ranges, as one might stick a needle into a bolster, in many places; for no one can lay claim to a really intimate knowledge of the Himalaya alone, as understood in the mountaineering sense at home.

(C.G. Bruce, *Twenty Years in the Himalaya* v)

The Himalaya is a mass greater than all the mountains of Europe, including the Caucasus, put together. Set down its western end at London, and its eastern end would reach almost to Moscow.

(Kenneth Mason, *Abode of Snow* 4)

The Himalaya

In 1854, when Frances Isabella Duberly accompanied her officer husband to the Crimea, she briefly resided on board the *Himalaya*, anchored 160 miles from Sebastopol. That a naval vessel stationed in the Black Sea should bear the name of these remote Central Asian mountains demonstrates the extent to which the Himalaya belonged to the imperial imagination and had become an integral part of the campaign to establish, extend, or test the borders of the British Empire. Ever since the early part of the nineteenth century, when British officers in northern India had encouraged soldiers and had eventually trained pundits (Indians in the service of the British), between 1865 and 1885, to survey and map the high passes and peaks of the Indian Himalaya, the tactical importance of these mountains, including the vast glacial system of the Karakoram range, had become increasingly significant. If the imperialistic project were to succeed and Britain extend its political and economic power, these mountains *must be pierced* (Younghusband 184).

As early as 1818, two officers of the Indian army, William Lloyd and Alexander Gerard, had reached more than 19,000 feet. Their accomplishment was at the time unusual, but a few decades later, scores of mapmakers and surveyors in the course of their task were to match their achievement and to reach heights that most climbers in the Alps would have thought almost impossible. The Himalaya that separated British territory from hostile forces in Nepal or Chinese-controlled Tibet were especially important in the building of empire. From the early part of the century on, naturalists, sportsmen, missionaries, or adventurers as well as border commissioners (often disguised as merchants, fakirs, or "Mussalmen") had crossed the Himalaya in attempts to explore and secretly map these forbidden lands. With difficulty and at enormous risk, they had sometimes penetrated into Nepal and Tibet, territories that were either permanently or periodically closed to the British. All, in their own way, were interested in establishing a footing and extending their influence beyond the established boundaries. As a result, by the mid-1850s, when Mrs. Duberly was on board the *Himalaya* and on her way to Balaklava, most of these giant mountains had been named and numbered, and their heights determined trigonometrically.

These early explorations into the Himalaya naturally caught the attention of the Alpine climbers who, searching for new challenges and places unspoiled by the polluting multitudes crowding the all-too familiar regions, were already "Mountaineering Beyond the Alps" (Freshfield, "Mountaineering Beyond the Alps" 290–316) and ascending peaks in such places as Norway, Japan, Africa, North America, and South America.[1] In particular, the Alpine Club was eager to be associated with this new territory – perhaps to satisfy the organization's own imperialistic fantasies as well as to show off its members' mountaineering skills. In the 1870s, officers of the organization conjectured: "The day will undoubtedly come when mountain-climbing will extend to the Himálaya, and our Club will have 'sections' at Simla and Calcutta." They advised: "English Alpine climbers, blessed with time and money, would do well to reflect that Simla is now only 3½ days from Bombay, or 3 weeks from England." ("Review and Notices," *The Alpine Journal* 7 [1875]: 341). Almost a decade later Major J.W.A. Mitchell addressed the Alpine Club and proposed sponsoring an expedition to the Himalaya. He declared: "I see no reason why an expedition to the Himalayas, under the auspices of the Alpine Club, should not succeed, even if an attempt were made to scale Kinchinjunga (altitude 28,156 feet)" (Mitchell, "Twenty Years' Climbing and Hunting in the Himalayas," *The Alpine Journal* 11 [1883]: 215). Around the same time some members expressed interest in helping out with the training of those who were mapping the region. The idea that these soldier-surveryors' mountaineering skills and techniques could be improved by Alpine experience, however, was not always welcomed. In "Himálayan and Alpine Mountaineeering" Douglas Freshfield reported that the recommendation that survey officers could benefit from the tutelage of Alpine guides was "taken in very bad part by persons of many years' experience in Himálayan travel and residence in India" – particularly by W. Robert of the Sikkim Survey (*The Alpine Journal* 12 [1884]: 99).[2] Robert was merely an

---

[1]   For instance, Douglas W. Freshfield went to the Caucasus in 1868; Edward Whymper to the Andes in 1871, Elizabeth Le Blond to Norway in the 1880s, and Edward A. Fitzgerald to South America in order to climb Aconcagua in 1896.

[2]   In "Himálayan and Alpine Mountaineering," Douglas W. Freshfield points out that W. Robert of the Sikkim survey cast doubt on one of the member's Himalayan climbs, and claimed that W. W. Graham, who had gone to the Himalaya for the purpose of climbing, had never made the ascent he described. From Robert's point of view, Graham's ascent of

assistant surveyor to H.C.B. Tanner, an army officer, but apparently Robert did most of the actual work.[3]

Given the Alpine Club's desire to be attached to the Himalaya and all its challenges, it was not long before its members were paying attention to W.H. Johnson's series of spectacular climbs in the 1860s. As a member of the Kashmir survey team, Johnson often went above 20,000' and slept at 22,000'. It was only a matter of time before people like W.W. Graham, accompanied by his Swiss guides, would come specifically to climb – and not to survey – as well as to incur risks that few had confronted.[4] In 1883 Graham went to northern India more for sport and adventure than for the advancement of scientific knowledge. His example reminded his fellow climbers of the remarkable possibilities that were available to them. By the 1890s, other well-known mountaineers, such as Douglas W. Freshfield, J. Norman Collie, Geoffrey G. Hastings, William Martin Conway, and A.F. Mummery, all well known for their Alpine feats, mounted ambitious expeditions – one sponsored by the Royal Geographical Society – and attempted difficult ascents. (On 24 August 1895, Mummery and two Gurkhas were killed in an attempt to reach the 26,630' peak of Nanga Parbat – the ninth highest mountain in the world. Their bodies were never recovered.)

These mountaineers soon found that conditions were just not the same as those experienced elsewhere. Even the trivia of a climb altered. If something got lost or damaged, whether insignificant or momentous, there was absolutely no means of replacing it – of descending a few thousand feet or retracing a few miles to buy or find what had been spoiled or misplaced. Odd though it may seem, now, instead of casually pausing to admire the view while taking a gentlemanly puff from one's pipe, as one often did on an Alpine ascent, one sometimes had desperately to shape a pipe out of snow – in Cowley Lambert's case this inadequate substitute for his lost pipe lasted long enough for him to gain a few precious puffs (Lambert 50). Members of the Conway expedition also ran into trouble when their cigarette paper got soaked; eager for a smoke, they pried tissue from the top of medicine bottles and used it for rolling their tobacco (McCormick 103).[5] By the turn of the century, though, in spite of these rather minor annoyances as well as far more serious difficulties, such as horrendous weather, diarrhea, accidents, altitude sickness, and even ruined or burned boots (a result of trying to dry them on a fire), many more attempts, some of which had been successful, had been made. Among

---

Kabru was nothing but a fiction, that he had mistaken a neighboring ridge for the real thing (see *The Alpine Journal* 12 [1884]: 99–108).

[3]   See Derek John Waller's *The Pundits: British Exploration of Tibet and Central Asia*, 188.

[4]   Graham was accompanied by M. Décle, a French member of the Alpine Club as well as by Joseph Imboden, his Swiss guide, who became homesick and left. Imboden was replaced by two other familiar Swiss guides: Emil Boss and Ulrich Kauffman.

[5]   In his book about climbing and exploring with William Martin Conway in the Himalaya, A.D. McCormick describes their desperate attempts to roll a cigarette.

these are ascents accomplished by the Americans Fanny Bullock Workman and William Hunter Workman (he was a member of the Alpine Club) who made six expeditions among the higher Himalaya in the northern frontier of India. In 1906 Fanny Bullock Workman, as I mentioned in Chapter 3, reached the highest point ever attained. Their book *The Call of the Snowy Hispar* (1910) describes these Himalayan adventures

A climb in the Himalaya was more like a campaign than an Alpine mountaineering expedition, requiring hundreds of sheep, horses, and porters (some of whom could be rebellious and unsuited to the demands of the journey) as well as a prodigious amount of supplies and time. Leslie Stephen, perhaps jealous of these new exploits, poked fun at Asian mountaineering, which seemed to him much more like a military expedition or a Gargantuan scientific experiment than a sport (Stephen, *Men, Books, and Mountains* 10). There were, of course, no day trips or one-night stays in mountain huts in the Himalaya. Even the approach to the mountains was prolonged, for, rather than starting almost immediately upon an ascent, as one did in the Alps, surveyors, naturalists, and climbers in the Himalaya had to walk and scramble for long dreary days of unbroken routine and endure severe night frosts in order to begin an ascent, and then had to face a series of steep passes before reaching their destination.[6] And death was more visible: frozen carcasses of horses that had fallen over steep precipices, skeletons of traders who had missed their footing, and at 13,500', the dead body of a boy who had been working for the Anglo-Indian army with its survey of a particular pass. Much to J.G. Gerard's disappointment, his field notebook with the measurements was not to be found:

> We came upon the body of the little boy who carried the field-book and all the
> papers of the route. He was half buried under the snow. He lies at 13,500 feet. We
> searched in vain for traces of the books, so that they are for ever lost. This being
> a chief object of my tour, and one I had much at heart, it made me look forward
> to the rest of it with less interest, but I had determined to ascertain the correct
> elevation of the cave, and continued descending. (Lloyd and Gerard 314)

Gerard's pragmatic reporting of the boy's demise reveals how common death in the mountains was.

Many informative studies have been written about these earlier scientific and later climbing expeditions. Among these, Kenneth Mason's 1955 *Abode of Snow: A History of Himalayan Exploration and Mountaineering* gives one a thorough sense of the history. And most recently, Maurice Isserman and Stewart Weaver's *Fallen Giants: A History of Himalayan Mountaineering* (2008) offers engaging,

---

[6] If I may insert a personal note here, in 1982, it took me two strenuous weeks to walk, up and down, in an attempt to reach the foothills of Ganesh Himal in Nepal. I ran out of time and had to turn round and face another two weeks' walk back to the road where I was going to be picked up.

indeed riveting, accounts of some of these early climbs within their cultural and historical context. In addition, the early surveyors, adventurers, missionaries, and entrepreneurs published narratives, detailing the particulars of their experiences. (The bibliography at end of this book offers but a glimpse of the numbers of books written about the Himalaya in the nineteenth century. It is interesting to note that one publisher, William Longman, was a founding member of the Alpine Club.)

The Raw Sublime

In this closing chapter, though, I am not interested in either repeating or contributing to this well-documented and often complex history. Rather, I want to concentrate upon the sublime as experienced by those who ventured into the Himalaya during the second half of the nineteenth century. Challenged by so much physical difficulty and preoccupied with the arduous and exacting task of surveying these mountains, did these explorers ever find a moment or an opening in which to register any sensitivity to the grandeur around them? Given their circumstances, was the sublime relevant? And what was their sense of it?

Invariably and for good reasons, when one reads about these early years of exploration in the Himalaya, one's attention is drawn toward the struggles for British control of certain regions, and to the nation's subsequent efforts to map this unwieldy mountain range so as to know it strategically as well as geographically – as Robert Macfarlane observes, "to gain logistic power over it" (186). But what gets lost in this inevitable concentration upon conquest and control, or upon Britain's "imperial project" in the Himalaya, is the aesthetic sensibility that accompanied it. Forgotten is the reality that these explorers were frequently overwhelmed by the sheer sublimity of their surroundings. At the same time as these nineteenth-century adventurers were measuring, surveying, and battling high altitudes as well as finding stocks of local people ("coolies") willing to carry their equipment, or dealing with the difficulties of hostile tribal groups, they were also enthralled by the "stupendous grandeur of the view ... overwhelming in its magnitude" (Tanner, "The Great Peaks of the Himalaya," *The Alpine Journal* 12 [1886]: 446).

Reading through accounts of their journeys among the Himalaya, from William Lloyd and Alexander Gerard's 1841 *Narratives of a Journey from Caunpoor to the Boorendo Pass in the Himalaya Mountains* all the way to William Martin Conway's 1894 *Climbing in the Himalaya: Maps and Scientific Reports*, and A.D. McCormick's 1895 *An Artist in the Himalaya*, or Frank E. Younghusband's 1896 *The Heart of the Continent*, one realizes that these individuals were as much guided by an aesthetic sensibility that encouraged them to respond to the way the light played upon the landscape as well as to yield to the stern, solitary, oppressive, and mysterious vastness of the mountains as they were involved in the project at hand and "the glory of our Empire" (Knight 528). Amidst the trials of his midsummer ramble in the Himalaya, J.F. Cheetham, who kept a sketchbook that is now in the Alpine Club Archives, took time to linger and look toward the north where "the mist, lifting for a moment, disclosed ... a striking glimpse of sunshine lighting up a deep and most desolate valley, across which rose wild rocky mountains too steep and smooth for the most part to hold much snow" (Cheetham, "The Tibetan Route from Simla to Srinágar," *The Alpine Journal* 3 [1867]: 129). Cheetham was an accomplished explorer who, in the summer and autumn of 1859, led an expedition through Tibet. This trek lasted from 4 July to late September and took him over many difficult passes, including Larsa (17,750'), Lunga Larch (16,750'), Bara Lacha (16,500'), and Photo La (13,600').[7]

Contrary to what most might believe, the imperial imperative did not necessarily negate or replace the sublime tradition. Indeed, in some strange way, the two were linked. On the one hand, the sublime not only legitimized but also added glory and force to the authority of their effort to define and extend the borders of empire. In a sense, the majesty and sheer power of the mountains reflected the grandeur of Britain's strength and reach. Yet, on the other hand, contrary to what Mary Louise Pratt suggests in her *Imperial Eyes*, this aesthetic dimension also detracted from these explorers' sense of mastery or domination, and, paradoxically stood side by side as a humbling moment in which the very force and immense scale of the surroundings put these invaders in their place. They were, consequently, never really part of a "Master-of-all-I-survey" scene.[8] The sublime might reflect the strength of empire but, simultaneously, it also subdued such self-congratulatory thoughts by reducing the viewer to scale and reminding him of his own littleness. There was no way to possess such a landscape. As a result, William Martin Conway might open his book on exploring and climbing in the Karakoram-Himalaya by speaking about the "prestige of England's imperial power," but soon his attention is absorbed by the overpowering scene before him: "It was beyond all comparison the finest view of mountains it has ever been my lot to behold ... I forgot headache, food, everything, in the overwhelming impression the majestic scene produced upon me" (Conway 377–78). Conway, and other surveyors before and after them, felt themselves in the presence of something larger that may have reinforced their sense of power but also, paradoxically, humbled them.

Throughout the nineteenth century narratives and diaries of exploration in the Himalaya pay homage to the sublime. At mid-century, the concept was an active force in Joseph Dalton Hooker's *Himalayan Journals*, chronicling his 1849 botanical expedition in Sikkim and the Nepal Himalaya. His diary is replete with expressions of awe for the "stupendous ice-crowned precipices that shot up to the summit" (244). Hooker exclaims: "I have never before or since seen anything which for sublimity, beauty, and marvelous effects could compare with what I gazed on that evening from Choonjerma pass." Attempting to compare the play of light on the scene to a Turner painting and to a series of magic-lantern slides, he adds:

---

[7] A watercolor sketch from J.F. Cheetham's trek can be seen in Peter Mallalieu's *The Artists of the Alpine Club*, 30–31.

[8] For a discussion of "The Monarch-of-all-I-see" genre or scene, see Mary Louise Pratt's *Imperial Eyes: Studies in Travel Writing and Transculturation*, 201–208.

In some of Turner's pictures I have recognized some effects, caught and fixed by a marvelous effort of genius; such are the fleeting hues over the ice, in his "Whalers," and the ruddy fire in his "Wind, Steam, and Rain," which one almost fears to touch. Dissolving views give some idea of the magic creation and dispersion of the colours, but any combination of science and art can no more recal [*sic*] the scene, than it can the feelings of awe that crept over me, during the hour I spent in solitude amongst these stupendous mountains. (254)

Hooker is defeated. He cannot master the scene, as Pratt suggests others did, by *estheticizing* the landscape or painting it (Pratt 204). Not even Turner could possess it fully.

Even when fatigue was overwhelming, the sublime could overcome the individual. When F.D. Brocklehurst traveled the Sooroo Route from Leh to Cashmere in 1861, he remarked that the amazing mountain peaks, computed to be at least 23,600', "quite riveted our attention, jaded as we were with the fatigue of a very rough twenty-four miles' march; nor could we cease from gazing at it till darkness overshadowed everything, and it faded out of sight like some mysterious dissolving view" (Brocklehurst, "The Sooroo Route from Leh to Cashmere," *The Alpine Journal* 4 [1869]: 198).

At the end of the century, the sublime was still very much a part of explorers' accounts. In Younghusband's 1896 *The Heart of a Continent*, the sense of awe of being among the "stately mountains" is a constant companion, even when he is determined to "pierce" their seemingly impregnable array (184). This sensitivity goes with him. When he fails in his search for the Shimshal Pass, a place no European has been near, he finds consolation and satisfaction through his aesthetic response to the landscape. The presence of the sublime has eradicated thoughts of his own mastery and, for the moment, altered his perspective:

But though I had not found the pass I was seeking, I could never regret spending those six days on the glacier in the heart of the mountains. The glacier itself was marvellously beautiful, and the mountains from which it flowed, and which towered above it, formed the main range of the Himalayas ... When I can free my mind from the overpowering sense of grandeur which the mountains produce, and from the thoughts of the stern hard work we had to go through ... I think of the beauty of that glacier scenery, the delicate transparency of the walls of ice, the exquisite tinting of the blues and greens ... and the pinnacles of ice, as forming a spectacle unsurpassed in its purity of loveliness. Other scenes are beautiful, and yet others are impressive by their grandeur ... But it is high up among the loftiest mountain summits, where all is shrouded in unsullied whiteness, where nothing polished dares pollute, that the very essence of sublimity must be sought for. It is there indeed that the grand and beautiful unite to form the sublime. (250–51)

And it was the sublime that kept pulling the ambitious Workmans back into the Himalaya. In their *The Call of the Snowy Hispar*, they explain:

With the conclusion of our Nun Kun Expedition in 1906 we thought we had
finished our work of exploration among the higher Himalayas. We had borne
the expense, the heat, the burden, the responsibilities and trials, and had been
rewarded by the pleasures and successes, of five expeditions among its [*sic*] ice-
clad peaks and glaciers, and had no intention of undertaking a sixth.

   But we had breathed the atmosphere of that great mountain-world,
had drunk of the swirling waters of its glaciers, and feasted our eyes on the
incomparable beauty and majesty of its towering peaks, and, as time passed, its
charms asserted their power anew and called to us with irresistible, siren strains
to return yet once again to those regions, the grandeur of which satisfies so fully
the sense of the beautiful and the sublime. (1)

The sublime, which had elsewhere diminished and fallen hostage to tourism,
commerce, familiarity, social pressures, and personal vanity or ambition, especially
in the Alps, was still available in the Himalaya – as one explorer noted, "without the
cockney element" (Webber 74). A new sense of space, scale, distance, proportion,
and shape did more than recall the earlier, pristine days of traveling in the Alps;
it also exceeded that experience and intensified or altered these individuals' sense
of the sublime. As if these Himalayan adventurers not only trespassed and crossed
political as well as physical boundaries when traversing the mountain passes, they
also entered a territory, where, as two early surveyors observed, "sublimity sits
filtered to desolation" (Lloyd and Gerard 143). The result was a raw and immediate
sense of the concept that not only recalled the earliest Alpine experiences but also
fixed attention on the unknown, the stern, desolate landscape, as well as on the
melancholy of the endless snows. There was no escaping from it, and no gossip at
the *table d'hôte* to censor or muffle it. Completely surrounded by an overwhelming
sense of the greatness of dimension and feelings of astonishment and potential
doom, these surveyors and climbers, in spite of all their technical, martial, and
scientific apparatus, reverted to the state of mind that had been experienced in
the presence of mountains before mountaineering had become a way of life and a
sport – before commercialism and empire had compromised their imagination.

   Making their way through the labyrinths of passes and immense, jagged
peaks, they came face to face with the very exemplars of Edmund Burke's theory.
Among the Himalaya, their understanding of the vastness, the awe, the chaos, the
danger, and the apparent infinity transcended any example of these qualities they
had known before, even among those who, later in the century, had arrived with
international experience. Whether surveying or climbing, these nineteenth-century
explorers were to experience the sublime again as something more intense and
immediate. Outside the authority of their own culture, they did not need to elicit
the mediation of the Romantic poets nor did they have to recall Longinus's words
to help them sense the sublimity before them. They had come to a culture that did
not depend upon the matrix of clichés and pre-formed ideas; it was as if they were
looking at a mountainous landscape for the first time. They had journeyed to a
space that was alien to any they had known before. As A.D. McCormick remarked

in 1895: "The feeling of strangeness never quite left me through all the journey" (19). He and others who ventured into the bleak and imposing interior had moved into a different dimension, exemplified, in part, by the pragmatic fact that the indigenous people measured distance in ways that were alien to Westerners. Some of their guides determined the length of a journey according to the number of times they stopped to smoke,[9] and the explorers themselves occasionally calculated the length of an area they had walked by counting beads hidden within prayer wheels – especially when they were in Chinese Tibet and were having not only to disguise themselves as holy men but also to hide the fact that they were mapping the hostile territory (see Mason 86).

So strong was the sense of crossing a boundary into another reality that even though they were engaged in systematic mapping, those who were doing the work felt that the region was actually too large and unwieldy to survey. At the turn of the century, C.G. Bruce was quick to explain that he had not been able, during his nineteen years in the Himalaya, "to do more than pierce these vast ranges, as one might stick a needle into a bolster, in many places; for no one can lay claim to a really intimate knowledge" of them (v).[10] In many respects, these surveyors and early climbers had moved away from anything that was recognizable. Mummery's attempts in the late 1890s to treat the Himalaya as an outsized version of the Alps only made him more vulnerable to its dangers. (He was crushed under the force of an avalanche while he was attempting to reach the summit of Nanga Parbat.) The experience with European ranges was not applicable to this new and alien territory.

But, in spite of this disturbing reality, many Westerners chose to describe their surroundings by comparing them to the Alps simply because this was their closest available frame of reference. As if to bring their raw experience of the sublime into their own familiar world and come to terms with this new and threatening sense of scale and proportion, these Victorian adventurers turned to the familiar to help them deal with the untried and the mysterious. This practice not only helped them communicate these mountains' character to the readers of their narratives but also offered them, personally, a metaphor for what otherwise might be elusive or too oppressive. The examples are numerous. James Atkinson in his 1839–40 *The Expedition into Afghanistan* recalls how the ground was "cracked in various large shapes, and the openings so wide and deep as to render it dangerous to walk over in the dark ... The deep irregular fissures in the alluvial soil produced by the heat of the sun, furnished me with a miniature resemblance of the *Mer de Glace* at

---

[9] William Simpson remarks: "The coolies in this region do not measure distance by 'cos' (miles), but by 'choories,' or so many smokes, because they take a smoke at each rest. They do not use pipes, but make a hole in the ground, and another hole connected with it, by which they suck through the smoke" ("List of Marches from the Ganges, near Maicha, to Chini; Also from Simla to Chini, And from Chini through Tibet to Cashmere," *The Alpine Journal* 7 [1875]: 260).

[10] C.G. Bruce, who taught soldiers and pundits climbing techniques, knew the region especially well, and, furthermore, was fluent in Nepalese.

Chamouni, in Switzerland" (69). Several years later, W.W. Graham, in an account of his recent expedition continues the convention when he frames his entire article on travels and ascents in the Himalaya by comparing the height of the mountains, the length of its glaciers, and the depth of its gorges to those found in the Alps. To stress just how astonishing the Himalaya are, he reminds his Alpine Club readers of the obvious fact that this Central Asian range "exceed[s] all Alpine rivals in extent and number as they do in height" ("Travel and Ascents in the Himálaya", *The Alpine Journal* 12 [1884]: 27). Their "peaks are wild and savage in the extreme" (28). He adds, the Matterhorn is a "mere dwarf" next to these giants (41).

Throughout the literature, comparisons between the height of Mont Blanc and a particular peak or mountain pass are common. It is not unusual to find a writer using the expression "I was now about the height of Mont Blanc." In *Among the Himalaya* (1898), L.A. Waddell asks his readers to "imagine Mont Blanc rearing its full height abruptly from the sea-shore, bearing on its summit Ben Nevis, the highest mountain in Great Britain, and above all that, two Snowdons, one on the top of the other" (34). In the same decade, E.F. Knight remarked: "even the very valley-bottoms are higher above the sea than the summit of Mont Blanc" (183). And in the late 1890s, when Annie Taylor was traveling through the Himalaya on her way to Tibet, she gave her audience a similar sense of the height of the pass she had just climbed by observing that it was "one of the easiest and lowest" and was "nearly as high as Mont Blanc" (Carey 25).

Height was not the only point of comparison between the two ranges. Many accounts also attempted to come to terms with the vastness of the Himalaya (unlike the populous Alps) by focusing on the utter sense of isolation in the Himalaya, the lack of a panoramic view – so admired and sought after in the Alps, the tangle or labyrinth of inexhaustible peaks, and the absence of established routes, reliable maps, discernible names, or inns to orient and comfort the traveler. Henry Strachey's 1853 article in the *Journal of the Royal Geographical Society* speaks of the barbaric, oblique, and inaccessible Himalaya that shut out all extended views: "On ascending the highest passes, we can seldom see anything but a contracted view of mountain tops on all sides, looking very like chaos: no general view of the range under our feet is ever obtainable" (Strachey 28 [1853]: 22).

In the Himalaya, one must readjust to a new sense of space and leave the Alpine scales behind. J. Norman Collie's reaction is typical: "That which in winter on a Scotch hill would be a slide of snow, and in the Alps an avalanche, becomes amongst these giant peaks an overwhelming cataclysm shaking the solid base of the hills, and capable with its breath alone of sweeping down forests" (2). And William Martin Conway remarks: "In no part of the Alps is there anything like the amount of rock ruin" (235). Later he notes: "The Aiguilles of Chamonix are wonderful, and possess a grace of outline all their own; but these needles outjut them in steepness, outnumber them in multitude, and outreach them in size" (386).

Having been repeatedly conquered, measured, and named, the Alps suffered from a sense of limit and order. In addition, they lacked the overwhelming monotony of the Himalaya, for glorious vegetation broke the dullness, and expanses of deep blue water or grand waterfalls cut through meadows and fell from the crags. Furthermore, the mountains were a spectacle with observers; a climber was rarely out of view or away from contact with a human element. But, of course, this was not possible in the Himalaya, where one can easily be a two-week walk away from a road. As Conway put it, the Himalaya are "Things wasting their splendour where there is none to admire" (276). Leslie Stephen's 1894 review of Conway's book summed up many of these differences:

> In the good old days an Alpine expedition meant a walk from a comfortable inn, a stiff climb or so up a peak of reasonable size .. perhaps, a night passed in a chalet or possibly on the rocks, and then a return with heightened appetite to a good *table d'hôte*, and a delicious evening talk, in which we recounted our performances with such modesty as we could command to like-minded friends. To travel half around the world ... to organize a whole army of porters and a system of supplies ... may be a good investment of energy; but it does not at present suggest a new sport accessible to the tired barrister or the university don in his vacation. It will be a long time before K2 will be as accessible as Mont Blanc is at present. (Stephen, *Men, Books, and Mountains* 209)

It was this isolation that protected the Himalaya and made it possible, even in the late-nineteenth century for Europeans to feel again the presence of the *Ur*-sublime, for want of a better word, in its original, most intense state. Aware, though, that an infusion of tourists could spoil and compromise this experience, no matter how chaotic, threatening, and gloomy the Himalaya could be, those who had worked in and traveled to India, Tibet, Afghanistan, and Nepal worried that one day too many visitors would come. Anxiously they awaited their invasion – an incursion that for some was possibly more threatening than the Russian presence and Chinese hostility. Fearing that one day the Himalaya would be spoiled as the Alps had been, they predicted: "this track will ere long be trodden ground" (E.G. Wilson 1). And, indeed claiming that it is usually the Englishman who has led the way, and that the love of travel and sport is an inherited characteristic of the nation, officials such Sir Richard Temple and Major Mitchell did warmly encourage tourists "to try" the Himalayas (Mitchell, "Twenty Years of Climbing and Hunting in the Himalayas," *The Alpine Journal* 11 [1883]: 205) – an invitation that Alpine Club members thought premature in the 1880s, even though they were among those who thirsted for fresh fields of adventure.

Other than the climbers, surveyors, missionaries (Annie Taylor and Isabella Bishop [Bird]), and naturalists, as well as eccentrics (an American was seen bicycling his way through the Himalaya), the occasional tourist did explore the Himalaya, especially those who were stationed at posts in northern India. Among these were Mrs. Hervey, Constance Frederick Gordon Cumming, Bruce's wife (she wrote "Camp Life from a Lady's Point of View"), and Elizabeth Sarah Mazuchelli, who, in the 1870s, with her husband, a chaplain with the Anglo-Indian army, took a two months' tour into the interior of the eastern Himalaya. It is significant that as early as the late 1870s, when Mazuchelli was reflecting upon these travels, she wondered: "Was it likely that these beautiful solitudes would remain uninvaded much longer?" She was, as she writes, "haunted by tourist apparitions" – a fear that seems extraordinary at this time. She imagines:

> I saw hosts of them bearing down upon us: English tourists, hot and eager, Murray and alpenstock in hand; lanky American tourists come *to do* the Himalayas, singing "U-pi-dee"; lively French tourists, shouting "*Vivent les Alpes Indiennes!*" heavy Prussians and German students, with ponderous spectacles on nose – undemonstrative but admiring, *Ach Himmel! Wie wunderschön!* With frequent, prolonged, and deeper mutterings of "*Ja wohl*" ... poetic Italian tourists, with large grave eyes, gazing in silent wonder. On they came – they came – and still they came, till the most distant tourist was but a mere speck on the horizons. (102)

If we can forgive her stereotyping, we have to admit that Mazuchelli's prediction unfortunately turned out to be correct. If anyone has recently been in Kathmandu searching for a place to eat in the polluted air and crowded, filthy streets, has attempted to trek the Annapurna circuit, has even set out on routes to less popular destinations, such as Ganesh Himal, he or she will readily recognize the aptness of Mazuchelli's fantasy. The sublimity associated with the Himalaya has been diminished or, at least, compromised, by international commercialization and by the garbage and dead bodies in various states of decay above Camp IV on Mt. Everest.[11] It is strange to think, a mountain that had just barely been identified, measured, and named by the mid-nineteenth century should now be soiled and the subject of eco expeditions that attempt to pick up the tons of refuse left on its slopes. Perhaps the contemporary public's outrage about these conditions speaks to a persistent desire for the sublime. If so, this longing would link us to those early nineteenth-century explorers, in both the Alps and the Himalaya, who responded to a reality that was at once vast, isolated, astonishing, and risky.

---

[11]   There are a number of websites dedicated to informing readers about the amount of garbage on Mt. Everest. See, for instance, "From Conquering to Cleaning up Mt. Everest" from *The Christian Science Monitor* 30 May 2003, <http://www.csmonitor.com/2003>

Bibliography

Adams, James Eli. *Dandies and Desert Saints: Styles of Victorian Manhood.* Ithaca: Cornell University Press, 1995.

Adams, William Davenport. *Celebrated Women Travellers of the Nineteenth Century.* New York: E. P. Dutton, 1903.

Adams, William H. *Alpine Climbing: Narratives of Recent Ascents of Mont Blanc; the Matterhorn, the Jungfrau, and other Lofty Summits of the Alps.* London: T. Nelson and Sons, 1881.

Addison, Joseph. "The Pleasure of the Imagination." *Spectator.* Ed. Donald F. Bond. Oxford: Clarendon Press, 1965. 3–412.

Adorno, Theodor W. *The Culture Industry: Selected Essays on Mass Culture.* London: Routledge, 1991.

Adult Health Advisor 2005.4: "Eye Flashes and Floaters." University of Michigan Health System. 25 Apr 2008. <http://www.med.umich.edu/1libr/aha/aha_flashflo_oph.htm.>

Adventures of the Economical Family. London: Larner and Blackbourn, 1873.

"Aesthetics among the Alps." *Blackwoods Magazine* 8.491 (Mar 1851): 272.

Allbutt, T. Clifford. M.A., M.D. "On the Health and Training of Mountaineers." *The Alpine Journal* 8 (1876): 30–40.

Alpine Club Archives

"The Alpine Club Exhibition of Pictures and Photographs, 1892." By C.D. [Clinton Dent]. *The Alpine Journal* 16 (1893): 342–47.

"The Alpine Court at the Liverpool Jubilee Exhibition." *The Alpine Journal* 13 (1887): 337–40.

"Alpine Notes." *The Alpine Journal* 5 (1871): 274–79.

"Alpine Notes." *The Alpine Journal* 9 (1879): 297–311.

"Alpine Notes." *The Alpine Journal* 14 (1888): 162–72.

"Alpine Notes." *The Alpine Journal* 15 (1890): 323–32.

Altick, Richard. *The Shows of London.* Cambridge, MA: Harvard University Press, 1978.

Alvarez, Al. "Getting High on the Himalayas." *New York Review of Books* 56:11 (2 Jul 2009): 27–29.

Anderson, Eustace. *Chamouni and Mont Blanc: A Visit to the Valley and an Ascent of the Mountain in the Autumn of 1855.* London: James Cornish, 1856.

Andrews, Malcolm. *The Search for the Picturesque: Landscape Aesthetics and Tourism in Britain, 1760–1800.* Stanford: Stanford University Press, 1989.

Arata, Stephen. "Realism" in *The Cambridge Companion to the Fin de Siècle.* Ed. Gail Marshall. Cambridge: Cambridge University Press, 2007. 169–87.

Armstrong, Isobel. *Victorian Glassworlds: Glass Culture and the Imagination 1830–1880*. Oxford: Oxford University Press, 2008.

"The Ascent of Mont Blanc." *The Illustrated London News* 22 (25 Dec 1852): 565.

Atkinson, James. *The Expedition into Afghanistan: Notes and Sketches Descriptive of the Country Contained in a Personal Narrative during the Campaign of 1839 & 1840, up to the Surrender of Dost Mahomed Khan*. London: W.H. Allen & Co., 1842.

Auldjo, John. *Narrative of an Accent to the Summit of Mont Blanc*. 2nd edn. London: Longman, Rees, Orme, Brown, and Green, 1830.

Austin, Linda M. "Aesthetic Embarrassment: The Reversion to the Picturesque in Nineteenth-Century English Tourism." *ELH* 74 (2007): 629–53.

Baedeker, Karl. *Switzerland and the Adjacent Portions of Italy, Savoy, and Tyrol: Handbook for Travellers*. Leipzig: Karl Baedeker Publisher, 1911.

Bain, Alexander. *The Senses and the Intellect*. Ed. Daniel N. Robinson. Vol. 4. Washington, DC: University Publications of America, 1977.

Ball, Patricia M. *The Science of Aspects: The Changing Role of Fact in the Work of Coleridge, Ruskin and Hopkins*. London: The Athlone Press, 1971.

Ballantyne, R.M. *Rivers of Ice*. [1875] Kessinger Publishing. www.kessinger.net

Band, George. *Summit: 150 Years of the Alpine Club*. London: Collins, 2006.

Banfield, Marie. "Darwinism, Doxology, and Energy Physics: The New Sciences, the Poetry and the Poetics of Gerard Manley Hopkins." *Victorian Poetry* 45.2 (2007): 175–94.

Barnes, G.S. "The Dents des Bouquetins." *The Alpine Journal* 13 (1888): 529–38.

Barry, Martin. *Ascent to the Summit of Mont Blanc in 1834*. Edinburgh: William Blackwood & Sons, 1836.

Baudrillard, Jean. *The Spirit of Terrorism and Other Essays*. London: Verso, 2002.

Beacham, Richard C. *Spectacle Entertainment of Early Imperial Rome*. New Haven: Yale University Press, 1999.

Beattie, William. *Switzerland: Illustrated in a Series of Views Taken on the Spot and Expressly for this work by W.H. Bartlett*. London: George Virtue, 1836.

Beecroft, Mrs. and Miss [Laura]. MS 6338. "Journal of a Tour to France and Switzerland." National Library of Scotland.

Beer, Gillian. "Helmholtz, Tyndall, Gerard Manley Hopkins: leaps of the prepared imagination." *Comparative Criticism* 13 (1992): 117–45.

"Bell." *Haps and Mishaps of the Simpleton Family Abroad*. London: Simpkin, Marshall, & Co., 1863.

Bell, Gertrude. The Gertrude Bell Archive. http://www.gerty.ncl.ac.uk/letters

Bellanca, Mary Ellen. *Daybooks of Discovery: Nature Diaries in Britain, 1770–1870*. Charlottesville: University of Virginia Press, 2007.

Bernard, Paul P. *Rush to the Alps: The Evolution of Vacationing in Switzerland*. New York: Columbia University Press, 1978.

Bernstein, Jeremy. *Ascent: Of the Invention of Mountain Climbing and its Practices* New York: Random House, 1965.

Bicknell, John W., ed. *The Selected Letters of Leslie Stephen.* 2 Vols. 1882–1904. Houndmills: Macmillan, 1996.

Birchall, Heather. "Contrasting Visions: Ruskin – The Daguerreotype and the Photograph." *Living Pictures: The Journal of the Popular and Projected Image before 1914* 2.1 (2003): 2–20.

Blunt, Alison and Gillian Rose. *Writing Women and Space: Colonial and Postcolonial Geographies.* New York: The Guildford Press, 1994.

Bodenheimer, Rosemarie. *Knowing Dickens.* Ithaca: Cornell University Press, 2007.

Bonney, Professor T.G. "Address." *The Alpine Journal* 11 (1884): 373–82.

Boorstin, Daniel J. *The Image: A Guide to Pseudo-Events in America.* New York: Harper & Rowe, 1961.

"A Boy's Ascent of Mont Blanc." *The Boy's Birthday Book: A Collection of Tales, Essays, and Narratives of Adventure.* London: Published for the Proprietors, 1864. 9–145.

[Bradford, Louisa Mary]. *Journal of a Tour in the Pyrenees During the Summer of 1872.* Liverpool: David Marples, Melvill Chambers, Lord Street, 1873.

Brockedon, William. *Journals of Excursions in the Alps: The Penine, Graian, Cottian, Rhetian, Lepontian, and Bernese.* London: James Duncan, 1845.

Brocklehurst, F.D. "The Sooroo Route from Leh to Cashmere." *The Alpine Journal* 4 (1869): 193–203.

Brown, Rebecca A. *Women on High: Pioneers of Mountaineering.* Boston: Appalachian Mountain Club Books, 2002.

Browne, Rev. G.F. "How We Did Mont Blanc." *Cornhill Magazine* (1865): 717–31.

Bruce, C.G. *Twenty Years in the Himalaya.* London: Edward Arnold, 1910.

A Budget of Letters or Things Which I Saw Abroad. Boston: William D. Ticknor and Company, 1847.

Bump, Jerome. "Hopkins' Drawings," *All My Eyes See: The Visual World of Gerard Manley Hopkins.* R.K.R. Thornton. Sunderland: Ceolfrith Press, 1973. 69–87.

"Bunny." *A Holiday Tour; Being a Few Weeks Passed among the Swiss and Italian Lakes.* London: William Brown & Co., 1868.

Burd, Van Akin, ed. *The Ruskin Family Letters: The Correspondence of John James Ruskin, His Wife, and Their Son, John 1801–1843.* 2 vols. Ithaca: Cornell University Press, 1973.

Burford, Robert. *Description of a View of Mont Blanc, the Valley of Chamounix, and the Surrounding Mountains, now exhibiting at the Panorama, Leicester Square.* London: T. Bretell, 1837.

Burke, Edmund. *A Philosophical Enquiry into the Origin of Our Ideas of the Sublime and the Beautiful. The Longman Anthology of British Literature,* 3rd ed. Gen. Ed. David Damrosch."The Romantics and their Contemporaries." Ed. Susan Wolfson and Peter Manning. 2A: 33–39. New York: Longman, 2006.

Butler, Samuel. *The Way of All Flesh.* Ed. James Cochrane. London: Penguin Books, 1966.

Buxton, E.N. "The Glaciers of the Bernina." *The Alpine Journal* (Sep 1864) 343–45

Buzard, James. *The Beaten Track: European Tourism, Literature, and the Ways of Culture, 1800–1918.* Oxford: Clarendon Press, 1993.

Carey, William. *Miss Annie R. Taylor's Remarkable Journey from Tau-Chau to Ta-Chien-Lu Through the Heart of the Forbidden Land.* London: Hodder and Stoughton, 1902.

Chater, William. "Switzerland 1865." MS Diary. Thomas Cook Archives.

Cheetham, J.F. "The Tibetan Route from Simla to Srinágar." *The Alpine Journal* 3 (1867): 118–53.

Cheever, George B. *The Pilgrim in the Shadow of the Jungfrau Alp.* New York: Wiley & Putnam, 1846.

Clark, Ronald. *The Victorian Mountaineers.* London: B.T. Bradford, 1953.

[Cole, Mrs. H.W.] *A Lady's Tour Round Monte Rosa: with Visits to the Italian Valleys of Anzaica, Mastalone, Camasso, Sesia, Lys, Challant, Aosta, and Cogne. In a Series of Excursions in the Years 1850–56–58.* London: Longman, Brown, Green, Longmans, and Roberts, 1859.

Coleridge, Samuel Taylor. *The Complete Poetical Works of Samuel Taylor Coleridge including Poems and Versions of Poems now Published for the First Time.* Ed. Ernest Hartley Coleridge. 2 Vols. V. 1: The Poems. Oxford: Clarendon Press, 1912.

Coleridge, Samuel Taylor. *Coleridge's Verse: A Selection.* Ed. William Empson and David Price. London: Faber and Faber, 1972. See "Chamouny; the Hour before Sunrise," 197–200.

Colley, Ann C. "Gerard Manley Hopkins and the Idea of Mapping," *The Search for Synthesis in Literature and Art: The Paradox of Space.* Athens: The University of Georgia Press, 1990. 67–100.

Colley, Ann C. "Recent Studies in the Nineteenth Century." *Studies in English Literature* 48 (Autumn 2008): 935–1010.

Collie, J. Norman. *Climbing in the Himalaya and Other Mountain Ranges.* Edinburgh: David Douglas, 1902.

Colvin, Sidney, ed. *The Letters of Robert Louis Stevenson.* V. 2 (1880–87). New York: Charles Scribner's Sons, 1911.

Conway, Derwent. *Switzerland, the South of France and the Pyrenees.* V. 1 of *Constable's Miscellany of Original and Selected Publications in the Various Departments of Literature, Science, and the Arts.* V. 66. Edinburgh: Constable & Co., 1831.

Conway, Martin. "How to Climb the Alps." *Daily Chronicle* (30 Dec 1893). Scrapbook, Alpine Club Archives.

Conway, William Martin. *Climbing and Exploration in the Karakoram-Himalaya.* London: T. Fisher Unwin, 1894.

Conway, William Martin. *Climbing in the Himalaya: Maps and Scientific Reports*. London: T. Fisher Unwin, 1894.

Cook's Tourist's Handbook: Switzerland via Paris. London: Thomas Cook & Son, 1874.

Coolidge, W.A.B. "Alpine Games." *The Alpine Journal* 14 (1888): 61–63.

Copjec, Joan. *Read My Desire: Lacan against the Historicists*. Cambridge, MA: MIT Press, 1994.

Cowell, J.J. Esq. "The Graian Alps and Mount Iseran." *Vacation Tourists and Notes on Travel in 1860*. Ed. Francis Galton. Cambridge: Macmillan & Co., 1861. 239–63.

Crane, J. Miriam, ed. *Swiss Letters and Alpine Poems by the Late Frances Ridley Havergal*. London: James Nisbet & Co., n.d., [1881].

Crary, Jonathan. "Modernizing Vision." *Vision and Visuality*. Ed. Hal Foster. Seattle: Bay, 1988. 29–48.

Crary, Jonathan. "Spectacle, Attention, Counter-Memory." *October* 50 (autumn, 1989): 96–107.

Crary, Jonathan. *Techniques of the Observer: On Vision and Modernity in the Nineteenth Century*. Cambridge, MA: MIT Press, 1991.

Curiosities of Modern Travel: A Year Book of Adventure. London: David Bogue, 1847.

Davidson, Lillias Campbell. *Hints to Lady Travellers at Home and Abroad*. London: Iliffe & Son, 1889.

Dearden, James S. "General Physical Appearance." *John Ruskin: A Life in Pictures*. Sheffield: Academic, 1999. 4–11.

De Beer, G.R. *Alps and Men: Pages from Forgotten Diaries of Travellers and Tourists in Switzerland*. London: Edward Arnold & Co., 1868.

Debord, Guy. *The Society of the Spectacle*. Trans. Donald Nicholson-Smith. New York: Zone Books, 1994.

Dent, C. [Clinton] T. "The Rothhorn from Zermatt." *The Alpine Journal* 6 (1873): 268–74.

Dent, Clinton [T.]. *Above the Snow Line: Mountaineering Sketches between 1870 and 1880*. London: Longmans, Green, and Co., 1885.

Dent, Clinton [T.]. "The Search Expedition to the Caucasus." *The Alpine Journal* 14 (1889): 432–36.

Dent, Clinton [T.]. "Presidential Address to the Alpine Club." *The Alpine Journal* 15 (1890): 3–16.

Dent, C. [Clinton] T. *Mountaineering*. 3rd ed. London: Longmanns, Green, and Co., 1900.

De Selincourt, Ernest, ed. *William Wordsworth: The Prelude; or the Growth of a Poet's Mind*. 2nd ed. rev. Helen Darbishire. Oxford: Clarendon Press, 1959.

Dickens, Charles. "Foreign Climbs." *All the Year Round* 2 (Sep 1868): 135–37.

Dickens, Charles. *David Copperfield*. Introd. Jeremy Tambling. London: Penguin Books, 1996.

Donkin, W.F. "Photography in the High Alps." *The Alpine Journal* 11 (1882): 63–71.

Doyle, Richard. *The Foreign Tour of Messrs Brown, Jones, and Robinson: Being the History of What they Saw and Did in Belgium, Germany, Switzerland, & Italy.* London: Bradbury, Evans, & Co., 1855.

"'An Easy Day for a Lady': Lily Bristow's Letters written while climbing with A.F. Mummery in 1893." *The Alpine Journal* 53 (1942): 370–74.

Edwards, Amelia B. *A Midsummer Ramble in the Dolomites.* London: George Routledge and Sons, 1889 [1873].

Engel, Claire-Elaine. "Early Lady Climbers." *The Alpine Journal* 54 (1943): 51–59.

Evans, Joan. *John Ruskin.* New York: Oxford University Press, 1954.

The Excurtionist. "Mount Cenis Train." 8 (1868): 8.

Eye Advisor 2007.2: Flashes and Floaters. 25 Apr 2008. <http://www.fairview.org/healthlibrary/content/ea_flashflo_oph.htm>

"Fatal Accidents in the High Alps." *The Alpine Journal* 11 (1882): 86–89.

"Fatal Accident to Irish Ladies in Switzerland." *The Alpine Journal* 2 (1866): 367–68.

Fedden, Robin. "Russell and the Vignemale." *The Alpine Journal* 65 (1960): 80–84.

Feeney, Joseph J., S.J. "His Father's Son: Common Traits in the Writing of Manley Hopkins and Gerard Manley Hopkins." *Gerard Manley Hopkins and Critical Discourse.* Ed. Eugene Hollahan. New York: AMS Press, 1993. 277–92.

Fellows, Jay. *The Failing Distance: The Autobiographical Impulse in John Ruskin.* Baltimore: Johns Hopkins University Press, 1975.

Fisher, Alden F., ed. *The Essential Writings of Merleau-Ponty.* New York: Harcourt, Brace & World, Inc., 1969.

Fitzsimons, Raymond. *The Baron of Piccadilly: The Travels and Entertainments of Albert Smith 1816–1860.* London: Geoffrey Bles, 1967.

Freedgoood, Elaine. *Victorian Writing about Risk: Imagining a Safe England in a Dangerous World.* Cambridge: Cambridge University Press, 2000.

Freshfield, Douglas W. "Himálayan and Alpine Mountaineering." *The Alpine Journal* 12 (1884): 99–108.

Freshfield, Douglas W. "Mountaineering Beyond the Alps." *Mountaineering.* Ed. C.T. Dent. London: Longmans, Green, and Co., 1900. 290–316.

[Freshfield, Mrs. Henry]. *Alpine ByWays or Light Leaves Gathered in 1859 and 1860.* By a Lady. London: Longman, Green, Longman, and Roberts, 1861.

Frith, Henry. *Ascents and Adventures: A Record of Hardy Mountaineering in Every Quarter of the Globe.* London: George Routledge and Sons, 1884.

Frow, John. *Time and Commodity Culture: Essays in Cultural Theory and Postmodernity.* Oxford: Oxford University Press, 1997.

Furby, Miss J. [Mary Jane]. "Switzerland and Italy 1877" MS Diary. D.8. Thomas Cook Archives.

Galton, Francis. "The Avalanche of the Jungfrau." *The Alpine Journal* 1 (1863). 184–88.

Gardner, W.H. *Gerard Manley Hopkins: A Selection of his Poems and Prose.* Harmondsworth: Penguin Books, 1958.

Gates, Barbara T. *Kindred Nature: Victorian and Edwardian Women Embrace the Living World.* Chicago: University of Chicago Press, 1998.

"Gay Man Climbs Mount Everest in Mink & High Heels." *Weekly World News: America's Extreme Magazine* 11 Apr 2005: 36–37.

Gaze, Henry. *Switzerland: How to See It for Ten Guineas by One Who Has Done It.* London: W. Kent & Co. n.d.

George, H[ereford]. B[rooke]. *The Oberland and its Glaciers: Explored and Illustrated with ice-axe and Camera, with twenty-eight photograph illustrations by Ernest Edwards and a map of the Oberland.* London: Alfred W. Bennett, 1866.

George, H[ereford]. B[rooke]. "Notes on Photography in the High Alps." *The Alpine Journal* 4 (1870): 402–10.

Gernsheim, Helmut and Alison. *L.J.M. Daguerre: The History of the Diorama & the Daguerreotype.* London: Seeker& Warburg, 1968.

Gittings, Christopher E., Ed. *Imperialism and Gender.* London.: Dangaroo Press, 1996.

"Good News for Cockney Travellers." *Punch* 27 (Jul–Dec 1854): 110.

Graham, W.W. "Travel and Ascents in the Himálaya." *The Alpine Journal* 12 (1884): 25–52.

Gray, Thomas. "Journal in a Letter to Dr. Wharton, October 18th 1769." Thomas West. *Guide to the Lakes.* 2nd edn. London, 1780. 199–204.

Green, Muriel M., ed. *A Spirited Yorkshirewoman: The Letters of Anne Lister of Shibden Hall, Halifax, b. 1791–d. 1840.* 1939.

Greenwood, Grace [Sarah Jane Lippincott]. *Haps and Mishaps or a Tour in Europe.* London: Richard Bentley, 1854.

Grierson, Janet. *Frances Ridley Havergal: Worcestershire Hymnwriter.* Worcester: The Havergal Society, 1979.

Grierson, Rev. Thomas. *Autumn Rambles among the Scottish Mountains or Pedestrian.* Edinburgh: Paton and Ritchie, 1850.

Grove, F.C. "Address to the Alpine Club." *The Alpine Journal* 13 (1887): 213–20.

Guide to Cook's Tours in France, Switzerland and Italy. London: Thomas Cook Tourist Manager, 1865.

A Hand-Book of Mr. Albert Smith's Ascent of Mont Blanc. Illustrated by Mr. William Beverley. 4th ed. London: Saville & Edwards, 1858.

Hansen, Peter Holger. "Albert Smith, the Alpine Club, and the Invention of Mountaineering in Mid-Victorian Britain." *The Journal of British Studies* 34.3 (1995). 300–24.

Hansen, Peter Holger. "British Mountaineering, 1850–1914." Dissertation. Department of History, Harvard University, 6 Sep 1991.

Hawkins, F. Vaughn. "Partial Ascent of the Matterhorn" in *Vacation Tourists and Notes on Travel in 1860*. Ed. Francis Galton. Cambridge: Macmillan & Co., 1861.

Hayman, John, ed. *John Ruskin: Letters from the Continent 1858*. Toronto: University of Toronto Press, 1982.

Heard, C.G. MS "Diary of Mr. C.G. Heard: Switzerland and Italy 1865." Thomas Cook Archives.

Heath, R.C. "Letter Diary of R.C. Heath" (Typescript). Alpine Club Archives.

Helsinger, Elizabeth. *Ruskin and the Art of the Beholder*. Cambridge, MA: Harvard University Press, 1982.

Hinchliff, Thomas W. *Summer Months among the Alps: with the Ascent of Monte Rosa*. London: Longman, Brown, Green, Longman, & Roberts, 1857.

Hobday, Stephen Reginald. MS "The Call of the Mountains" [1896] [1899]. Alpine Club Archives.

Hood, Thomas. "An Assent to the Summut of Mount Blank." *Comic Annual*. London: Charles Tilt, 1839. 49–55.

Hooker, Joseph Dalton. *Himalayan Journals, Notes of a Naturalist in Bengal, the Sikkim and Nepal Himalaya, the Khasia Mountains etc.* New ed. 2 Vols. London: John Murray, 1855.

Hopkins, Gerard Manley. *Further Letters of Gerard Manley Hopkins*. Ed. Colleer Abbott. London: Oxford University Press, 1938.

Hopkins, Gerard Manley. *The Journals and Papers of Gerard Manley Hopkins*. Ed. Humphry House. Completed by Graham Storey. London: Oxford University Press, 1959.

Hopkins, Gerard Manley. *The Letters of Gerard Manley Hopkins to Robert Bridges*. Ed. with notes and an introduction by Claude Colleer Abbott. London: Oxford University Press, 1959.

Hopkins, Gerard Manley. *Poems of Gerard Manley Hopkins*. Ed. W.H. Gardner and N.H. MacKenzie 4th edn. Oxford: Oxford University Press, 1967.

Hopkins, Gerard Manley. *The Early Poetic Manuscripts and Note-Books of Gerard Manley Hopkins in Facsimile*. Ed. Norman H. Mackenzie. New York: Garland Publishing, Inc., 1989.

Horkheimer, Max and Theodor W. Adorno. *Dialectics of Enlightenment*. Trans. John Cumming. New York: Herder and Herder, 1969 [1944].

H.[Hornby], E.[Emily]. *Mountaineering Records*. Liverpool: J.A. Thompson, 1907.

How We Did Them in Seventeen Days! To Wit: Belgium, the Rhine, Switzerland, and France. Described and Illustrated by One of Ourselves [i.e. Richard Marrack]*; Aided, Assisted, Encouraged, and Abetted by the Other* [i.e. Edmund G. Harvey]*!* Truro: Lake and Lake, n.d. [1876].

"How, When and Where? Or, The Modern Tourist's Guide to the Continent." *Punch* 31 Oct 1863: 182.

Hunt, John Dixon. *The Wider Sea: A Life of John Ruskin*. New York: Viking, 1982.

Hyde, Ralph. *Panoramania: Art and Entertainment of the All-Embracing View.* London: Trefoil association with Barbican Art Gallery, London, 1988.

Ingham, Vivien. "Anne Lister's Ascent of Vignemale." *The Alpine Journal* 73 (1968): 199–206.

Isabella Bird Catalogue Spring 2005.

Isserman, Maurice and Stewart Weaver. *Fallen Giants: A History of Himalayan Mountaineering.* New Haven: Yale University Press, 2008.

Jackson, Mrs. E.P. "A Winter Quartette." *The Alpine Journal* 14 (1889): 200–210.

James, Sir William. *The Order of Release: The Story of John Ruskin, Effie Gray and John Everett Millais Told for the First Time in Their Unpublished Letters.* London: John Murray, 1947.

Jones, E.D. Wynne. *General Description of My Late Tour through France, Switzerland and Germany.* Rhyl: J. Morris, 1867.

Kant, Immanuel. *Critique of Judgement.* New York: Hafner Publishing Company, 1972.

Keenlyside, Francis. *Peaks and Pioneers: The Story of Mountaineering.* London: Paul Elek, 1975.

Kemble, Frances Anne. *The Adventures of Mr. John Timothy Homespun in Switzerland.* Full Text <http://lion.chadwyck.com:8085/frames/drama>

King, H. Seymour. "The First Ascent of the Aiguille Blanche de Peuteret." *The Alpine Journal* 12 (1886): 431–38.

King, Rev. S.W. *The Italian Valleys or the Penine Alps: A Tour through all the Romantic and less-frequented "Vals" of Northern Piedmont, from the Taventaise to the Gries.* London: John Murray, 1858.

Knight, E.F. *Where Three Empires Meet: A Narrative of Recent Travel in Kashmir, Western Tibet, Gilgit, and the Adjoining Countries.* London: Longmans, Green, and Co., 1894.

Kracauer, Siegfried. "Sport as Spectacle; Swimming in Victorian and Edwardian Britain." *Cahiers victoriens & edouardien* 59 (2004): 101–16.

Lambert, Cowley. *A Trip to Cashmere and Ladâk.* London: Henry S. King, 1877.

Leaf, Walter. "Climbing with a Hand-Camera." *The Alpine Journal* 15 (1891): 472–79.

[Le Blond, Elizabeth] Mrs. Fred Burnaby. *The High Alps in Winter, or, Mountaineering in Search of Health.* London: Sampson Low, Marston, Searle, & Rivington, 1883.

[Le Blond, Elizabeth] Mrs. Fred Burnaby. *High Life and Towers of Silence.* London: Sampson Low, Marston, Searle, & Rivington, 1886.

[Le Blond, Elizabeth] Mrs. Aubrey Le Blond. *True Tales of Mountain Adventure for Non-climbers Young and Old.* London: T. Fisher Unwin, 1903.

[Le Blond, Elizabeth] Mrs. Aubrey Le Blond/ Mrs. Main. *Adventures on the Roof of the World.* London: T. Fisher Unwin, 1904.

[Le Blond, Elizabeth] Mrs. Aubrey Le Blond. *Mountaineering in the Land of the Midnight Sun.* London: Fisher Unwin, 1908.

[Le Blond, Elizabeth] Mrs. Aubrey Le Blond. *Day In, Day Out*. London: John Lane the Bodley Head Limited, 1928.

[Le Blond, Elizabeth] Mrs. Main. *Hints on Snow Photography*. London: Sampson Low, Marston & Company, n.d.

Leslie, Marion. "Women Mountaineers." *The Woman at Home* 1903: 310–19.

Lever, Charles. *The Dodd Family Abroad*. New York: Harper & Brothers, 1854.

Levine, George. *The Realistic Imagination: English Fiction from Frankenstein to Lady Chatterly*. Chicago: The University of Chicago Press, 1981.

Lloyd, Major Sir William and Captain Alexander Gerard. *Narrative of a Journey from Caunpoor to the Boorendo Pass in the Himalaya Mountains*. London: J. Madden & Co., 1841.

Lockett, W.G. *Robert Louis Stevenson at Davos*. London: Hurst & Blackett, Ltd. n.d.

Longinus. "On the Sublime." *The Great Critics: An Anthology of Literary Criticism*. Ed. James Harry Smith and Edd Winfield Parks. New York: W.W. Norton, 1939. 62–111.

[Longman, William and Henry Trower] W.L. and H.T. *Journal of Six Weeks' Adventures in Switzerland, Piedmont, and on the Italian Lakes, June, July, August, 1856*. London: Spottswoods and Co., 1856.

Lunn, Arnold. *A Century of Mountaineering*. London: Longmans, Green, and Co., 1900.

MacCannell, Dean. *The Tourist: A New Theory of the Leisure Class*. New York: Schocken, 1976.

Macfarlane, Robert. *Mountains of the Mind*. New York: Pantheon Books, 2003.

Mackenzie, Norman H. "Hopkins and Science." *Gerard Manley Hopkins and Critical Discourse*. Ed. Eugene Hollahan. New York: AMS Press, 1993. 81–95.

Maclachlan, Jill Marie. "Peak Performances: Cultural and Autobiographical Constructions of the Victorian Female Mountaineer." Dissertation. Department of English, University of British Columbia, 2004.

Maitland, Frederic William. *The Life and Letters of Leslie Stephen*. London: Duckworth & Co., 1906.

Mallalieu, Peter. *The Artists of the Alpine Club: A Biographical Dictionary*. London: The Alpine Club and the Ernest Press, 2007.

Mannoni, Laurent. *The Great Art of Light and Shadow: Archaeology of the Cinema*. Trans. Richard Crangle. Exeter: University of Exeter Press, 2000.

Mason, Kenneth. *Abode of Snow: A History of Himalayan Exploration and Mountaineering*. London: Rupert Hart-Davis, 1955.

Mathews, C.E. "The Jägerhorn and the Luskamm from Gressonay." *The Alpine Journal* 4 (1868): 65–73.

Mathews, C.E. "The Growth of Mountaineering." *The Alpine Journal* 10 (1881): 251–63.

Mayhew, Henry and Athol Mayhew. *Mont Blanc: A Comedy in Three Acts*. London: Printed for Private Circulation, 1874.

Mazel, David, ed. *Mountaineering Women: Stories of Early Climbers*. College Station: Texas A & M University Press, 1994.

[Mazuchelli, Elizabeth Sarah]. *The Indian Alps and How We Crossed Them. Being a Narrative of Two Years' Residence in the Eastern Himalaya and Two Months' Tour into the Interior*. London: Longmans, Green, and Co., 1876.

McCormick, A.D. *An Artist in the Himalaya*. London: T. Fisher Unwin, 1895.

"The Meije by the Eastern Ridge." *The Alpine Journal* 12 (1885): 460–62.

Michie, Helena. *Victorian Honeymoons: Journeys to the Conjugal*. Cambridge: Cambridge University Press, 2006.

Middletton, Dorothy. *Victorian Lady Travellers*. Chicago: Academy Press, 1993. [1965].

Miell, Alfred. MS "Swiss Tour 11–25 August, 1865." Thomas Cook Archives.

Miller, Luree. *On Top of the World: Five Women Explorers in Tibet*. Paddington, N.S.W.: Paddington Press, 1976.

Milne, Mrs. Robert. *Notes of a Tour on the Continent in August and September, 1869. Written for her Children*. Printed by Private Publication, 1871.

Miss Jemima's Swiss Journal: The First Continental Tour of Switzerland. London: Putnam, 1963 [1863].

"Mr. Perk's Mountain Experience, Parts I and II." *Punch* (27 Sep/11 Oct, 1856): 130, 150.

Mitchell, Major J.W.A. "Twenty Years' Climbing and Hunting in the Himalayas." *The Alpine Journal* 11 (1883): 193–215.

Mitchell, Robert. *Plans and Views in Perspective of Buildings Erected in England and Scotland*. London: Wilson & Co., 1801.

Moir, Esther. *The Discovery of Britain: the English Tourist 1540 to 1840*. London: Routledge & Kegan Paul, 1964.

"Mont Blanc by Telescope." *The Daily News*. Scrapbook, Alpine Club Archives.

"Mont Blanc has Become a Positive Nuisance." *The Times* (6 Oct 1856): 8.

Moore, A.W. *The Alps in 1864: A Private Journal*. Ed. Alex B.W. Kennedy. Edinburgh: David Douglas, 1902.

Mummery, A.F. *My Climbs in the Alps and Caucasus*. Oxford: Basil Blackwell, 1936 [1895].

"New Expeditions." *The Alpine Journal* 14 (1889): 479–519.

Nicolson, Marjorie Hope. *Mountain Gloom and Mountain Glory: The Development of the Aesthetics of the Infinite*. New York: W.W. Norton, 1959.

Nixon, Julie V. "'Death blots black out': Thermodynamics and the Poetry of Gerard Manley Hopkins." *Victorian Poetry* 40.2 (2002): 131–55.

Noë, Alvin. *Action in Perception*. Cambridge, MA: MIT Press, 2004.

Norman [Dowie], Ménie Muriel. *A Girl in the Karpathians*. London: George Philip & Son, 1891.

"Observatory on the Summit of Mont Blanc." *The Alpine Journal* 2 (1865): 220–21.

Oetterman, Stephan. *The Panorama: History of a Mass Medium*. New York: Zone Books, 1997.

O'Gorman, Francis. "'The Mightiest Evangel of the Alpine Club': Masculinity and Agnosticism in the Alpine Writing of John Tyndall." *Masculinity and Spirituality in Victorian Culture*. Ed. Andrew Bradstock, Sean Gill, Anne Hogan, and Sue Meyer. Basingstoke: Palgrave Macmillan, 2001. 134–48.

"The Passage of the Sesia-Joch from Zermatt to Alagna by English Ladies." *The Alpine Journal* 5 (1872): 367–72.

Pater, Walter H. *Studies in the History of the Renaissance*. London: Macmillan & Co., 1873.

A Peep at the Mountains: The Journal of a Lady. For Private Circulation only. Leicester: F. Hewitt, 1871.

A Peep at the Pyrenees by a Pedestrian: Being a Tourist's Note-Book. London: Whitaker & Co., 1867.

Penell, Elizabeth Robins. *Over the Alps on a Bicycle*. London: T. Fisher Unwin, 1898.

Phillips, Catherine. *Gerard Manley Hopkins and the Victorian Visual World*. Oxford: Oxford University Press, 2007.

Plunket, Frederica. *Here and There Among the Alps*. London: Longmans, Green, and Co., 1875.

Pollock, Frederick. "The Library of the Alpine Club." *The Alpine Journal* 12 (1880): 425.

Pope, Alexander. "Peri Bathous, Or Of the Art of Sinking in Poetry." *Selected Poetry and Prose*. Introd. William K. Wimsatt, Jr. New York: Rinehart & Co., 1967. 306–60.

Port, R.F. and T. Van Gelder. *Mind as Motion: Exploration in the Dynamics of Cognition*. Cambridge, MA: MIT Press, 1995.

Pratt, Mary Louise. *Imperial Eyes: Studies in Travel Writing and Transculturation*. New York: Routledge, 1992.

"Proceedings of the Alpine Club." *The Alpine Journal* 17 (1894): 85–88.

Rabb, Jane M. "John Ruskin." *Literature and Photography: Interactions 1840–1990*. Albuquerque: University of New Mexico Press, 1995. 110–15.

Radcliffe, Anne. *A Journey made in the Summer of 1794 through Holland and the Western Frontier of Germany, with a Return down the Rhine, to which are added Observations During a Tour of the Lakes in Westmorland and Cumberland*. London, 1795.

"Reviews and Notices." *The Alpine Journal* 7 (1875): 338–44.

"Reviews and Notices." *The Alpine Journal* 11 (1883): 305–307.

Richardson, Mary. Diaries of Mary Richardson. Typescript of Diaries. T 48 (1833), T 49 (1840–41). Ruskin Library, University of Lancaster.

Richardson, Mary, and John Ruskin. "A Tour to the Lakes in Cumberland." Photocopy. Ruskin Library, University of Lancaster.

Ring, Jim. *How the English Made the Alps*. London: John Murray, 2000.

Ritchie, Hester, ed. *Letters of Anne Thackeray Ritchie*. London: John Murray, 1924.

Robertson, David. "Mid-Victorians Amongst the Alps." *Nature and the Victorian Imagination*. Ed. U.C. Knoepflmacher and G.B. Tennyson. Berkeley, CA: University of California Press, 1977. 113–36.

Robinson, Jane. *Wayward Women: A Guide to Women Travellers*. Oxford: Oxford University Press, 1990.

Rosenberg, John D. *The Darkening Glass: A Portrait of Ruskin's Genius*. New York: Columbia University Press, 1961.

Ruskin, John. Ms Letters to Mother. Ruskin Library. University of Lancaster.

Ruskin, John. *The Works of John Ruskin*. Ed. E.T. Cook and Alexander Wedderburn. Library Edition. Vols. 1, 4, 5, 6, 8, 15, 20, 26, 36, 37. London: George Allen, 1903.

Ruskin, John. *The Diaries of John Ruskin*. Ed. Joan Evans and John Howard Whitehouse. Vols. 1–3. Oxford: Clarendon Press, 1956.

Ruskin, John. *The Stones of Venice*. Ed. J.G. Links. New York: Da Capo, 1960.

Ruskin, John. *Ruskin in Italy: Letters to his Parents 1845*. Ed. Harold L. Shapiro. Oxford: Clarendon Press, 1972.

Ruskin, John. *Ruskin's Letters from Venice 1851–1852*. Ed. John Lewis Bradley. Westport: Greenwood, 1978.

Ruskin, John. *Praeterita: The Autobiography of John Ruskin*. Oxford: Oxford University Press, 1989.

Saville, Julia. *A Queer Chivalry: The Homoerotic Asceticism of Gerard Manley Hopkins*. Charlottesville, University Press of Virginia, 2000.

Sawyer, Paul L. "Ruskin and Tyndall: The Poetry of Matter and the Poetry of Spirit." *Victorian Science and Victorian Values: Literary Perspectives. Annals of the New York Academy of Sciences*. V. 360. New York: The New York Academy of Sciences, 1981. 217–46.

Schiller, Friedrick von. *Two Essays by Friedrich von Schiller: Naïve and Sentimental Poetry and On the Sublime*. Trans. Julius A. Elias. New York: Frederick Ungar Publishing Co., 1966.

Schwartz, Vanessa R. *Spectacular Realities: Early Mass Culture in Fin-de-Siècle France*. Berkeley: University of California Press, 1998.

Scriven, G. "The Prevention of Snow-Burning and Blistering." *The Alpine Journal* 13 (1887): 389–90.

Sewell, Miss. *A Journal Kept During a Summer Tour for the Children of a Village School*. London: Longman, Brown, Green and Longmans, 1852.

Shaw, Philip. *The Sublime*. London: Routledge, 2006.

Simpson, William. "List of Marches from the Ganges, near Maicha, to Chini; Also from Simla to Chini, And from Chini through Tibet to Cashmere." *The Alpine Journal* 7 (1875): 259–63

Sketchley, Arthur [George Rose]. *Mrs. Brown on the Grand Tour*. London: George Routledge and Sons, n.d. [1871].

Slack, Darryl and J. Macgregor Wise. *Culture and Technology: A Primer*. New York: Peter Lang, 2005.

Smith, Albert. "Loose Leaves from the Travellers Album at Chamouni." *Bentley's Miscellany*. 10. London: Richard Bentley, 1841.

Smith, Albert. *The Adventures of Mr. Ledbury and His Friend Jack Johnson*. 3 Vols. London: Richard Bentley, 1844.

Smith, Albert. *Christopher Tadpole*. London: George Routledge and Sons, 1848.

Smith, Albert. *The Miscellany: A Book for the Field or the Fire-side: Amusing Tales and Sketches*. London: David Bogue, 1850.

Smith, Albert. "Mont Blanc." *Blackwood's Magazine* 71 (Jan 1852): 35–54.

Smith, Albert. *The Story of Mont Blanc*. London: David Bogue, 1853.

Smith, Lindsay. *Victorian Photography, Painting and Poetry: The Enigma of Visibility in Ruskin, Morris and Pre-Raphaelites*. Cambridge: Cambridge University Press, 1995.

Smith, William. *Adventures with my Alpen-Stock and Carpet-Bag or a Three Weeks' Trip to France and Switzerland*. London: E. Pitman, 1864.

Smith, William, Jr. *A Yorkshireman's Trip to Rome in 1866*. London: Longmans, Green, Reader, and Dyer [c. 1868].

Smythe, F.S. *British Mountaineers*. London: Collins, 1946.

Snow, Robert. "Passage of the Col de Géant." *Memorials of a Tour on the Continent August, 1844* in *The Recreation: A Gift Book for Young Readers with Engravings*. Edinburgh: John Menzies, 1847. 89–100.

Sowka, Joseph W. and Alan G. Kabat. "How to Make Sense of Flashes and Floaters." *Review of Optometry* 15 Jun 2000: 67–72.

Stephen, Leslie. "The Allelein-Horn." *Vacation Tourists and Notes on Travel in 1860*. Ed. Francis Galton. Cambridge: Macmillan & Co., 1861. 264–81.

Stephen, Leslie. "The Joungfrau-Joch and Viescher-Joch, Two New Passes in the Oberland." *The Alpine Journal* 1 (1863): 97–112.

Stephen, Leslie. "The Peaks of Primiero." *The Alpine Journal* 4 (1870): 385–402.

Stephen, Leslie. *The Playground of Europe*. London: Longmans, Green, and Co., 1871.

Stephen, Leslie. *Studies of a Biographer*. V. 3. London: Duckworth & Co., 1902.

Stephen, Leslie. "A Critical Essay on Robert Louis Stevenson." *The Works of Robert Louis Stevenson*. V. 9. New York: The Davos Press, 1906. 1–23.

Stephen, Leslie. *Men, Books, and Mountains: Essays by Leslie Stephen*. Ed S.O.A. Ullmann. London: The Hogarth Press, 1956.

Stevenson, Robert Louis. *Memories and Portraits*. New York: Charles Scribner's Sons, 1897.

Stevenson, Robert Louis. "A Quiet Corner of England." *The Works of Robert Louis Stevenson*. V. 9. New York: The Davos Press, 1906. 251–54.

Stevenson, Robert Louis. *The Silverado Squatters* in *The Works of Robert Louis Stevenson*. V. 6. The Vailima Edition. New York: P.F. Collier & Son, 1912.

Stevenson, Robert Louis. *Essays on Literature, on Nature; Juvenilia*. New York: Charles Scribner's Sons, 1925.

Stevenson, Robert Louis. *Travels with a Donkey in the Cévennes and The Amateur Emigrant*. Ed. Christopher Maclachlan. London: Penguin Books, 2004.

Strachey, Captain Henry. "Physical Geography of Western Tibet." *Journal of the Royal Geographical Society* 28 (1853): 1–69.

Strasdin, Kate. "'An Easy Day for a Lady': The Dress of Early Women Mountaineers." *Costume* 38 (2004): 72–85.

Styles, Showell. *On Top of the World: An Illustrated History of Mountaineering and Mountains*. New York: Macmillan, 1967.

"Summary of New Expeditions During the Summer of 1863, up to August 12." *The Alpine Journal* 1 (1863): 134–38.

"Summary of New Expeditions." *The Alpine Journal* 1 (1863): 196–202.

"Summary of New Expeditions" *The Alpine Journal* 1 (1864): 429–37.

SummitPost—Buet (Mont). 25 Apr 2008. <http://www.summitpost.org/mountain/rock/151207/buet-mont.html>

Sussman, Herbert. *Victorian Masculinities: Manhood and Masculine Poetics in Early Victorian Literature and Art*. Cambridge: Cambridge University Press, 1995.

Swinglehurst, Edmund. *Cook's Tours: The Story of Popular Travel*. Poole: Blandford Press, 1982.

Swiss Notes By Five Ladies: An Account of Touring and Climbing in 1874. Ed. Peter A. Marshall and Jean K. Brown. Lancaster: Peter A. Marshall, 2003.

Symonds, John Addington. *The Letters of John Addington Symonds*. V. 2. Ed. Herbert M. Schueller & Robert L. Peters. Detroit: Wayne State University Press, 1968.

Symonds, John Addington and his daughter Margaret. *Our Life in the Swiss Highlands* London: Adam and Charles Black. 1892.

Tanner, H.C.B. "The Great Peaks of the Himalaya." *The Alpine Journal* 12 (1886): 438–60.

"There I stood, the Terrible Abyss Yawning at my feet." *Punch* 23 (Jan 1897).

Thomas, Hilary M. *Grandmother Extraordinary: Mary De La Beche Nicholl: 1839–1922*. Barry: Stewart Williams, n.d.

Thomas, Sophie. "Gothic Technologies: Visuality in the Romantic Era: Making Visible: The Diorama, the Double and the Gothic Subject." <http://www.re.umd.edu/praxis/gothic/thomas/thomas.html>

Thompson, Alfred. *Linda of Chamouni, or not "Formosa": an Operatic Incongruity*. London [n.p.] [n.d.] [First produced at the Gaiety Theatre, Strand, on Monday, 13 Sep 1869].

Thorington, J. Monroe. *Mont Blanc Sideshow: The Life and Times of Albert Smith*. Philadelphia: The John C. Winston Company, 1934.

Thornton, R.K.R. "The People Hopkins Knew." *All My Eyes See: The Visual World of Gerard Manley Hopkins*. Sunderland: Ceolfrith Press, 1975. 33–52.

Trench, F.M. *A Journal Abroad in 1868. For Young Friends at Home*. London: Richard Bentley, n.d.

Trollope, Anthony. "The Alpine Club Men." *Travelling Sketches*. London: Chapman and Hall, 1866. 84–97.

Trollope, Anthony. "The Unprotected Female Tourist," *Travelling Sketches*. London: Chapman and Hall, 1866. 29–42.

Tuckett, Elizabeth. *How We Spent the Summer or "A Voyage en Zigzag."* 3rd. ed. London: Longmans, Green, Reader & Dyer, 1866.

Tuckett, Elizabeth. *Beaten Tracks, or, Pen and Pencil Sketches in Italy*. London: Longmans, Green, and Co., 1866.

Tuckett, Elizabeth. *Pictures in Tyrol and Elsewhere*. London: Longmans, Green, and Co., 1867.

Tuckett, Elizabeth. *Zigzagging Amongst Dolomites*. London: Longmans, Green, Reader & Dyer, 1871.

Tuckett, F[rancis] F[ox]. *A Pioneer in the High Alps: Alpine Diaries and Letters of F.F. Tuckett 1856–1874*. London: Edward Arnold, 1920.

"Turgidus Alpinus." *The Eagle* 6.3 (Dec 1869): 221–24.

Twain, Mark [Samuel Clemens]. *A Tramp Abroad; Illustrated by W.Fr. Brown, True Williams, B. Day and Other Artists – With Also Three or Four Pictures Made by The Author of this Book, Without Outside Help; in all Three Hundred and Twenty-Eight Illustrations*. Hartford: American Publishing Company, 1880.

Tyndall, John. *The Glaciers of the Alps: Being a Narrative of Excursions and Ascents, an Account of the Origin and Phenomenon of Glaciers, and an exposition of the physical principles to which they are related*. Boston: Ticknor and Fields, 1861.

Tyndall, John. *Mountaineering in 1861: A Vacation Tour*. London: Longman, Green,Longman, and Roberts, 1862.

Ullman, James Ramsey. *The Age of Mountaineering*. London: J.P. Lippincott, 1954.

Ury, John. *The Tourist Gaze: Leisure and Travel in Contemporary Societies*. London: Sage, 1990.

Waddell, L.A. *Among the Himalaya*. Kathmandu: Ratria Pistak Bhandar, 1978.

Walker, Joseph. "Grand Tour in 1850 by Joseph Walker." Typescript. Alpine Club Archives.

Waller, Derek John. *The Pundits: British Exploration of Tibet and Central Asia*. Lexington, KY: The University Press of Kentucky, 1990.

Webber, Thomas W. *The Forests of Upper India and their Inhabitants*. London: Edward Arnold, 1902.

Wells, H.G. "Little Mother up the Mörderberg." *The Complete Short Stories of H.G. Wells*. London: Ernest Benn, 1970. 575–86.

Weston, Rev. Walter. *Mountaineering and Exploration in the Japanese Alps*. London: John Murray, 1896.

Whistler, James Abbott McNeill. "Ten O'Clock Lecture." *The Longman Anthology of British Literature*, 3rd ed. Gen. Ed. David Damrosch. V. 2B. *The Victorian Age*. Ed. Heather Henderson and William Sharpe. New York: Longman, 2006. 2067.

White, Norman. "The Context of Hopkins' Drawings." *All My Eyes See: The Visual World of Gerard Manley Hopkins*. Sunderland: Ceolfrith Press, 1975.

White, Norman. *Hopkins: A Literary Biography*. Oxford: Clarendon Press, 1992.

Whitwell, Thomas. "Alpine Log." MS 6343. National Library of Scotland.

Whymper, Edward, ed. *A Guide to Chamonix and the Range of Mont Blanc*. London: John Murray, 1905.

Whymper, Edward. *Scrambles Amongst the Alps in the Years 1860–69*. London: John Murray, 1871.

Wildman, Stephen. "Ruskin, Switzerland and the Alps: A Loan Exhibition of Watercolours and Drawings from the Ruskin Foundation." Ruskin Library, University of Lancaster.

Williams, Cicely. *Women on the Rope: The Feminine Share in Mountain Adventure*. London: George Allen & Unwin, 1973.

Willink, H.G.W. "Alpine Sketching." *The Alpine Journal* 12 (1885): 361–80.

[Willink] H.G.W. "Exhibition of Mr. Donkin's Photographs." *The Alpine Journal* 14 (1889): 309–11.

Wilson, Andrew. *The Abode of Snow: Observations on a Journey from Chinese Tibet to the Indian Caucasus, through the Upper Valleys of the Himalaya*. 2nd ed. Edinburgh: William Blackwood and Sons, 1876.

Wilson, Eric G. *The Spiritual History of Ice*. New York: Palgrave, 2009.

Winkworth, Susanna, ed. *The Letters and Memorials of Catherine Winkworth*. Privately Printed, 1883.

Withey, Lynne. *The Grand Tours and Cook's Tours: A History of Leisure Travel, 1750 to 1915*. New York: William Morrow and Company, 1997.

Workman, Fanny Bullock and William Hunter Workman. *The Call of the Snowy Hispar*. London: Constable and Company, 1910.

Yates, Mrs. Ashton. *Letters Written During a Journey to Switzerland in the Autumn of 1841*. 2 Vols. London: Duncan and Malcolm, 1843.

Young, Geoffrey Winthrop. *On High Hills: Memories of the Alps*. New York: E.P. Dutton and Company, 1926.

Younghusband, Frank E. *The Heart of a Continent: A Narrative of Travels in Manchuria, across the Gobi Desert, through the Himalayas, the Parners, and Chitral, 1884–1894*. London: John Murray, 1896.

Zaniello, Tom. "Alpine Art and Science: Hopkins' Swiss Adventure." *The Hopkins Quarterly* 27.1/2 (2000): 3–17.

Zaniello, Tom. *Hopkins in the Age of Darwin*. Iowa City: University of Iowa Press, 1988.

Index

For Product Safety Concerns and Information please contact our
EU representative GPSR@taylorandfrancis.com Taylor & Francis
Verlag GmbH, Kaufingerstraße 24, 80331 München, Germany

For Product Safety Concerns and Information please contact our
EU representative GPSR@taylorandfrancis.com Taylor & Francis
Verlag GmbH, Kaufingerstraße 24, 80331 München, Germany